STUDY GUIDE

MARKETING TODAY
Second Edition

STUDY GUIDE

Constantine G. Petrides
Borough of Manhattan Community College

MARKETING TODAY
Second Edition

David J. Rachman
Baruch College

THE DRYDEN PRESS
Chicago   New York   San Francisco
Philadelphia   Montreal   Toronto
London   Sydney   Tokyo

ISBN 0-03-013569-9
Printed in the United States of America
789-066-987654321

Address orders:
111 Fifth Avenue
New York, NY 10003

Address editorial correspondence:
One Salt Creek Lane
Hinsdale, IL 60521

The Dryden Press
Holt, Rinehart and Winston
Saunders College Publishing

To my father James and in memory of my mother
Venetia who toiled to establish themselves in
the new land armed with an earnest faith in God
and the ideals of their Hellenic Heritage

Who labored to find the spirit to sustain
themselves and future generations

And who passed on this legacy to their children
that we may keep their dream alive for a
brighter tomorrow

This book is dedicated with deep
respect and gratitude.

CONTENTS

This <u>Study Guide</u> has been prepared for the purpose of assisting and reinforcing your understanding of <u>Marketing Today</u>, Second Edition, by David Rachman. It is an integral part of a total teaching/learning package and will enable you to learn the text material better. This edition has been updated to include additional supportive material that can help you to improve your overall perspective on the content as is found in the text chapters.

This <u>Study Guide</u> follows the sequence of <u>Marketing Today</u> and contains eighteen chapters divided into six sections. Each section provides a complete learning unit for a specific topic. You are advised to read the chapter summary, learning goals, and key concepts and then work through the programmed review before attempting to complete the marketing riddle, experiential exercise, and self-quiz.

The <u>Chapter Summary</u> reviews, in order of their appearance, the main points of each chapter, including the key terms. I suggest that you read the chapter summary before reading the chapter in the textbook because the summary can act as a guide and make you aware of the major topics and relationships presented in the chapter.

The <u>Learning Goals</u> identify the major points in each chapter. Your ability to discuss these points will reflect how well you understand the chapter material.

The <u>Key Concepts</u> should be used as a check to see if you understand the important terms in each chapter. Answers to the Key Concepts are provided at the end of each chapter. Check your answers only after filling in all the blanks. Any incorrect answers suggest the need for further review.

The <u>Programmed Review</u> reinforces what you have previously learned. It is an excellent method of learning and retaining the various concepts and information presented in the text. You should hold an index card or piece of paper over the answer column on the left-hand side of the page. Then, as you read the various learning frames on the right-hand side, write what you believe are the correct answers in each blank space. You will find the correct response printed in the margin to the left of the question.

The <u>Marketing Riddles</u>. See enclosed information on page xv.

The <u>Experiential Exercises</u> present a variety of unique business experiences based on the principle of "learning by doing."

The <u>Self-Quiz</u> includes several multiple-choice and true-false questions. The questions are designed to test your comprehension of the material presented in the chapters. You should answer these questions and then check

them in the solution section at the end of the chapter. These questions provide you with one final opportunity to see how well you understand the major
ideas in each chapter.

The proper use of this <u>Study Guide</u> along with <u>Marketing Today</u> will provide
you with the knowledge to better understand the strategic function of marketing and explore the potential for a successful marketing career.

Good luck!

                              Constantine G. Petrides

CONTEST DETAILS
SOLVE MARKETING RIDDLES
WIN VALUABLE PRIZES

In each chapter you will find a challenging game of riddles that represent a
new and exciting attempt to reinforce marketing concepts. Each riddle gives
you an opportunity to apply the chapter context by supplying the missing
word. You will find statements that require you to make a response by filling in the blank, or blanks, for the appropriate missing word(s). Each
statement contains a key letter which, when combined with other key letters,
will provide you with the solution to the riddle. By solving all of the
riddles correctly, you qualify for a drawing that will give you a chance to
win one of the prizes listed on the entry form below.

Entry Form

MARKETING TODAY

Study Guide Contest

sponsored by THE DRYDEN PRESS

Chapter Riddles

1. _____   10. _____
2. _____   11. _____
3. _____   12. _____
4. _____   13. _____
5. _____   14. _____
6. _____   15. _____
7. _____   16. _____
8. _____   17. _____
9. _____   18. _____

Student's name: _____

College address & phone: _____

Home address & phone: _____

**PRIZE

(check one)

☐ AM/FM Stereo Radio Cassette Recorder

☐ 2" Watchman (mini-TV)   MAIL ENTRIES TO:

☐ 35 mm camera   Prof. Constantine G. Petrides
                                           Manhattan Community College
☐ $100.00 Gift Certificate   199 Chambers Street, S660
                                           New York, NY   10007
☐ Compact refrigerator

☐ Microwave oven

** All entries must be postmarked by June 30, 1989. Drawing will take place
   August 1, 1989. Three winners will be notified by October 1, 1989.

CHAPTER 1
THE IMPORTANCE AND SCOPE OF MARKETING

CHAPTER SUMMARY

1. Marketing is an important part of our economic system that can be
    found in both profit and nonprofit organizations. Marketing represents
    an exciting, challenging, and rewarding business activity that affects
    our lives each and every day. At one time marketing was defined as all
    the steps necessary in providing goods and services to others. This
    definition gave one the impression that marketing activities began
    once a product was produced. Today, marketing is concerned not only
    with the distribution of goods and services but also in their devel-
    opment. <u>Marketing</u> consists of those activities performed by individ-
    uals, businesses, and nonprofit organizations that satisfy needs and
    wants through the process of exchange. <u>Exchange</u> is the process by
    which two or more parties freely give something of value to one another
    to satisfy some of their needs or wants. Therefore, marketing can
    include advertising, market research, selling, distribution, produce
    development, and a great many other activities. Marketing is dynamic,
    exciting, and challenging, with room for almost every skill and talent.

2. In marketing terms a <u>product</u> refers to a good, service, and an idea
    offered for exchange that provides benefits for consumers. Products
    can either be goods or services. A <u>service</u> refers to the intangible
    benefit exchanged in marketing. The increase in the level of services
    by an economy is characteristic of an affluent society. In the United
    States about 50 percent of the average family's budget is spent on
    services. The many services we use in our society can be highlighted
    when we consider the amount of money spent in such areas as shelter,
    medical care, recreation, and travel. In addition, consumers use a
    large number of services provided by nonprofit organizations which
    they pay for with taxes and contributions. These services can be found
    in such areas as education, government, health care, religion, and
    culture. As businesses prosper the demand for industrial services
    grows. The increasing complexities of business often contribute to
    firms' hiring the services of numerous specialists who can often provide
    better quality services at lower costs. Businesses often hire a
    specialist in such areas as maintenance, security, food supply, and
    accounting.

3. By producing and marketing goods and services, marketers provide society
    with want-satisfying utility. Want-satisfying utility refers to the
    act of making goods useful. In other words, all societies must market

their goods and services--that is, satisfy needs. This is accomplished through complex marketing activities. Of course, in the U.S., most marketing activities are performed by the private enterprise system pursuing a profit. Thus, utility, or usefulness, is the major function of marketing activity. In marketing we can identify form utilities.

4. Form Utility is given to a product by converting raw materials into finished goods. This function is not directly marketing related. Basically, form utility is a production function. Bread is made from wheat, sugar, yeast, salt, and water; perfume is made from the essential oils of flowers, alcohol, water, and artificial colors; and a brassiere is made from nylon, lace, elastic, metal clips, and at times, foam padding. The producer assembles these raw materials and uses capital, machines, and labor to create a product.

5. Time Utility refers to the value added to a product by making it available when buyers need it. Referring to the previously mentioned products in form utility, day old bread is unacceptable; most perfume is sold during the Christmas holidays; and brassieres must constantly be available. The necessary marketing activities for making these products available when consumers want them adds value to these goods.

   Fresh bread requires rapid transportation, selling, buying, credit, and promotion. These activities add utility to products. How would you like the imposition of ordering bread two weeks in advance?

6. Place Utility refers to the value added to a product by making it available where buyers want it. Do you want to travel 300 miles each time you need a loaf of bread, a bottle of perfume, or a brassiere? Marketing does the job for consumers. Transportation, credit, selling, buying, and risk taking all make goods available where consumers want them.

   Products are generally produced in specific geographic areas that specialize in concentrated production. Autos are produced in Detroit, clothing in New York City, shoes in St. Louis, oranges in Florida and California, furniture in the Carolinas, and so it goes. However, consumers want goods where they live, not necessarily where they are manufactured. Oranges do not grow in Chicago, but residents there drink an enormous amount of orange juice. Place Utility is the process of creating value in products by having them available where consumers want them.

7. Ownership Utility refers to the value added to a product by giving consumers a way of obtaining ownership of it. Ownership utility refers to the value added to a product when a means of transferring title to it is provided. Selling, credit, and promotion are essential in creating usefulness for the owner; transferring possession and title to goods can be complex and time consuming. These essential tasks demand great marketing effort.

2

Title can be passed to bread through a cash transaction, and perfume may be purchased "on credit." Possession may be transferred personally in a retail store, through the mail, or at a designated pick-up point. Title and possession are achieved through marketing efforts--"ownership utility" is the result.

8. Marketing can also be described by its functions which help create and bring about exchanges. Marketing functions can include searching out buyers and sellers, matching goods, services, and other offerings to the needs of customers, finding an acceptable price in the marketplace, informing buyers and sellers of product availability and convincing them to purchase, transporting and storing goods, settling details for the final exchange, and assuming risks.

9. The identification of marketing as an essential business activity that aids in the production, distribution, and selling of goods and services is reflected by its long history. Marketing is probably as old as civilization itself. Marketing has existed since the days of the cavemen. The Industrial Revolution, which began in the late 1700s, marked the beginning of marketing as we've come to know it. The history of marketing can best be described by the production concept, sales concept, and marketing concept. The production concept emphasized the importance of producing goods. From the beginning of our country until about 1929, most American companies were production oriented. Since demand was greater than supply and there was minimum competition, most manufacturers produced whatever goods they could; buyers for their products were easily found. Demand was greater than supply--it was a seller's market. Consumers often had limited variety and purchased whatever was available. Firms believed that the consumers would buy their products no matter what. Therefore, the emphasis was on producing, rather than on selling. The production concept assumed that anything that can be produced can be sold, that the most important task of management is to keep the cost of production down, and that a company should produce only certain basic products.

10. Beginning in the 1920s and continuing until about 1950, the strong consumer demand for products subsided. The sales concept increased production and competitive capability caused manufacturers to realize changes were in order. They not only wanted to produce quality products but also to develop the necessary sales expertise to outsell competition. The major problem during these years was a lack of consumer purchasing power. The "Great Depression" limited consumer demand, although producers were capable of supplying sufficient goods and services. A major task during this period was for management to convince buyers to purchase the output of their particular firm. In fact, goods had to be pushed by an enormous selling effort until consumers became more prosperous after World War II. Sales-oriented businesses emphasized that finding buyers was the chief concern, and that management's main task was to convince buyers--through varying degrees of persuasion-- to purchase a firm's output.

3

11. After World War II and the return to a peace-time economy, consumer income increased dramatically. Manufacturers began to realize the importance of marketing for satisfying consumer needs. At this stage of time the economy shifted from a seller's market to a buyer's market and a new approach to business--the marketing concept--was formulated. A seller's market is one in which there is a shortage of goods and services. A buyer's market is one in which there is an abundance of goods and services. Businesses began to acknowledge the importance of the consumer in the marketplace. With the realization that you cannot force consumers to purchase something they do not want or need, the consumer's role in the marketplace was assured by the switch from production dominance to marketing dominance. The marketing concept stated that companies should produce only what customers want, that management must integrate all company activities to develop programs to satisfy those wants, and that long-range profit goals rather than "quick" sales should guide management decisions. In order to achieve the marketing concept a company should discover what customers want, mobilize the entire organization to meet those wants, and pursue long-term profit.

12. Since the marketing concept affects all types of business activities, a business must pay close attention to three basic points or ideas. The first point reflects an understanding of consumers' wants and needs. Management must develop an information system that will enable it to seek out consumer purchasing power and opinions about products.

   The second point recognizes the need to reorganize its staff to reflect changes in the way it conducts business. Top management must establish goals and objectives, which may often necessitate the elimination of some departments and the creation of others. The marketing mix specifies the policies a firm intends to adopt. The marketing mix consists of four major components. The product reflects the offering (a good, service, or idea) that embodies benefits consumers seek. Pricing reflects the value placed upon the product by the firm. Promotion reflects the firm's communications with customers to inform, persuade, and remind them of the product's benefits. Placement, also called distribution, is the means of delivering the product and sometimes title to it.

   The third point necessary for the successful implementation of the marketing concept requires the understanding of long-term profit. No business can survive without making a profit. Businesses should think in terms of the long run. They may have to sacrifice profits in the present for a better return in the future.

   A marketer must realize that adoption and implementation of the marketing concept does present some criticism. Most of the complaints center around such areas as consumerism, profit orientation, and long-term competitiveness. Consumerism is a movement to increase the influence, power, and rights of consumers in their dealings with institutions of all types. Advocates of consumerism believe that companies must bear in mind their social responsibility to make products that are safe and do not harm the environment. Profit orientation critics believe that conflicts between providing customer satisfaction and the basic goal of any business to make a profit may be at odds. The long-term competitiveness critics have accused the marketing concept of diverting attention from the product to advertising, selling, and promotion.

13. One of the most difficult problems marketers will face in the coming years is striking a balance between the needs and wants of individuals and those of society at large. A new marketing concept, called societal marketing, has recently emerged. This concept attempts to balance concerns for profits, satisfying individual wants, and meeting overall societal needs. Social responsibility within a company involves philanthropic giving; total compliance with international, federal, state, and local laws; and moral and ethical standards under which the company will operate, stated in terms of what the company will and will not tolerate. As more business people become aware of their social responsibilities and an increasing number of individuals and groups pressure business to be responsive to societal needs, we can expect more organizations to seek a careful blend of these issues with the quest for profit.

LEARNING GOALS

After reading this chapter, you should be able to:

1. Define marketing.
2. Differentiate between products, goods, and services.
3. Describe how marketing adds value to a product and differentiate between form, time, place, and ownership utility.
4. Describe the functions of the marketing sector.
5. Discuss the history of marketing and describe the events that took place during the production concept, sales concept, and marketing concept.
6. Identify and explain the key elements of the marketing concept.
7. Describe the 4 Ps of marketing.
8. Describe three areas of criticism surrounding the marketing concept.
9. Discuss marketing and society including the importance of social responsibility.

KEY CONCEPTS

From the list of lettered terms, select the one that best fits in the blank of the numbered statements that follow. Write the letter of that choice in the space provided.

(Answers to the key concepts appear at the end of the chapter.)

a. Time utility
b. Marketing
c. A seller's market
d. Consumerism
e. Pricing
f. Societal marketing
g. Form utility
h. Placement
i. Ownership utility
j. Sales orientation
k. The four "Ps"

l. Production orientation
m. An exchange
n. Promotion
o. Profit
p. The marketing concept
q. The marketing mix
r. Place utility
s. Goods
t. A service
u. A buyer's market
v. A product

1. _____ refers to the value added to a product by converting raw materials into a finished good.

2. _____ is the process by which two or more parties freely give something of value to one another to satisfy needs and wants.

3. _____ is defined as the activities performed by individuals, businesses, and not-for-profit organizations that satisfy needs and wants through the process of exchange.

4. _____ refers to the intangible benefit exchanged in marketing.

5. _____ is the business philosophy emphasizing that (1) finding buyers for products is management's chief concern; (2) management must integrate all company activities to develop programs to satisfy those wants; and (3) long-range profit goals should guide management.

6. _____ is a movement to increase the influence, power, and rights of consumers in their dealings with institutions of all types.

7. _____ refers to a good, service, or idea offered for exchange that provides benefits for customers.

8. _____ refers to the value added to a product by giving consumers a way to obtain ownership of it.

9. _____ consists of a plan that specifies what will be offered to customers (the product) and how (its price, promotion, and placement).

10. _____ is the business philosophy emphasizing that (1) anything that can be produced can be sold; (2) the most important managerial task is to keep the cost of production down; and (3) a company should produce only certain basic products.

11. _____ is the placing of a value on a product.

12. _____ refers to value added to a product by making it available where buyers want it.

13. _____ is what remains for a business after expenses are deducted from revenues or income.

14. _____ is the means of delivering a product (also called distribution).

15. _____ is the concept that balances concern for profits with concern for satisfying individual wants and social needs.

16. _____ refers to communication that is designed to inform, persuade, and remind customers of a product's benefits.

17. _____ is a market in which there is a shortage of goods and services.

18. _____ are the elements of the marketing mix, which are product, price, promotion, and placement.

19. _____ is a business philosophy emphasizing that (1) companies should produce only what customers want; (2) management must integrate all company activities to develop programs to satisfy those wants; and (3) long-range profit goals should guide management.

20. _____ are tangible objects exchanged in marketing.

21. _____ refers to the value added to a product by making it available when buyers need it.

22. _____ is a market in which there is an abundance of goods and services.

PROGRAMMED REVIEW

The following self-teaching exercises consist of short statements that require you to make a response by filling in the blank (or blanks) provided. You will find the correct response printed in the margin to the left of the question.

tangible

1. In marketing terms, _____ items received in an exchange are goods.

50

2. The United States is now a service economy. About _____ percent of the average family's budget is spent on services.

7

a. Anything that can be produced can be sold.
b. The most important task of management is to keep the cost of production down.
c. A company should produce only certain basic products.

3. What were the three assumptions basic to the production concept or orientation?

a. _____
   _____

b. _____
   _____
   _____
   _____

c. _____
   _____
   _____

works

4. Commitment to the marketing concept requires top management to completely reorganize how the company _____ .

a. product
b. price
c. promotion
d. placement or distribution

5. The marketing mix specifies the policies a firm intends to adopt with respect to:

a. _____
b. _____
c. _____
d. _____

influence
power
rights

6. Consumerism has been defined as a movement to increase the _____ , _____ , and _____ of consumers in their dealings with institutions of all types.

two

7. An exchange is the process by which _____ or more parties freely give something of value to one another.

Indirect participation

8. _____ includes product delivery, communication of product availability, or research into demand for products.

a. concerns for profits
b. satisfying individual
   wants
c. meeting overall
   societal needs

9. What are the three areas of concern that societal marketing attempts to balance?

   a. _____
   _____

   b. _____
   _____

   c. _____
   _____

when

10. Marketing creates time utility by making goods and services available _____ consumers want them.

a. finding buyers is
   the chief concern
b. management's main task is
   to convince buyers--
   through various degrees of
   persuasion--to purchase a
   firm's output

11. What were the two points that a sales-oriented business emphasized?

   a. _____
   _____

   b. _____
   _____
   _____
   _____
   _____

want
need

12. A product is the marketing term for anything offered to meet a _____ or _____.

where

13. Marketing creates place utility by making goods and services available _____ they are accessible to consumers.

seller's
buyer's

14. At the end of World War II, the economy shifted from a _____ market to a _____ market.

9

a. Companies should produce only what consumers want.
b. Management must integrate all company activities in order to develop programs to satisfy those wants.
c. Long-range profit goals, rather than "quick" sales, should guide management decisions.

15. What are the three basic ideas that the marketing concept addresses?

a. _____
_____
_____

b. _____
_____
_____
_____
_____

c. _____
_____
_____
_____

needs and wants
society

16. One of the most difficult problems marketers will face in the coming years is striking a balance between the _____ _____ of individuals and those of _____ at large.

40 to 60

17. It has been estimated that between _____ cents of every dollar the consumer spends helps to pay for marketing costs.

a. form utility
b. time utility
c. place utility
d. ownership utility

18. What are the four kinds of utilities or values that can be added to a product?

a. _____
b. _____
c. _____
d. _____

owning
using

19. Marketing creates ownership utility by giving the consumer a way to obtain the rights of _____ and _____ a product.

a. consumerism
b. profit orientation
c. long-term competitive-
   ness

20. What are the three areas of criticism
    that have been centered around the
    marketing concept?

    a. _____

    b. _____

    c. _____

Marketing

21. _____ may be defined
    as activities performed by individuals,
    businesses, and nonprofit organizations
    that satisfy needs and wants through the
    process of exchange.

raw materials
finished good

22. Marketing provides form utility which is
    given to a product by converting
    _____ into a
    _____.

a. philanthropic giving
b. total compliance with
   international, federal,
   state, and local laws
c. moral and ethical standards under which the
   company will operate,
   stated in terms of what
   the company will and
   will not tolerate

23. What are the three areas of concern
    that social responsibility within a com-
    pany involves?

    a. _____
       _____

    b. _____
       _____
       _____

    c. _____
       _____
       _____
       _____
       _____
       _____

a. discover what customers
    want
b. mobilize the entire
    organization to meet
    those needs
c. pursue long-term profit

24. What are the three basic principles that
    are needed in a successful implementa-
    tion of the marketing concept?

    a. _____
        _____

    b. _____
        _____

    c. _____
        _____

psychological

25. When you buy almost any product, you are
    buying certain symbolic or
    _____ benefits
    along with the product itself.

MARKETING RIDDLE

The purpose of this exercise is to find the missing word that solves the
riddle. Each of the statements requires you to make a response by filling in
the blank (or blanks) for the appropriate missing word. Each statement contains a key letter which, when combined with the other key letters, will provide you with the solution to the riddle. Correct solutions to the riddle
questions can lead to valuable prizes. See instructions for more information.

        Marketing is important to each of us in many ways. To be
        successful, our marketing system will only work if we are able
        to exchange our surpluses for the goods and services as they are
        needed. By establishing a marketing system, people are given
        the freedom to

        __ __ __ __ __ __ __ __ __ __ .
        1 2 3 4 5 6 7 8 9 10

1. The ☐ __ __ __ __ orientation prevailed from 1920 to about 1950.

2. Many companies find it worthwhile to spend dollars to achieve brand
    loyalty if in the long term they may __ __ __ __ __ ☐ their initial
    investment many times over.

3. In the late 1700s, the __ __ __ __ __ __ __ __ __ __ __
    __ ☐ __ __ __ __ __ __ __ __ brought the beginning of modern marketing.

4. The sales concept developed after World War I.
    ☐ __ __ __ __ __ __ __ __ __ __ __ grew, and there were more goods to sell
    than demand warranted.

12

5. Besides requiring customer orientation and an integrated effort, the marketing concept also stresses the importance of long-term __ __ __ __ ☐ __.

6. Most marketing experts agree that a substantial part of any marketing exchange involves __ __ __ ☐ __ __ __ __ __ __ elements, even when the thing exchanged is as unmistakably solid as a car.

7. Pricing reflects the __ __ ☐ __ __ placed upon the product by the firm.

8. When a company adopts the marketing concept, it often finds it must __ __ __ __ __ __ __ ☐ __ __ staff to reflect changes in the way it conducts business.

9. Marketing orientation includes evaluating the position of the __ __ __ __ __ __ ☐ __ __ __ __ __ as well as that of consumers.

10. Unless marketers respond to consumer criticism, they may be subject to government __ ☐ __ __ __ __ __ __ __ __.

EXPERIENTIAL EXERCISE

In our business environment, we have seen many different companies adopt marketing as a major area of concern. Within the past decade we have seen more and more nontraditional marketing organizations recognize its potential.

Describe how the following groups or organizations have shown an interest in marketing.

1. Lawyers

   _____
   _____
   _____
   _____

2. Accountants

   _____
   _____
   _____
   _____

13

3. Doctors

_____
_____
_____

_____

4. Colleges

_____
_____
_____

_____

5. Textbook Publishers

_____
_____
_____

_____

SELF-QUIZ

Multiple Choice

_____ 1. The United States is now a service economy. About _____ percent of
            the family's budget is spent on services.
            a. 25
            b. 35
            c. 50
            d. 85

_____ 2. The best key to successful marketing is
            a. good promotion.
            b. good products.
            c. an exchange.
            d. good sales people.

_____ 3. A market in which there is a shortage of goods and services is
            known as a
            a. buyer's market.
            b. consumer market.
            c. distribution market.
            d. seller's market.

_____ 4. The concept that resulted from the seemingly boundless supply of customers and natural resources was known as
   a. the sales concept.
   b. the production concept.
   c. the natural concept.
   d. the marketing concept.

_____ 5. A firm's communications with customers to inform, persuade, and remind them of the product's benefits is known as
   a. promotion.
   b. distribution.
   c. pricing.
   d. placement.

_____ 6. The utility that puts value to a product by the conversion of raw materials into a finished good is known as
   a. time utility.
   b. form utility.
   c. place utility.
   d. ownership utility.

_____ 7. Societal marketing is a belief that a firm
   a. should attempt to maximize profits.
   b. should produce what consumers want.
   c. should balance concerns for profits, satisfying individual wants, and meeting overall societal needs.
   d. should have integration of all functions in the organization in such a way as to meet consumer needs.

_____ 8. Which of the following is not considered a function of marketing?
   a. actual production of the tangible good
   b. selling
   c. transporting
   d. risk taking

_____ 9. The marketing mix component that is concerned with the delivering of a product is known as
   a. pricing.
   b. product.
   c. promotion.
   d. placement or distribution.

_____ 10. It has been estimated that between _____ cents of every dollar the consumer spends helps to pay for marketing costs.
   a. 10 to 20
   b. 30 to 40
   c. 40 to 60
   d. 50 to 60

_____ 11. At the end of World War II, the economy shifted from a buyer's market to a seller's market.

_____ 12. According to the sales concept, consumers must be persuaded to buy a product.

_____ 13. Increased competition and increased affluence in the 1950s caused a change in management's attention from the consumer to the product.

_____ 14. An important function of a firm's marketing department is to develop the proper combination and use of the marketing mix.

_____ 15. The marketing concept says that businesses should think in terms of the long run.

_____ 16. Place utility occurs when value is added to a product by making it available when buyers need it.

_____ 17. Marketing is concerned with the ability to buy goods and services that consumers really do not want or need.

_____ 18. Customers must be sought out not only for their purchasing power, but for their opinions about products.

_____ 19. Marketing may be defined as activities performed by individuals, businesses, and nonprofit organizations that satisfy needs and wants through the process of exchange.

_____ 20. In an exchange process, what is given or received must be either a physical product or money.

CHAPTER SOLUTIONS

Key Concepts

1. g	6. d	11. e	16. n	21. a
2. m	7. v	12. r	17. c	22. u
3. b	8. i	13. o	18. k	
4. t	9. q	14. h	19. p	
5. j	10. l	15. f	20. s	

Self-Quiz

1. c	5. a	9. d	13. F	17. F
2. c	6. b	10. c	14. T	18. T
3. d	7. c	11. F	15. T	19. T
4. b	8. a	12. T	16. F	20. F

CHAPTER 2
MARKETING MANAGEMENT AND PLANNING

CHAPTER SUMMARY

1. The strength and weakness of an organization can be identified and analyzed by observing performance trends, capabilities, and resources. The
   marketing department is often concerned with the generation of sales
   revenue. The size and profitability of this revenue depends upon the
   nature of the offer that the firm designs and its reception by the
   market.

   A marketing manager, or chief marketing executive, is the person who
   coordinates all of the work of a marketing department. Every marketing
   manager engages in certain basic tasks, such as planning, implementing,
   and evaluating. The first stage consists of strategic marketing planning
   which typically takes a long-range view of an organization's objectives.
   It is the process of establishing an organization's overall goals,
   assessing opportunities, and developing marketing objectives. The marketing manager should establish marketing goals in accordance with the
   rest of the company's objectives. He should assess opportunities as they
   develop and capitalize on them when warranted. He should develop
   marketing objectives which specify what the marketing department intends
   to accomplish through marketing activities. A marketing strategy is a
   plan for achieving the marketing objectives. It describes the marketing
   mix that the company will use to reach a selected part of the market.
   The second stage is implementing. To implement a plan is to put it into
   action. The marketing manager should organize, coordinate and direct
   the marketing activities. The third stage in the management of marketing
   activities is evaluating, which is the means by which a manager can
   ensure that the department is meeting its objectives and revises its
   plans if something goes wrong.

2. All managers are involved in a company's strategic planning. They set
   objectives, develop plans, execute those plans, and evaluate their
   success. However, marketing managers face certain challenges unique to
   their jobs. They include the highly changeable nature of the market,
   geographical complexities of the market, people variables, the need to
   rely on people outside the firm, a wide number of alternatives, and
   marketing's influence on the success of the firm.

3. Marketing plans can be short run (typically one year), intermediate or
   moderate length (two to five years), or long run (five years and
   beyond). Many firms rely on a combination of these plans. The first
   step in establishing plans is to define the mission and objectives. A
   mission is concerned with an organization's commitment to a business
   activity and its place in the market. It is a firm's overall reason for
   existing. A mission must be translated into specific objectives.

18

Organizational objectives specify goals for the organization to pursue as a whole. Goals are used to describe objectives that have been made specific in size and time.

4. Most marketing plans cover the following elements: (1) a market analysis, which includes information on demand, competition, environmental climate, resources of the firm, distribution factors, and political and legal constraints; (2) problems and opportunities; and (3) a marketing strategy which includes marketing objectives and marketing mix decisions.

5. A market analysis is concerned with the organization's ability to identify marketing opportunities. Demand helps determine the organization's markets. A market segment is a group of individuals, groups, or organizations in a market that share similar characteristics that cause them to have similar wants or needs. Market segments can be identified as either the consumer market or industrial market. The consumer market consists of individuals who buy either for their own or their families' personal consumption. The industrial market is made up of individuals who buy for business, government, or institutional use mainly for the purpose of resale or re-exchange. Competition both within and between industries is keener today than ever. Part of the reason for this is the increasing strength of foreign marketers at home and abroad. Environment analysis involves examining the environment and identifying the circumstances and conditions that can cause the greatest problems or offer the greatest opportunities. The internal, or micro, environment is the most immediate and controllable environmental level. It is the level that contains factors that are outside the control of marketing manager but within the organization as a whole. Problems often arise when products or services are developed that may be good for some producers and consumers but may not be good for society as a whole. The operating environment consists of individuals and organizations outside the organization that help shape marketing plans and can, to a limited extent, be shaped by them. The general, or macro, environment includes the national and global conditions that affect the success or failure of marketing plans. The macro environment is the least subject to marketing control and is affected by social, political, regulatory, economic, or technological conditions.

6. The success of marketing plans often depends largely on the resources of an organization. Tangible resources include the physical plant, financial reserves, and raw materials. Differential advantage is the special edge over competition a company may have or develop. Intangible resources include a firm's public image with customers, stockholders, suppliers, and others. Distribution is also an important part of the marketing plan. Middlemen, or dealers, are needed to deliver the product from the consumer to industrial user. Their cooperation is of vital importance. Marketers should establish and maintain good relations with dealers. Marketers must also be conscious of the political and legal climate. Marketers today must take into account antitrust laws, antipollution laws, truth-in-lending laws, truth-in-advertising laws, and many other laws and regulations.

7. Once the market analysis is complete, the next element is to list the problems and opportunities that have been uncovered in the course of developing the preliminary phase of the plan.

8. The next element is to develop a strategy by which the various components of the marketing mix are employed to meet established goals. Marketing objectives include the need to determine the market segments to be targeted, sales volume, market share, and profit. A marketing plan should then take into consideration the components of the marketing mix--product, price, promotion, and placement--which should be carefully and thoroughly evaluated in order to achieve maximum results from the target market. The marketing manager should try to systematically blend or bring together all the elements into a workable plan. The rewards may be great for a job skillfully done.

LEARNING GOALS

After reading this chapter, you should be able to:

1. Describe who the marketing manager is and note the responsibilities associated with the position.
2. Discuss the marketing manager's basic tasks which often center around planning, implementing, and evaluating.
3. Discuss the importance of strategic marketing planning.
4. Describe challenges that the marketing manager often faces.
5. Define a mission and objectives.
6. Know the steps in creating a marketing plan and differentiate between a market analysis, problems and opportunities, marketing strategy, and marketing mix decisions.

KEY CONCEPTS

From the list of lettered terms, select the one that best fits in the blank of the numbered statements that follow. Write the letter of that choice in the space provided.

(Answers to the key concepts appear at the end of the chapter.)

a. Goals
b. A market segment
c. Strategic marketing planning
d. Marketing objectives
e. The general (macro) environment
f. Organizational objectives
g. An environment analysis
h. The marketing manager

i. Target markets
j. Marketing strategy
k. The consumer market
l. The operating environment
m. Differential advantage
n. The internal (micro) environment
o. The industrial market
p. A market

1. _____ is concerned with the examination of the environment and identification of the circumstances and conditions that can cause the greatest problems or offer the greatest opportunities.

2. _____ involves individuals who buy either for their own or for their family's personal consumption.

3. _____ are stated goals of the marketing department that specify quantitatively how marketing will contribute to meeting overall organizational objectives.

4. _____ are market segments that an organization designs its marketing mix around in order to reach because that segment is considered likely to demand the product being marketed.

5. _____ are organizational objectives that have been made specific with regard to size and time.

6. _____ refers to the special edge over competition an organization may have or develop by working with the elements of this marketing mix.

7. _____ for businesses are those individuals who are willing to buy a firm's output and have the purchasing power to do so; for non-profit firms, those who have an interest in a product and are willing to exchange something in return (whether monetary or non-monetary).

8. _____ is the process of establishing organization's goals, assessing its opportunities, and developing marketing objectives; results in marketing strategies.

9. _____ is the chief marketing executive who coordinates the work of the members of a marketing department.

10. _____ consists of the factors in an organization (such as financial resources and employees) capable of being influenced but not totally controlled by marketing managers.

11. _____ are the overall goals a firm pursues, such as increasing sales or maintaining a quality image.

12. _____ is a group of individuals, groups, or organizations in a market that share similar characteristics that cause them to have similar wants or needs.

13. _____ consists of purchasers who buy for business, government, or institutional use, mainly for the purpose of resale or re-exchange.

14. _____ consists of the economic, technological, legal, and social forces that are largely outside the control of marketers and that affect the success or failure of marketing plans.

15. _____ consists of individuals and organizations outside a firm (such as dealers and competitors) that help shape marketing plans and can, in turn, be shaped by them to some extent.

16. _____ consists of the concrete plans for achieving marketing objectives by using a specified marketing mix to reach a specified target market.

PROGRAMMED REVIEW

The following self-teaching exercises consist of short statements that require you to make a response by filling in the blank (or blanks) provided. You will find the correct response printed in the margin to the left of the question.

demand

1. Marketing managers are unique in that they direct their department's activities toward the goal of maintaining _____ for the firm's products.

a. the highly changeable nature of the market
b. geographical complexities of the market
c. people variables
d. the need to rely on people outside the firm
e. wide numbers of alternatives
f. marketing's influence on the success of the firm

2. While marketing managers share certain functions with other department heads, what are some of the challenges which are unique to the marketing manager's job?

a. _____
   _____
b. _____
   _____
c. _____
   _____
d. _____
   _____
e. _____
   _____
f. _____
   _____

marketing mix

3. A marketing strategy is a plan for achieving marketing objectives. It describes the _____ that the company will use to reach a selected part of the market.

22

departments

4.A marketing manager must know the problems and capabilities of the other
_____ in the
company.

a. sales volume
b. market share
c. profits

5.What are the three factors that marketing objectives generally include?

a. _____

b. _____

c. _____

a. planning
b. implementing
c. evaluating

6.What are the three basic tasks that
every marketing manager engages in?

a. _____

b. _____

c. _____

national
global

7.The general, or macro, environment level
includes the _____ and
_____ conditions that
affect the success or failure of marketing plans.

operating

8.The _____ environ-
ment consists of individuals and organizations outside the organization that
help shape marketing plans and can, to
a limited extent, be shaped by them.

coordinates

9.A marketing manager, or chief marketing
executive, is the person who
_____ the work of a
marketing department.

a. market analysis
b. problems and oppor-
tunities
c. marketing strategy

10.What are the three elements that are
generally included in most marketing
plans?

a. _____

b. _____

c. _____

characteristics

11. A market segment is a group of individuals, groups, or organizations in a market that share similar _____ that cause them to have similar wants and needs.

a. the physical plant
b. financial reserves
c. raw materials

12. What are the three tangible organizational resources contributing to marketing success?

a. _____
b. _____
c. _____

clearly
time limits

13. In determining marketing objectives, the marketing manager should state the objectives _____ and set _____ for them.

actual
forecasts

14. A sales analysis measures _____ sales against _____ of sales.

quantified

15. To be effective, marketing objectives should be _____.

a. establishing an organization's overall goals
b. assessing opportunities
c. developing marketing objectives

16. What are the three factors involved in strategic marketing planning?

a. _____
_____
b. _____
_____
c. _____
_____

personal

17. The consumer market consists of individuals who buy either for their own or their families' _____ consumption.

outside
within

ongoing
continuous

Intangible

Differential

a. demand
b. competition
c. environmental climate
d. resources of the firm
e. distribution factors
f. political and legal
   constraints

specific

resale
re-exchange

ensure
revises

18. The internal, or micro, environment con-
    tains factors that are _____
    the control of marketing managers but
    _____ the organization
    as a whole.

19. Marketing planning is an _____
    and _____ process.

20. _____ resources
    include a firm's public image with
    customers, stockholders, suppliers, and
    others.

21. _____ advantage
    is the special edge over competition
    that a company may have or develop.

22. What are six factors that help with an
    analysis of the market?

    a. _____

    b. _____

    c. _____

    d. _____

    e. _____

    f. _____

    _____

23. Goals are organizational objectives
    that have been made _____
    with regard to size and time.

24. The industrial market is made up of
    purchasers who buy for business, gov-
    ernment, or institutional use mainly
    for the purpose of _____ or
    _____.

25. Evaluating is the means by which a man-
    ager can _____ that the
    department is meeting its objectives,
    and that the department _____
    its plans if something goes wrong.

MARKETING RIDDLE

The purpose of this exercise is to find the missing word that solves the riddle. Each of the statements requires you to make a response by filling in the blank (or blanks) for the appropriate missing word. Each statement contains a key letter which, when combined with the other key letters, will provide you with the solution to the riddle. Correct solutions to the riddle questions can lead to valuable prizes. See instructions for more information.

Marketing goals and objectives are subordinate to those of the organization. They should be __ __ __ __ __ __ __ __ __ __ with
1 2 3 4 5 6 7 8 9 10
the latter and should contribute to their achievement.

1. Marketing goals specify what the marketing department intends to
__ __ ☐ __ __ __ __ __ __ __ through marketing activities.

2. One typical method of evaluation is the sales analysis, which measures actual sales against __ ☐ __ __ __ __ __ __ __ of sales.

3. __ __ ☐ __ __ __ is the one element on which much of the marketing plan hinges.

4. Few organizations know every ☐ __ __ __ __ __ __ __ __ customer's exact wants and needs.

5. To implement a plan is to put it into ☐ __ __ __ __ __.

6. A well-defined sense of mission is important, but it is not enough. The mission must be __ __ __ __ __ __ __ ☐ __ __ into specific objectives.

7. The marketing department can meet its objectives most efficiently by __ __ __ __ __ ☐ __ __ on the part of the total market most likely to want or need the company's products.

8. Some companies have made major marketing mistakes by ignoring their __ __ __ __ __ __ __ ☐ __ __ assets, such as company reputation.

9. Marketing managers cannot set __ __ __ ☐ __ __ __ __ __ objectives without knowledge of the market they want to serve.

10. To be effective, marketing objectives should be __ __ __ __ __ __ __ __ ☐ __.

EXPERIENTIAL EXERCISE

As indicated, a marketing plan is a written statement detailing time parameters for carrying out the marketing strategy. A market analysis is the section of the marketing plan which provides information and background regarding many factors.

Select a fast-food business (Burger King, McDonald's, etc.) that you believe to be marketing oriented and develop a realistic market analysis for the firm. Make whatever assumptions that you believe are necessary to support your views (library research and an interview with a store manager can be helpful).

Market Analysis

Demand (who are you going to serve?)

_____

_____

_____

_____

Competition (the number and types of)

_____

_____

_____

_____

Environmental Climate (internal, general, operating)

_____

_____

_____

_____

Resources of the Firm (tangible and intangible)

_____

_____

_____

_____

Distribution Factors (delivery of product)

_____

_____

_____

_____

Political and Legal Constraints (regulations and laws)

_____

_____

_____

_____

SELF-QUIZ

Multiple Choice

_____ 1. The environment that consists of individuals and organizations outside the firm that can help shape marketing plans and can, to a
limited extent, be shaped by them is known as the
a. environment.
b. general environment.
c. internal environment.
d. operating environment.

_____ 2. Probably the most important task of the marketing manager is to
a. implement.
b. plan.
c. evaluate.
d. control.

_____ 3. Groups of individuals who share qualities that make them the target
of a marketing effort are called
a. market segments.
b. consumer markets.
c. industrial markets.
d. people markets.

_____ 4. The first step in establishing plans is to
a. staff your organization.
b. evaluate your organization.
c. define the organization's mission and objectives.
d. select a sample.

_____ 5. The special edge over competition an organization may have, or
develop, by working with the elements of the marketing mix is known
as a
a. mission.
b. market segment.
c. differential advantage.
d. competitive edge.

6. Short-term market plans are usually
   a. 2 years.
   b. 5 years.
   c. a year or less.
   d. 3 years.

7. The section of the marketing plan which provides information and background regarding demand for an organization's product or service, competition, the environmental climate, etc., is known as
   a. a market analysis.
   b. a market survey.
   c. strategic planning.
   d. a mission.

8. The level that contains factors that are outside the control of marketing managers but within the organization as a whole is known as the
   a. marketing environment.
   b. macro environment.
   c. environmental analysis.
   d. micro environment.

9. A firm's resource that includes a firm's public image with customers, stockholders, suppliers, and others is known as
   a. intangible resources.
   b. differential advantage.
   c. public resources.
   d. tangible resources.

10. The marketing manager's task that is concerned with ensuring a department's objectives and revising plans if something goes wrong is called
    a. observing.
    b. evaluating.
    c. implementing.
    d. planning.

True-False

11. The general, or macro, environment is the level that includes the national and global conditions that affect the success or failure of marketing plans.

12. Strategic marketing planning typically takes a short-range view of an organization's objectives.

13. Organizational objectives specify goals for the organization to pursue as a whole.

14. Most businesses prefer oral marketing plans over written plans.

_____ 15. Competition both within and between industries is keener today than ever. Part of the reason for this is the increasing strength of foreign marketers at home and abroad.

_____ 16. Marketing planning should not be an ongoing, continuous process.

_____ 17. The consumer market is made up of individuals who buy for business, government, or institutional use.

_____ 18. Long-run plans generally run five years and beyond.

_____ 19. A mission is concerned with an organization's commitment to a business activity and its place in the market.

_____ 20. A market analysis is concerned with marketing objectives, target markets, and marketing mix decisions.

CHAPTER SOLUTIONS

Key Concepts

1. g	5. a	9. h	13. o
2. k	6. m	10. n	14. e
3. d	7. p	11. f	15. l
4. i	8. c	12. b	16. j

Self-Quiz

1. d	5. c	9. a	13. T	17. F
2. b	6. c	10. b	14. F	18. T
3. a	7. a	11. T	15. T	19. T
4. c	8. d	12. F	16. F	20. F

CHAPTER SUMMARY

1. Marketers must be conscious of those external environmental forces that can affect their decision-making abilities. The competitive, legal and political, social, economic, and technological environments represent a few of the most important areas of concern. Unlike the marketing mix variables, marketers cannot totally control the environment. Marketers have to recognize and adapt to the environmental issues as they carry out their mission.

2. Marketers realize that competition is part of our capitalistic society. There are four general categories of competitive markets. Pure competition occurs when products are uniform and there are many buyers and sellers. Because of this, there is little opportunity to influence price. The agriculture industry is an example of pure competition. Oligopoly exists when a few companies dominate an industry and have great control over the product's price. The automobile, cereal, ciga-rette, and steel industries operate under oligopolistic competition. Monopolistic competition describes a market in which there are many prod-ucts and many sellers and each firm tries to gain exclusive possession of a share of the market. Buyers perceive products as being diverse, so firms stress differential advantages such as product style, design, or technology. A monopoly exists when one company is the exclusive provider of a product or service. A pure monopoly is rare but can exist as a government monopoly, as a regulated monopoly, and temporarily as a private monopoly by holding a patent on a product. To be successful, a firm must be able not only to prepare marketing programs, but also to prepare itself as a sophisticated competitor. The firm must be able to select the type of competitive environment in which it wishes to operate.

3. Businesses are often restricted by the legal environment in which they must operate. The legal environment consists of laws and interpretations of laws that compel business to operate under competitive conditions and to observe various consumer rights. Procompetitive legislation is simply laws enacted to sustain and protect competition. The Sherman Act of 1890 prohibits contracts or conspiracies that would restrain trade and for-bids attempts at creating a monopoly. Subsequent laws have prohibited price fixing, bid rigging, and boycotts, as well as mergers within the same industry.

4. The enforcement of laws is affected by the prevailing political climate and by public opinion. Marketers must be constantly alert to subtle shifts in public and political attitudes toward business in general and their products in particular. In general, regulatory laws attempt to make the marketing process fairer to both buyers and sellers. The

Federal Trade Commission (FTC), established in 1914, was the first governmental body formed specifically to investigate cases of unfair competition. Besides the FTC, the Justice Department is the principal agency for handling antitrust matters. Antitrust laws provide for punishment of violators, restitution to injured competitors, and relief from further violations. To prevent further injury, the government may seek an injunction, or court order, to refrain from a practice. A consent decree, or voluntary agreement, reflects the company's decision to abide by the rules of business behavior. A dissolution, or divestiture decree, is an order to break up. Other federal regulatory agencies include the Food and Drug Administration, the Interstate Commerce Commission, the Consumer Product Safety Commission, the Civil Aeronautics Board, the Federal Communications Commission, the Environmental Protection Agency, and the Office of Consumer Affairs.

5. A marketer must also recognize the many constraints imposed by the political environment because it often affects legislation. When a new administration takes office, the power and influence of many agencies is often altered. This in turn can cause debates and discussions in such areas as consumerism, tax cuts, wage rates, unemployment, etc. A cost-benefit analysis is a system for weighing economic costs against economic benefits. Many interest groups often look after the rights of particular segments of the population. In addition, many industries have formed self-regulating bodies to oversee the activities of their members. The National Advertising Review Board (NARB) was founded in 1971 to monitor national advertising for truth and accuracy. The Direct Marketing Association (DMA) is made up of companies engaged in direct mail, telephone, and direct response broadcast marketing. The Council of Better Business Bureaus (CBBB) is an international association of national and local businesses whose goal is to ensure consumer confidence in the marketplace. This bureau, which is supported by local businesses, also tries to influence business conduct, and uses the media to inform the public of businesses in the community that use unethical business practices.

6. Marketers must evaluate the state of the social environment. The consumer movement developed and was fostered as a result of increased education and income in the 1960s, a greater complexity of products, and by the influence of writers and activists. Consumerism led to charges against business of deficiencies in product quality, lack of information, unfair pricing practices, and environmental pollution. Often product improvements were trivial, but manufacturers promoted them as major changes. Other products were unsafe or nutritionally deficient. In response to such complaints the Consumer Product Safety Commission (CPSC) was established with the power to order the recall, repair, or replacement of any product thought to be a risk to the consumer and to set safety standards for industry groups to meet. Recall is the power of certain federal agencies to require manufacturers to notify customers that a product may be hazardous and may be exchanged or repaired. Often

consumers complained about what appeared to be a lack of information in such areas as product labels that presented incomplete information and pictorials that exaggerated product quality. The FTC now requires marketers to provide documentation to support advertising claims and to run corrective ads when false claims are made. Consumers questioned prices that were higher as a result of excessive marketing expenditures and that marketing activities gave firms the power to increase prices and make excessive profits. Consumers also believed that middlemen would add to the cost of distribution and ultimately raised prices without providing anything in return. As a result of unfair pricing practices, Congress enacted the Equal Credit Opportunity Act and the truth-in-lending law in an attempt to protect consumers against credit abuses. Consumers believed that many manufacturers would create interest in products that polluted the environment. Today, the Environmental Protection Agency (EPA) has been given the power to enforce federal anti-pollution laws. The agency was established and assigned the responsibility to set up environmental standards, sue polluters, and impose fines on those who delay pollution control orders. In addition, various special interest groups were formed to inform the public of consumer issues and to exert pressure on business and government. Other social areas of concern to the marketer include the changing U.S. household, geographic changes, and the state of transition in our culture and ethnicity.

7. Businesses must accept social responsibility for their actions. Social responsibility refers to the moral obligation of businesses to consider the effects of their decisions on society and to accomplish social benefits. Managers must consider the effects of their decisions on the external world so as to accomplish social benefits as well as traditional economic ones. The degree to which businesses should become socially responsive will probably be debated for a long time to come. On the other hand, consumers should be knowledgeable and aware of their rights. Consumer's responsibility refers to the buyers' obligation to know their rights and to make informed judgments.

8. Our economy goes through business cycles which reflect economic growth over time. Prosperity is a period of generally high income, employment, and business growth. Recession is a phase of decreasing income, employment, and growth rate. Depression is a radical drop in business activity and consequent high unemployment and business failure. Recovery is an upswing characterized by a gradual rise in business and consumer economic well-being. A firm's marketing effort changes depending on the current stage of the business cycle. To determine the rate of economic growth in a region's or country's economy, economists turn to the GNP. The gross national product is the total dollar volume of goods and services produced in a country in any one year.

    Marketers must pay close attention to the amount of consumer spending. Disposable income consists of the amount of money remaining after taxes. Discretionary income consists of any money left over from disposable income that a family or individual is free to spend for luxuries or to save. How consumers spend their money is obviously very important to the marketer. He must continuously be prepared to change in relation to the economic climate.

9. _Technology_ applies science to the solution of practical problems. Technology is concerned with the development and use of products, machinery, and processes. Businesses must be aware of advancements in such areas as medicine, communication computers, electronics, and transportation. Developments in technology can have significant marketing implications because they can drastically alter industries.

LEARNING GOALS

After reading this chapter, you should be able to:

1. Determine the need for information about the competitive, legal and political, social, economic, and technological environments.
2. Discuss the competitive environment including the ability to differentiate between pure competition, oligopoly, monopolistic competition, and monopoly.
3. Define the legal environment and its ability to protect business and consumer rights.
4. Describe federal legislation designed to protect competition.
5. Describe federal regulatory agencies that have been designed to oversee specific industries.
6. Describe how industries regulate themselves.
7. Discuss the social environment and describe consumer dissatisfaction as it relates to deficiencies in product quality, lack of information, unfair pricing practices, and environmental pollution.
8. Describe various acts designed to protect consumers against misbranding and false or harmful advertising.
9. Discuss the importance of special interest consumer groups and the need for businesses to accept social responsibility for their actions.
10. Discuss the economic environment and describe economic cycles including the ability to differentiate between prosperity, recession, depression, and recovery.
11. Discuss the technological environment and how marketers can respond to its change.

KEY CONCEPTS

From the list of lettered terms, select the one that best fits in the blank of the numbered statements that follow. Write the letter of that choice in the space provided.

(Answers to the key concepts appear at the end of the chapter.)

a. Pure competition
b. Consumer responsibility
c. Recall
d. A depression
e. Technology
f. Procompetitive legislation
g. Social responsibility
h. Recovery
i. Discretionary income

j. Monopolistic competition
k. The legal environment
l. Social environment
m. A monopoly
n. Cost-benefit analysis
o. An oligopoly
p. Prosperity
q. Disposable income
r. A recession

1. _____ reflects the climate of public opinion that affects marketers' practices.

2. _____ refers to any money remaining from disposable income that a family or individual is free to spend for luxuries or save.

3. _____ is the phase of the business cycle characterized by a radical drop in business activity and consequent high unemployment and business failure.

4. _____ refers to the power of certain federal agencies to require manufacturers to notify customers that a product may be hazardous and may be exchanged or repaired.

5. _____ is the moral obligation of businesses to consider the effects of their decisions on society and to accomplish social benefits.

6. _____ refers to the buyers' obligation to know their rights and to make informed judgments.

7. _____ is a situation in which there are many sellers in a market who rarely engage in price competition but compete by trying to establish brand preferences among consumers.

8. _____ refers to laws that sustain and protect competition.

9. _____ is a situation in which one company is the exclusive provider of a product or service.

10. _____ is an upswing in the business cycle characterized by a gradual rise in business and consumer economic well-being.

11. _____ refers to any money that remains after taxes are paid and that is spent for necessities.

12. _____ is a situation in which there are many sellers, no seller dominates a market, and the products sold are interchangeable.

35

13. _____ refers to laws that compel businesses to operate under competitive conditions and to observe specified consumer rights.

14. _____ is the application of principles of science to the solution of practical problems.

15. _____ is a situation in which a few firms dominate the market, set similar prices, and make entry by other firms difficult.

16. _____ is a system for weighing economic costs against economic benefits.

17. _____ is a period in business cycle of generally high income, employment, and business growth.

18. _____ is a phase of the business cycle characterized by decreasing income, employment, and growth rate.

PROGRAMMED REVIEW

The following self-teaching exercises consist of short statements that require you to make a response by filling in the blank (or blanks) provided. You will find the correct response printed in the margin to the left of the question.

agriculture

1. An example of pure competition is the _____ industry.

a. increased education and income
b. greater complexity of products
c. writers and activists who drew national attention to environmental and consumer issues

2. What were three major causes in the rise of consumerism during the 1960s?

   a. _____
   _____

   b. _____
   _____

   c. _____
   _____
   _____

Environmental Protection Agency

3. The power to enforce anti-pollution laws is vested in the _____ _____.

a. pure competition
b. oligopoly
c. monopolistic competition
d. monopoly

4. What are the four general categories that competitive markets fall into?

a. _____

b. _____

c. _____

d. _____

Direct Marketing

5. The _____ Association is made up of companies engaged in direct mail, telephone, and direct response broadcast marketing.

a. prosperity
b. recession
c. depression
d. recovery

6. What are the four phases of an economic cycle?

a. _____

b. _____

c. _____

d. _____

the Federal Trade Commission

7. The first governmental body formed specifically to investigate cases of unfair competition was _____ _____.

a. deficiencies in product quality
b. lack of information
c. unfair pricing practices
d. environmental pollution

8. In the 1960s consumers voiced dissatisfaction about

a. _____ _____

b. _____

c. _____

d. _____

the Food and Drug Administration

9. The governmental agency which controls the product development, manufacturing, branding, labeling, and advertising of food and drugs is called _____ _____.

Political
economic

10. _____ and
    _____ thinking
    in the United States assumes that the
    economy benefits from competition
    among many firms.

competition

11. The type of _____
    a company faces will dramatically
    affect its marketing strategy.

a. the way a product is
   designed and manufac-
   tured
b. the design of and information on the product's
   packaging
c. the information in the
   advertising for the
   product
d. the price at which the
   product is sold

12. Congress has established several fed-
    eral regulatory agencies in an attempt
    to oversee

    a. _____
       _____
       _____
       _____
    b. _____
       _____
       _____
       _____
    c. _____
       _____
       _____
    d. _____
       _____
       _____

the Justice Department

13. Besides the Federal Trade Commission,

    _____
    is the principal agency for handling
    antitrust matters.

price
service

14. In providing product quality, marketers
    have had to face the challenge of try-
    ing to balance _____ and
    _____ to find a
    satisfactory mix.

a. an injunction
b. a consent decree
c. a dissolution

little
basically

a. products are uniform
b. there are many buyers
    and sellers

documentation
corrective

few

a. as a government
    monopoly
b. as a private regu-
    lated monopoly
c. temporarily as a pri-
    vate monopoly by holding
    a patent on a product

15. In an attempt to control business activ-
    ity, antitrust laws allowed the govern-
    ment to seek

    a. _____

    b. _____

    c. _____

16. In the case of pure competition, a com-
    pany typically invests _____
    in the market, because consumers view
    one company's products as being
    _____ the same as
    another's.

17. What are the conditions that character-
    ize pure competition?

    a. _____

    b. _____

    _____

18. The Federal Trade Commission requires
    marketers to provide _____
    to support advertising claims and to
    run _____ ads
    when false claims are made.

19. In an oligopoly we find a _____
    companies dominating an industry.

20. What are the three ways that a pure
    monopoly can exist?

    a. _____

    _____

    b. _____

    _____

    c. _____

    _____

    _____

self-regulating

21. Many industries have formed
_____ bodies
to oversee the activities of their
members.

difference

22. Under monopolistic competition, the
role of marketing is to establish a
brand _____ in
customers' minds.

the Sherman Act

23. The Act, passed in 1890, that prohibited contracts or conspiracies that
would restrain trade and forbid attempts
to create a monopoly was known as

_____.

a. to order the recall,
    or replacement, of
    any product thought
    to be a risk to the
    consumer
b. to set safety standards
    for industry groups to
    meet

24. What are the two primary powers of the
Consumer Product Safety Commission as
established in 1972?

a. _____
_____
_____
_____

b. _____
_____
_____

Council of Better Business
Bureaus (CBBB)

25. The _____
_____ is an
international association of national
and local businesses whose goal is to
ensure consumer confidence in the marketplace.

MARKETING RIDDLE

The purpose of this exercise is to find the missing word that solves the
riddle. Each of the statements requires you to make a response by filling in
the blank (or blanks) for the appropriate missing word. Each statement contains a key letter which, when combined with the other key letters, will provide you with the solution to the riddle. Correct solutions to the riddle
questions can lead to valuable prizes. See instructions for more information.

Marketing activities are influenced by major changes and trends in the economy. It is important that marketers understand significant economic developments and assess correctly their likely __ __ __ __ __ __ __ on their businesses.
‾1‾ ‾2‾ ‾3‾ ‾4‾ ‾5‾ ‾6‾

1. Under monopolistic competition, companies look for a __ __ __ __ __ __ __ __ __ ☐ __ __ advantage.

2. Because of pollution control laws, a company may find that it is more expensive to pollute than to __ __ ☐ __ __ __ with the law.

3. Consumers are concerned about the quality of the goods they buy and the quality of the services that __ __ __ __ __ ☐ __ __ __ those goods.

4. It might seem that price is one element of the marketing mix that has to be __ __ __ ☐ __ to buyers.

5. In light of the ☐ __ __ __ __ __ __ __ __ __ __ of modern products, consumers need information to make intelligent decisions.

6. The National Advertising Review Board (NARB) was founded in 1971 to monitor national advertising for ☐ __ __ __ __ and accuracy.

EXPERIENTIAL EXERCISE

Technological changes have a great impact on people's everyday lives. Technology affects our life-style and standard of living. The challenge to marketing will be to keep abreast of these changes and to carefully consider their long-range effects on our quality of life.

The purpose of this exercise is to assist you in determining some of the technological forces and their effects on market decisions and activities. In each of the forces listed below, describe what changes you foresee and what decisions a marketer should consider in relation to long-range potential.

1. Communication

_____

_____

_____

_____

2. Transportation

_____
_____
_____
_____

3. Computers

_____
_____
_____
_____

4. Energy

_____
_____
_____
_____

5. Medicine

_____
_____
_____
_____

SELF-QUIZ

Multiple Choice

_____ 1. A method of competition that exists when a few companies dominate
            the industry is known as
            a. a monopoly.
            b. monopolistic competition.
            c. pure competition.
            d. an oligopoly.

_____ 2. The law that prohibits contracts or conspiracies that would restrain trade and forbids attempts at monopolization is the
a. Clayton Act.
b. Wheeler-Lea Act.
c. Sherman Act.
d. Fair Packaging and Label Act.

_____ 3. The organization that is an international association of national and local businesses whose goal is to ensure consumer confidence in the marketplace is known as the
a. Direct Marketing Association.
b. Consumer Product Safety Commission.
c. Council of Better Business Bureaus.
d. Environmental Protection Agency.

_____ 4. Which of the following was established primarily to protect consumers, as contrasted to regulating competition?
a. Food and Drug Administration
b. Sherman Antitrust Act
c. Clayton Act
d. Wheeler-Lea Act

_____ 5. The first governmental body formed specifically to investigate cases of unfair competition was the
a. Wheeler-Lea Act.
b. Food and Drug Administration.
c. Interstate Commerce Commission.
d. Federal Trade Commission.

_____ 6. All of the following are examples of the changing social environment except
a. the increasing number of women in the work force.
b. the rate of inflation and rising interest rate.
c. the interest in conserving energy.
d. the desire to reduce gasoline consumption.

_____ 7. Which of the following businesses is most likely to prosper during good economic conditions?
a. shoe repair
b. self-service auto repair centers
c. nightclubs
d. door-to-door sales

_____ 8. The phase of the business cycle whereby we find decreasing income, employment, and growth rate is known as
a. a recession.
b. a depression.
c. a recovery.
d. prosperity.

_____ 9. A voluntary agreement by a company to abide by the rules of business behavior is known as
   a. a consent decree.
   b. an injunction.
   c. a dissolution.
   d. a cost-benefit analysis.

_____ 10. The competitive market that occurs when each firm tries to gain exclusive possession of a share of the market is known as
   a. a monopoly.
   b. monopolistic competition.
   c. pure competition.
   d. an oligopoly.

True-False

_____ 11. The agricultural sector is a very good example of pure competition.

_____ 12. A system for weighing economic costs against economic benefits is known as cost-benefit analysis.

_____ 13. Discretionary income reflects income that remains after taxes and is spent for necessities.

_____ 14. Social responsibilities reflect the moral obligation of businesses to consider the effects of their decisions and to accomplish social benefits as well as traditional economic ones.

_____ 15. A dissolution occurs when a court order provides for a company to refrain from a practice.

_____ 16. Changing political currents and their effects on regulation have no profound consequences for market decision making.

_____ 17. The Interstate Commerce Commission sets safety standards for products and imposes penalties for failure to meet the standards.

_____ 18. In recent years we have seen the Reagan administration emphasize deregulation of industries.

_____ 19. Rachel Carson and Ralph Nader drew national attention to environmental and consumer issues.

_____ 20. The Equal Credit Opportunity Act requires lenders to disclose the annual percentage rate of interest they charge.

CHAPTER SOLUTIONS

Key Concepts

1. l	5. g	9. m	13. k	17. p
2. i	6. b	10. h	14. e	18. r
3. d	7. j	11. q	15. o	
4. c	8. f	12. a	16. n	

Self-Quiz

1. d	5. d	9. a	13. F	17. F
2. c	6. b	10. b	14. T	18. T
3. c	7. c	11. T	15. F	19. T
4. a	8. a	12. T	16. F	20. F

CHAPTER 4
MARKET SEGMENTATION AND SALES FORECASTING

CHAPTER SUMMARY

1. The world is too large and filled with many different people and organizations for any single marketing mix to satisfy the needs of everyone. Before targeting a market, a marketing manager must first determine what, if any, factors can distinguish groups from the overall market. The first important decision that must be made is whether or not to target a market. In mass marketing all the customers in a particular market are thought of as having the same, or homogeneous, needs. Those needs are easily satisfied by a single product and a single marketing program or mix. Mass marketing works as long as customers demand no variety. Firms that mass market do so for one reason--to save money.

2. Target marketing refers to the practice of dividing the market into segments and devising a marketing mix to appeal to one or more targeted market segments. Target marketing stresses the fact that a marketing mix is tailored to fit some specific or narrow target customer unlike mass marketing which aims at everyone with the same marketing mix. The chief drawback of target marketing is that it raises costs. This occurs because various advertising campaigns have to be created, different sales specialists hired, and pricing structures established. The main advantage of target marketing is that it usually results in more sales than mass marketing.

3. After one studies the basis for target marketing, it becomes evident that identifying effective market segments can be difficult. The four primary ways a marketer can segment a consumer market are (1) by demographic factors, (2) by rate of product usage, (3) by perceived product benefits, and (4) by life-style, or psychographic, characteristics. Demographic segmentation groups customers on the basis of geographic proximity or some shared socioeconomic trait. The theory behind demographic segmentation is that customers who live in the same locale or belong to the same age, income, or other grouping have common needs and will buy similar products. Demographic segmentation is the most commonly used method of subdividing target markets. Usage-rate segmentation takes into account variations in demand among different groups and divides the market into heavy, light, and nonusers. Benefit segmentation seeks to identify the benefits people seek in a product as a basis for grouping them together. By determining the benefits that people want, marketers are able to divide people into groups that seek certain benefits. Once the benefits are known, it is often possible to develop the necessary

goods or services to reach the respective targets. Psychographic segmentation seeks to divide the market according to people's life-styles, or distinct approaches to living. The concept of life-styles refers to a person's pattern of living in the world as expressed in his or her activities, interests, and opinions. Marketers often administer lengthy questionnaires in their attempt to determine why consumers act and behave as they do. An understanding of life-styles can provide a marketer with information about how people live, their everyday facets of life, their beliefs about themselves, needs, motives, and how they spend their time. The psychographic method is expensive, and the problems in the areas of misinterpretation, cost, and standardization of procedures will first have to be resolved before the true effectiveness of psychographic segmentation can be totally recognized.

4. In the industrial market, the most common methods of segmentation are customer location, type of industry, company size, and end use of product. Companies seeking to market their products should concentrate their efforts in those geographic locations where several key customers can be found. Manufacturers and other related industries are often clustered in just a few locations in a given area. The marketer is also interested in the type of industries that can be serviced. The Standard Industrial Classification Code is a numbering system for categorizing business by economic activities and provides marketers with the opportunity to distinguish among the ten major industry groups as recognized by the government. A marketer may want to further segment the market on the basis of the size of possible customers. Industrial products may be used many different ways; thus, the marketer may want to segment a market by the way the product will be ultimately used. After a marketer has divided the market into segments, the next step is to decide which segments to target. Often the decision rests on whether to target a single market segment or appeal to several segments.

5. Concentrated marketing requires an organization to focus all its efforts on one segment with a single marketing mix. The advantage of concentrated marketing is that is allows a firm to know and understand its market well, and then be able to meet its specialized needs in a way that would not be possible with a more diversified strategy. In differentiated marketing an organization markets to many segments, each with a different marketing mix. A policy of differentiated marketing allows a firm to pull out of a segment that proves unprofitable and to rely on other segments. There are three questions that a marketer should consider in deciding how many segments to pursue. The first is concerned with the financial position of the firm. The second is concerned with competition, and the third relates to whether the market is new to the firm. A segment is a good candidate for target marketing if the market is identifiable, a market segment is accessible, and the market segment is large enough to be profitable.

6. The strategy of target marketing can succeed only if there is sufficient demand in the segment or segments under consideration to justify a

marketing program. <u>Forecasting</u> is the act of predicting demand in the marketplace over a given period of time. Forecasts may be short, medium, or long range. <u>Market potential</u> refers to the total of all sales that might be generated in a market segment. <u>Sales forecast</u> refers only to the prediction of actual sales a company can expect to make in a certain market or segment.

The economic, industry, and sales forecasts represent three important forecast types that a marketer should be familiar with. <u>Economic forecasts</u> can detect how changes in the national and international business climate will affect specific industries. The indicators (gross national product and the unemployment rate) needed to make an economic forecast are compiled by the government and reported in two government publications, the Survey of Current Business and the Federal Reserve Bulletin. An <u>industry forecast</u> is the prediction of likely sales for a class of products. Industry sales are affected by the amount of industry-wide marketing activity and the prevailing social and legal climate. In determining a <u>company sales forecast</u>, a marketer is interested in the company's <u>market share</u>, which refers to the percentage of the total industry sales that a particular firm can claim. A company's share of market demand is directly related to its marketing effort. The hardest part of sales forecasting is determining expected market share.

7. The key to any successful market plan is the ability to measure and forecast market demand. The methods for estimating demand can be simple or elaborate. All survey techniques estimate demand by relying on soliciting the opinions of some of the people involved in the marketing process. An <u>executive-panel survey</u> is often used when funds are limited or when a new product is being introduced. In a <u>sales-force survey</u> a company asks its salespeople to estimate sales in their territories in the upcoming year. <u>Customer sampling</u> is a survey of consumers' intentions to buy and can provide useful information regarding the strength of market demand.

8. Statistical methods, which make use of past data, attempt to take some of the guesswork out of demand estimation. <u>Time-series projections</u> uncover patterns of movement in past sales and project these patterns into the future. At least five years of past sales data is usually required for predictions of any accuracy. <u>Correlation analysis</u> is used to find factors that change in advance of changes in product demand. In <u>test marketing</u> a product is sold in a limited area chosen as a representative of the entire market. If the product does well in the test market, the company may then consider expanding its test in other representative cities or introduce the product to all. Accurate information is critical for marketing decision making. No organization can successfully operate without detailed information. Many companies use two or more survey techniques as a check on accuracy.

LEARNING GOALS

After reading this chapter, you should be able to:

1. Define mass marketing and target marketing.
2. Describe consumer market segmentation and differentiate between demographic factors, by rate of product usage, by perceived product benefits,
   and by psychographic or life-style characteristics.
3. Describe industrial market segmentation and differentiate between customer location, industry type, customer size, and end use of product
   characteristics.
4. Discuss the difference between concentrated marketing and differentiated
   marketing.
5. Describe the general criteria that should be used in determining a good
   candidate for target marketing.
6. Define forecasting and differentiate between economic, industry, and
   sales forecasts.
7. Discuss the techniques of demand estimation including the difference
   between the executive-panel survey, the sales-force survey, and customer
   sampling.
8. Discuss the importance of statistical methods as tools in forecasting
   and differentiate between time-series projections, correlation analysis,
   and market tests.

KEY CONCEPTS

From the list of lettered terms, select the one that best fits in the blank
of the numbered statements that follow. Write the letter of that choice in
the space provided.

(Answers to the key concepts appear at the end of the chapter.)

a. The executive-panel survey
b. Demographic segmentation
c. Target marketing
d. Benefit segmentation
e. A sales forecast
f. Forecasting
g. An industry forecast
h. Time-series projection
i. A correlation analysis
j. Customer sampling
k. The Standard Industrial Classification (SIC) Code
l. Mass marketing
m. Differentiated marketing
n. Usage-rate segmentation
o. An economic forecast
p. Test marketing
q. A market share

r. Psychographic segmentation
s. Concentrated marketing
t. Market potential
u. A sales-force survey
v. Life-style

1. _____ refers to the prediction of likely sales for a class of products.

2. _____ is the numbering system followed by the U.S. government for categorizing businesses by economic activity.

3. _____ refers to the prediction of how the economy will fare as a whole in light of changes in the national and international business climate.

4. _____ is the statistical method of forecasting used to find factors that change in advance of changes in product demand.

5. _____ reflects the percentage of total industry sales that a particular firm can claim.

6. _____ is the means for sales forecasting using opinions of company officials.

7. _____ is the prediction of actual sales a company can expect to make in a certain market or segment.

8. _____ refers to the practice of dividing the market into segments and devising a marketing mix to appeal to one or more targeted market segments.

9. _____ refers to the practice of marketing to many market segments, each with a different marketing mix.

10. _____ reflects total of all sales that might be generated in a market segment.

11. _____ refers to trial marketing in a limited area chosen as representative of an entire market.

12. _____ is predicting demand in the marketplace over a given period of time.

13. _____ reflects the division of a market into classes on the basis of geographic proximity or some shared socioeconomic trait.

14. _____ is a person's pattern of living expressed in activities, interests, and opinions.

15. _____ refers to the practice of dividing the market into market segments and selecting only one segment to serve with a marketing mix.

16. _____ is a statistical method for forecasting sales based on past patterns projected into the future.

17. _____ reflects division of the market into classes on the basis of the life-styles of members.

18. _____ is a survey conducted to sample customers' intentions to buy.

19. _____ reflects the division of a market into classes on the basis of benefits that members of each class seek.

20. _____ is the practice of directing the marketing mix at all potential buyers rather than a particular subgroup.

21. _____ is the means for sales forecasting using opinions of company officials.

22. _____ reflects the division of a market into classes on the basis of the rate at which members buy and use products.

PROGRAMMED REVIEW

The following self-teaching exercises consist of short statements that require you to make a response by filling in the blank (or blanks) provided. You will find the correct response printed in the margin to the left of the question.

a. A market segment must be identifiable.
b. A market segment must be accessible.
c. A market segment must be large enough to be profitable.

1. What are the three criteria necessary for effective market segmentation?

   a. _____
      _____

   b. _____
      _____

   c. _____
      _____
      _____

money

2. Firms who opt for the mass marketing approach do so because it saves _____.

51

heavy
light
nonusers

one
single

divides
different or heterogeneous

a. economic
b. industry
c. sales

a. customer location
b. type of industry
c. company size
d. end use of product

percentage

a. by demographic factors
b. by rate of product
    usage
c. by perceived product
    benefits
d. by psychographic, or
    life-style, character-
    istics

3. Usage-rate segmentation takes into
    account variations in demand among dif-
    ferent groups and divides the market into
    _____, _____,
    and _____.

4. Concentrated marketing occurs when an
    organization focuses all its efforts on
    _____ segment with a _____
    marketing mix.

5. Target marketing occurs when a company
    _____ the market into
    groups of customers with
    _____
    needs.

6. What are three types of forecasts com-
    monly used by marketers?

    a. _____

    b. _____

    c. _____

7. What are the four most common ways of
    segmenting an industrial market?

    a. _____

    b. _____

    c. _____

    d. _____

8. Market share is the _____
    of the total industry sales that a par-
    ticular firm can claim.

9. What are the four primary ways a marketer
    can segment a market?

    a. _____

    b. _____

    c. _____

    d. _____

        _____

52

many
different

advance

funds
new product

a. the amount of industry-
   wide activity
b. the prevailing social
   and legal climate

market share
new product

mass marketing

a. What is the financial
   condition of the
   firm?
b. What is the competition
   doing?
c. Is the market new to
   the firm?

10. Differentiated marketing occurs when an
    organization markets too _____
    segments, each with a _____
    marketing mix.

11. Correlation analysis is used to find
    factors that change in _____
    of changes in product demand.

12. An executive-panel survey is often used
    when _____ are limited
    or when a _____
    is being introduced.

13. In addition to the economic climate,
    what two factors affect industry sales?

    a. _____

       _____

    b. _____

       _____

14. The hardest part of sales forecasting
    is determining expected _____
    _____. This
    is especially difficult when the fore-
    cast is for a _____
    with no track record.

15. The main advantage of target marketing
    is that it usually results in more
    sales than _____.

16. What are three questions relevant to
    deciding how many market segments to
    pursue?

    a. _____

       _____

    b. _____

       _____

    c. _____

       _____

grouping

a. executive-panel survey
b. sales-force survey
c. customer sampling

why

a. the Gross National
   Product (GNP)
b. the unemployment rate

statistical
ideally

a. time-series projection
b. correlation analysis
c. market tests

past
projects

17. Benefit segmentation seeks to identify
    the benefits people seek in a product
    as a basis for _____
    them together.

18. What are three survey techniques used
    by marketers in an attempt to estimate
    demand?

    a. _____

    b. _____

    c. _____

19. The basic question left unanswered by
    demographic and usage-rate segmentation
    is _____ consumers purchase what
    they do.

20. What are the two most widely used eco-
    nomic indicators?

    a. _____

    b. _____

21. Often researchers must apply sophisti-
    cated _____ tools
    to distinguish between the benefits
    people see in marketed products and the
    benefits they would _____
    like to see.

22. What are three statistical methods used
    by marketers in an attempt to estimate
    demand?

    a. _____

    b. _____

    c. _____

23. Time-series projection uncovers patterns
    of movement in _____ sales
    and _____ these pat-
    terns in the future.

54

geographic
socioeconomic

24. Demographic segmentation groups customers on the basis of _____
proximity or some shared
_____ trait.

national
international

25. An economic forecast detects how
changes in the _____
and _____
business climate will affect specific
industries.

MARKETING RIDDLE

The purpose of this exercise is to find the missing word that solves the
riddle. Each of the statements requires you to make a response by filling in
the blank (or blanks) for the appropriate missing word. Each statement contains a key letter which, when combined with the other key letters, will provide you with the solution to the riddle. Correct solutions to the riddle
questions can lead to valuable prizes. See instructions for more information.

      Once firms have decided upon a segmentation strategy, specific
      information must be gathered to define the different types of
      customers for which __ __ __ __ __ __ marketing programs will be
                                       1 2 3 4 5 6
      prepared.

1. ☐ __ __ __ __ __ __ __ __ segmentation takes into account variations in
demand among different groups and divides the market into heavy, light,
and nonusers.

2. The SIC code is a ☐ __ __ __ __ __ __ __ __ __ system for categorizing
businesses by economic activity.

3. Rarely do marketers use only one socioeconomic factor to segment the market, because many __ __ __ ☐ __ __ __ __ __ can be found.

4. The market for many products is divided up ☐ __ __ __ __ naturally by
the benefits people see.

5. The increased acceptance of the marketing concept has resulted in the
rapid adoption of target marketing as the most productive strategy for
most companies to __ __ __ __ ☐ __.

6. The advantage of concentrated marketing is that it allows a firm to
thoroughly know and understand its market and thus to meet its specialized
needs in a way that would not be possible with a more
__ __ __ ☐ __ __ __ __ __ __ __.

EXPERIENTIAL EXERCISE

Market segmentation provides the industrial marketer with the opportunity of subdividing the market into various groups. In this way a group could be selected as a target market and be reached with a specific marketing mix.

If you were a supplier of automobile tires, describe what information you would need to successfully reach your target market taking into consideration the four common methods of industrial segmentation. Also describe where you would go to find this information.

1. Customer Location

_____

_____

_____

_____

_____

2. Type of Industry

_____

_____

_____

_____

_____

3. Company Size

_____

_____

_____

_____

_____

4. Product Application

_____

_____

_____

_____

_____

Multiple Choice

_____ 1. Which method segmentation is still in its infancy and needs further testing before it becomes more readily accepted?
a. demographic
b. rate of product usage
c. perceived product benefits
d. life-style, or psychographic

_____ 2. Which one of the following is not a common way of segmenting an industrial market?
a. customer location
b. type of industry
c. life-style
d. company size

_____ 3. A method that uncovers patterns of movement in past sales and projects these patterns into the future is known as
a. customer sampling.
b. correlation analysis.
c. test marketing.
d. time-series projection.

_____ 4. Which of the following is a government tool used by the industrial marketer?
a. the sales and marketing survey of industrial purchasing power
b. the directory of business
c. Standard and Poors Register
d. the Standard Industrial Classification Code

_____ 5. Which method of segmentation takes into account variation in demand among different groups and divides the market into heavy, light, and nonusers?
a. demographic
b. rate of product usage
c. perceived product benefits
d. life-style, or psychographic, characteristics

_____ 6. The forecasting method that attempts to predict the likely sales for a class of products is known as
a. industry forecasting.
b. economic forecasting.
c. sales forecasting.
d. company forecasting.

_____ 7. What is the term often used when all of the customers in a particular market are thought of as having the same, or homogeneous, needs?
a. forecasting
b. segmentation
c. survey techniques
d. mass marketing

_____ 8. By which one of the four primary ways of segmenting the consumer market can we find information more easily obtainable?
a. by demographic factors
b. by rate of product usage
c. by perceived product benefits
d. by life-style, or psychographic, characteristics

_____ 9. Which survey technique is often used when funds are limited or when a new product is being introduced?
a. a sales-force survey
b. an executive-panel survey
c. customer sampling
d. a company sales survey

_____ 10. Which statistical method is used to find factors that change in advance of changes in product demand?
a. a correlation analysis
b. time-series projection
c. test marketing
d. customer sampling

True-False

_____ 11. Differentiated marketing occurs when an organization focuses all its efforts on one segment with a single marketing mix.

_____ 12. Advocates of psychographic segmentation focus on potential consumers' life-styles and personality traits.

_____ 13. The Standard Industrial Classification Code is a government numbering system to categorize business by economic activity.

_____ 14. Demographic segmentation takes into account variations in demand among different groups and divides the market into heavy, light, and nonusers.

_____ 15. Forecasting is the act of predicting demand in the marketplace over a given period of time.

_____ 16. A marketing manager who must predict the sales of his or her own company's products must anticipate how the marketing activities of other companies may influence total demand.

_____ 17. An executive-panel survey is one in which a company asks its salespeople to estimate sales in their territories in the upcoming year.

_____ 18. Benefit segmentation seeks to identify the benefits people seek in a product as a basis for grouping them together.

_____ 19. A person's life-style groups customers on the basis of geographic proximity or some shared socioeconomic trait.

_____ 20. Market potential refers only to the prediction of actual sales a company can expect to make in a certain market or segment.

CHAPTER SOLUTIONS

Key Concepts

1. g	6. a	11. p	16. h	21. u
2. k	7. e	12. f	17. r	22. n
3. o	8. c	13. b	18. j	
4. i	9. m	14. v	19. d	
5. q	10. t	15. s	20. l	

Self-Quiz

1. d	5. b	9. b	13. T	17. F
2. c	6. a	10. a	14. F	18. T
3. d	7. d	11. F	15. T	19. F
4. d	8. a	12. T	16. T	20. F

CHAPTER SUMMARY

1. Identifying and collecting market information is an increasingly vital
    aspect of the total marketing function. Marketers need accurate and
    timely data in order to keep abreast of day-to-day operations and to
    gather facts on which to base important nonroutine decisions. Two sources
    of information often used in planning long-range and short-term goals
    are marketing information systems and marketing research. A market
    information system (MIS) is an orderly procedure for the regular col-
    lection of raw data, both internally and externally, and the conversion
    of that data into information for use in making marketing decisions.
    A useful marketing information system meets three criteria by providing
    data that are collected regularly, collecting the data from both inside
    and outside the organization, and converting the data into useful infor-
    mation. Market research involves collecting data in order to solve a
    particular marketing problem or take advantage of a particular oppor-
    tunity. Market research differs from an MIS in that researchers collect
    data once, the data collected are pertinent to a single problem or sit-
    uation, and much of the data must come from outside the firm.

2. The three reasons why marketers need more formal systems for gathering
    information include the movement from local to national marketing, from
    buyer needs to buyer wants, and from price to nonprice competition. A
    good market information system is often considered the nerve center of
    a company. Many large companies keep their own computerized data col-
    lection in data banks, which store and selectively retrieve data gathered
    from the internal and external environments.

3. An MIS is composed of three subsystems of information. They include an
    internal accounting system, a market intelligence system, and market
    research reports. In the internal accounting system, the chief source
    of internal data is the sales invoice, which records the customer's
    order. A series of sales analyses can break down sales according to
    product, territory, salesperson, and customer. Managers can apply the
    information provided by an internal accounting system by pinpointing
    reasons for sales decline, evaluating the progress of a promotional cam-
    paign, and by analyzing sales by market segments. The marketing
    intelligence system provides a wealth of information from external
    sources. Sources of information can include the sales force, government
    agencies, private organizations, and company libraries. Often marketers
    have to depend on in-depth marketing research studies to reveal the
    real causes of a problem. Market research is most useful when marketing
    researchers work as a partner with management, when they are able to do
    objective, professional work of the highest standard of integrity, when
    management is receptive to the value of research, and when researchers

and management share a sense of clearly identified research needs and wants. Besides seeking the underlying causes of specific problems, market research can be used to explore opportunities in the marketplace by measuring market potential, determining market characteristics, and by analyzing sales and market shares.

4. The market research process consists of five basic methods or stages systematically conducted in an attempt to gather information. They include problem identification, exploratory investigation, research design, data collection, and data interpretation. The first stage is problem identification, which is concerned with defining underlying causes or areas of opportunities without so narrowing the definition that final recommendations for action are trivial. The preliminary narrowing of the problem must be followed by a search for a statement of the problem that can be tested. Defining the problem provides the marketer with direction. He now knows the nature of the information that would have to be sought out.

5. The second stage is exploratory investigation, the purpose of which is to develop a hypothesis, or an educated guess about the relationship between things or what will happen in the future. Hopefully, it can describe the nature of the marketing problem. This may involve talking to informed people in informal interviews or investigating literature that may pertain to the possible problem areas. The focus group interview consists of a group of people with something in common who assemble with a moderator or interviewer to discuss a topic. The homogeneous group of about 8 to 10 people often provide information on such issues as new products, an advertising approach, or some other marketing concern of the company sponsoring the interview. Researchers often use literature reviews such as secondary data which consists of information that already exists somewhere, having been collected for another purpose. Organizations chiefly responsible for such information include the federal government, state and local governments, trade associations, magazine and newspaper publishers, computer-assisted literature sources, commercial market researchers, and consumer attitude and public opinion research. In the use of secondary data, researchers should be aware that the data may be collected for purposes other than the specific study, it may be unreliable because it is biased, and it may not be completely relevant to the problem at hand. On the positive side, secondary data provides savings of time and money. Properly conducted exploratory research can provide enough information for researchers to develop a hypothesis about the problem.

6. The third stage of market research is research design. At this step marketers prepare to collect primary data, which is original information produced specifically for the present study. Research design refers to the method of carrying out the study. The marketer must determine whether he can conduct the research himself or seek out outside specialists who would act as consultants. The observation, experimentation, or survey methods are often used individually or collectively. The correct method for doing the research depends on the project. The

observation method involves the collection of data either by personal or mechanical viewing of subjects or physical phenomena. Very often the one being observed is not aware that he or she is under investigation. The strength of observational research is that it reveals what is happening. Its weakness is in not revealing why something is occurring. Experimentation establishes cause and effect relationships between factors. It allows the researcher to alter one or two variables, while noting the effect of those changes on another variable. The strength of experimentation is in trying to duplicate realistic experiments both in lab settings and under real conditions in the field, thus the bias element can be minimized. Its weakness lies in the fact that experiments can be very expensive and time consuming. The most widely used and useful method for marketers is the survey research, which involves interviewing of people. The survey may directly ask consumers their reasons for buying or not buying, or it may use questions to uncover motives indirectly. The three basic survey methods are personal interviewing, mail surveys, and telephone interviewing. Personal interviewing is the most favored method for conducting a survey. Its strength lies in the fact that it can be long, and thus a good deal of data can be secured. It often provides the researcher with the opportunity to explore in-depth probing and open-ended response questioning. Doubts about question meaning can be clarified, and visual aids can be used to increase understanding. In addition, the interviewer can report on the social and economic status of those interviewed. Its weakness lies in the high cost of hiring personal interviewers and of training them so that they do not bias results by inappropriate remarks. Mail surveys are often used because they are less costly than personal interviews and can reach people who might otherwise be missed. Its weaknesses are in low response rates and the inaccuracy of mailing lists. In addition, respondents often misunderstand questions or skip them altogether. The telephone interview provides a good compromise between the face-to-face interview and the impersonal mail survey. Its strengths lie in providing interviewer probing, some respondent privacy, and immediate response. Problems with phone interviews include the fact that people tend to be more impatient over the phone, many people have unlisted numbers, and with questions pertaining to personal characteristics. The particular survey method selected should depend upon the nature of what must be probed. All surveys require a data collection form so that participants answer the same questions. Questionnaire writers should use simple, conversational language that can be understood by respondents.

7. The fourth stage of market research is data collection. Researchers must decide from whom they want information and how they want to go about collecting it. A census is data collected from every member of a population under study. A sample is collecting data from only part of the population, which may yield information about the larger group. Researchers recognize probability and nonprobability as two broad types of samples. In a probability sample, each member of a given population is selected on some objective basis not controlled by the researcher. In a random sample, each member of a population under study has an equal chance

of being selected from a list. In <u>stratified sampling</u>, important sub-groups are identified and then randomly sampled. <u>Cluster sampling</u> occurs when people are divided by geographic area, and then parts of the area may be sampled. <u>Nonprobability samples</u> involve personal judgments in the selection of sampled items. The researcher, rather than chance, decides who will be selected to participate in the study. In a <u>convenience sample</u>, members are selected because they are close at hand. In a <u>judgment sample</u>, experts, who are thought to be specially qualified in the area of interest, are chosen. In <u>quota samples</u>, participants are singled out by researchers on the basis of characteristics thought pertinent to the study.

8. The fifth step of market research is <u>data interpretation</u>. Good market researchers must convert raw data into usable information that can aid in the development of accurate marketing decisions. Market researchers should be able to carefully analyze data, be aware of the importance of intuition, be able to communicate clearly, and be able to present accurate conclusions and recommendations to marketing managers. All the efforts of the market research process should provide information toward solving the problem. If further information is needed, management should then act accordingly. All decisions should provide for a follow-up so that it can then be determined whether the decisions reached were accurate based upon the data collected.

LEARNING GOALS

After reading this chapter, you should be able to:

1. Describe the importance of gathering information in order to assist the marketer in making correct decisions on the routine and nonroutine operations of a business.
2. Define market information systems as a means of gathering information.
3. Define market research as a means of gathering information and describe how it contrasts with MIS.
4. Discuss the three subsystems of an MIS differentiating between an internal accounting system, a market intelligence system, and market research.
5. Discuss the scope of marketing research.
6. Describe the purpose of an exploratory investigation.
7. Identify and describe the five methods of conducting market research.
8. Differentiate between observation, experimentation, and the survey methods of research design.
9. Discuss the importance of sampling and differentiate between the various types of samples.
10. Discuss the importance of data interpretation including the role of analysis, intuition, and communication.
11. Describe the future of market research to many organizations.

KEY CONCEPTS

From the list of lettered terms, select the one that best fits in the blank of the numbered statements that follow. Write the letter of that choice in the space provided.

(Answers to the key concepts appear at the end of the chapter.)

a. A census
b. Survey research
c. A sample
d. A research design
e. A convenience sample
f. Experimentation
g. A nonprobability sample
h. A judgment sample
i. A focus group interview
j. Marketing research
k. Cluster sampling

l. A market information system (MIS)
m. A hypothesis
n. Stratified sampling
o. Primary data
p. Observation
q. A random sample
r. A data bank (also data base)
s. A sales analysis
t. Secondary data
u. A probability sample
v. A quota sample

1. _____ is a form of probability sample in which each member of a population under study has an equal chance of being selected.

2. _____ is a method of determining customer attitudes by interviewing a relatively homogeneous group assembled to discuss a topic.

3. _____ is the study using direct or indirect interviews.

4. _____ is an educated guess about the relationship between things or what will happen in the future.

5. _____ is a form of nonprobability sample in which subjects are chosen on the basis of convenience to the researcher.

6. _____ is the breakdown of a company's sales data by product or customer demand, territorial volume, and salesperson performance.

7. _____ refers to a sample that involves personal judgment in the selection of sampled items.

8. _____ is original information gathered for a specific research project.

9. _____ refers to probability sampling in which the population under study is divided into subgroups and then parts of the group are chosen at random to be sampled.

10. _____ is an orderly procedure for regular collection of raw data internally and externally and conversion of those data into information for use in making marketing decisions.

11. _____ is a sample in which each member of a given population is selected on some objective basis not controlled by the researcher.

12. _____ is the marketing information system's storehouse of information gathered from internal and external environments and used to retrieve data selectively.

13. _____ refers to a complete canvass of every member of a population under study.

14. _____ is a form of probability sampling in which subgroups are identified and then randomly sampled.

15. _____ is a method for carrying out a marketing study.

16. _____ refers to a limited canvass of a representative part of a population under study.

17. _____ is a research method that involves either the personal or mechanical viewing of subjects or physical phenomena.

18. _____ is a method for collecting, on a one-time basis, data pertinent to a particular marketing problem or opportunity.

19. _____ is a form of nonprobability sample composed of subjects chosen on the basis of characteristics thought pertinent to a study.

20. _____ refers to information that exists before a particular study is conducted and that was collected for another purpose.

21. _____ is a research method that establishes cause and effect relationships.

22. _____ refers to nonprobability sample composed of subjects who are specially qualified in the area of interest of a study.

PROGRAMMED REVIEW

The following self-teaching exercises consist of short statements that require you to make a response by filling in the blank (or blanks) provided. You will find the correct response printed in the margin to the left of the question.

a. the survey method
b. the observational method
c. the experimentation method

1. What are the three methods often used by researchers in seeking out primary data?

   a. _____

   b. _____

   c. _____

geographic area

a. product
b. territory
c. salesperson
d. customer

educated guess

a. the federal government
b. state and local
   governments
c. trade associations
d. magazine and newspaper
   publishers
e. computer-assisted
   literature searching
f. commercial market
   researchers
g. consumer attitudes and
   public opinion research

a. Complete counts are
   consuming and costly.
b. It is physically impossible to check all
   members of a population.

2. In cluster sampling, people are often
   divided by _____,
   and then parts of the area may be
   sampled.

3. In a sales analysis, what four ways can
   sales be broken down and thus provide a
   picture of how well a company is doing
   in sales?

   a. _____
   b. _____
   c. _____
   d. _____

4. A hypothesis is an _____
   _____ about the relationship
   between things or what will happen in
   the future.

5. What are seven sources of secondary data
   of most interest to researchers?

   a. _____
   b. _____
   c. _____
   d. _____
      _____
   e. _____
      _____
   f. _____
   g. _____
      _____

6. For what two reasons do market researchers
   prefer to sample rather than take a
   census?

   a. _____
      _____
   b. _____
      _____
      _____

subgroups
randomly

a. problem identification
b. exploratory investigation
c. research design
d. data collection
e. data interpretation

objective
random

a. The data are collected regularly.
b. The data collected come from both inside and outside the organization.
c. The data are converted into useful information.

quickly
limited

7. In stratified sampling, important _____ are identified and then _____ sampled.

8. What are the five basic steps in the market research process?

   a. _____

   b. _____

   c. _____

   d. _____

   e. _____

9. In a probability sample, each member of a given population is selected on some _____ basis not controlled by the researcher. This is called _____ selection.

10. What are the three criteria that a marketing information system meets?

    a. _____
       _____

    b. _____
       _____
       _____

    c. _____
       _____

11. Frequently researchers resort to non-probability samples because they must collect data _____ and work with _____ funds.

a. Researchers do objective,
   professional work of the
   highest standard of
   integrity.
b. Management is receptive
   to the value of research.
c. Researchers and management share a sense of
   clearly identified
   research needs and
   issues.

12. Marketing researchers are best able to
    adopt the role of partner with manage-
    ment when these three conditions are
    present.

    a. _____
       _____

    b. _____
       _____

    c. _____
       _____
       _____

probing
privacy

13. The telephone interview allows some
    _____ by the interviewer
    and still permits some _____
    for the respondent.

a. talking to informed
   people in informal
   interviews.
b. investigating litera-
   ture that may pertain
   to the possible problem
   areas.

14. An investigation, often called situation
    analysis, involves

    a. _____
       _____
       _____

    b. _____
       _____
       _____

inside
outside

15. In marketing information systems, data
    is collected regularly from both
    _____ and _____
    the firm, and analyzed for use in making
    everyday business decisions.

a. probability
b. nonprobability

16. What are two broad types of samples
    that researchers recognize?

    a. _____
    b. _____

68

internal
external

a. personal interview
b. mail surveys
c. telephone interviews

objectives
amount
quality

a. customers
b. middlemen
c. staff

original

a. an internal account-
   ing system
b. a marketing intelli-
   gence system
c. marketing research
   reports

variety

17. At the heart of a computerized MIS is
    the data bank which stores and selec-
    tively retrieves data gathered from the
    _____ and _____
    environments.

18. What are the three basic survey methods?

    a. _____

    b. _____

    c. _____

19. The organization's research
    _____, plus the
    _____ and _____
    of information gained from exploratory
    research, help the marketing manager
    decide whether to continue researching.

20. An exploratory investigation may con-
    sist of interviews with what three
    groups?

    a. _____

    b. _____

    c. _____

21. Primary data reflects _____
    information produced specifically for
    the present study.

22. What three kinds of information com-
    prises a marketing information system?

    a. _____

       _____

    b. _____

       _____

    c. _____

       _____

23. Focus groups provide information rele-
    vant to a _____ of
    situations.

a. to measure market
   potentials
b. to determine market
   characteristics
c. to analyze sales and
   market shares

24. Why do most firms use market research?

   a. _____
      _____
   b. _____
      _____
   c. _____
      _____

a. convenience
b. judgment
c. quota

25. What are three types of nonprobability
    samples?

   a. _____
   b. _____
   c. _____

MARKETING RIDDLE

The purpose of this exercise is to find the missing word that solves the
riddle. Each of the statements requires you to make a response by filling in
the blank (or blanks) for the appropriate missing word. Each statement contains a key letter which, when combined with the other key letters, will provide you with the solution to the riddle. Correct solutions to the riddle
questions can lead to valuable prizes. See instructions for more information.

   Essentially, market research is conducted to help the organization
   better ___ ___ ___ ___ ___ ___ ___ ___ and implement the marketing concept.
          1   2   3   4   5   6   7   8

1. A good research report must be readable, objective, and
   ☐ __ __ __ __ __ __.

2. The survey may directly ask consumers their reasons for buying or not
   buying, or it may use questions to __ __ __ __ __ __ ☐ motives indirectly.

3. The organization's research objectives, plus the amount and quality of
   information gained from __ __ __ __ __ __ ☐ __ __ __ __ research, help
   the marketing manager decide whether to continue researching.

4. The people chosen for __ __ ☐ __ __ group interviews are seldom scien-
   tifically selected; therefore, the results can be biased and should not
   be taken as conclusive.

5. Beginning researchers often mistake __ __ __ __ ☐ __ __ __.

6. In recent years experimentation, which establishes cause and effect relationships, has attracted more ☐ __ __ __ __ __ __ __.

7. Data collection by observation involves either the personal or __ __ __ __ __ __ __ ☐ __ __ viewing of subjects or physical phenomena.

8. Market researchers prefer to sample, rather than take a __ ☐ __ __ __ __, for many reasons.

EXPERIENTIAL EXERCISE

Market research is an organized method for gathering an analysis of information about marketing problems. Market research attempts to provide a manager with the information necessary to make the best decisions possible as to the size of a market it wishes to enter and its chance of success.

Assume you are employed by an automobile company and have been asked to conduct a market research investigation concerning the possibility of introducing and mass producing an electric/battery-operated car. By means of the market research process, what would you do and how would you go about gathering information to assist you in making the correct decision concerning the market potential of the car?

The Market Research Process

Problem Identification

_____
_____
_____
_____
_____
_____

Exploratory Investigation

_____
_____
_____
_____
_____
_____

Research Design

_____
_____
_____
_____
_____
_____

Data Collection

_____
_____
_____
_____
_____
_____

Data Interpretation

_____
_____
_____
_____
_____
_____

SELF-QUIZ

Multiple Choice

_____ 1. When each member of a given population is selected on some objective basis not controlled by the researcher, it is called a
    a. probability sample.
    b. stratified sample.
    c. cluster sampling.
    d. nonprobability sample.

_____ 2. Original information produced specifically for the present study is known as
a. secondary data.
b. primary data.
c. data base.
d. data information.

_____ 3. When researchers single out participants on the basis of character-istics thought pertinent to the study, it is called a
a. judgment sample.
b. cluster sample.
c. convenience sample.
d. quota sample.

_____ 4. The most widely used and useful method for marketers in gathering information for a primary investigation that involves the direct or indirect interviewing of people is known as the
a. experimentation method.
b. observation method.
c. survey method.
d. research method.

_____ 5. The method for collecting, on a one-time basis, data pertinent to a particular marketing problem or opportunity is known as
a. market information system.
b. market research.
c. sampling.
d. marketing intelligence system.

_____ 6. An example of a secondary data source would be
a. the federal government.
b. quota sample results.
c. cluster sample results.
d. convenience sample results.

_____ 7. The probability sampling technique in which a population under study is divided into subgroups and then parts of the group are chosen at random to be sampled is called
a. a stratified sample.
b. a random sample.
c. a judgment sample.
d. a cluster sample.

_____ 8. The research design which establishes cause and effect relationships is called
a. surveys.
b. personal interviews.
c. experimentation.
d. observation.

_____ 9. It has been estimated that new products fail about _____
of the time.
a. 80 percent
b. 60 percent
c. 50 percent
d. 30 percent

_____ 10. In a market information system, which one of the following does
not apply?
a. The data are collected regularly.
b. The data collected are pertinent to a single problem or opportunity.
c. The data are converted into useful information.
d. The data come from both inside and outside the organization.

True-False

_____ 11. Marketers do not need information from the world outside their
companies in order to make wise decisions.

_____ 12. At the heart of a computerized MIS are data banks, which store
and selectively retrieve data gathered from the internal and external environments.

_____ 13. Statistical techniques in themselves cannot ensure reliable
research results. Intuition can thus play an important role in
decision making.

_____ 14. The preliminary narrowing of the problem must be followed by a
search for a statement of the problem that can be tested.

_____ 15. In general, when presenting market research reports to management,
it is best to start with the hypothesis.

_____ 16. In an internal accounting system, the chief source of internal
data is the sample selected.

_____ 17. In a random sample, each member of a population under study has
an equal chance of being selected from a list.

_____ 18. Today the personal collection of all data is necessary.

_____ 19. In conducting market research, much of the data must come from
inside the firm.

_____ 20. The purpose of exploratory research is to develop a hypothesis.

CHAPTER SOLUTIONS

Key Concepts

1. q	6. s	11. u	16. c	21. f
2. i	7. g	12. r	17. p	22. h
3. b	8. o	13. a	18. j	
4. m	9. k	14. n	19. v	
5. e	10. l	15. d	20. t	

Self-Quiz

1. a	5. b	9. a	13. T	17. T
2. b	6. a	10. b	14. T	18. F
3. d	7. d	11. F	15. F	19. F
4. c	8. c	12. T	16. F	20. T

CHAPTER SUMMARY

1. A study of buyer behavior is essential to a successful marketing campaign. The buyer is the focal point around which all marketing activities
revolve. Buyer behavior is the discipline that provides marketing managers with an understanding of what is behind the decision to spend money,
time, and effort on consumption-related items. To better understand
consumers, marketers draw heavily on the findings of the social sciences.
Anthropology studies the culture of a society or part of a society.
Sociology studies human behavior as influenced by groups such as the
family and social class. Demography uses statistics to analyze various
population characteristics such as residence, age, education, occupation,
and income. Psychology studies the human mind and individual behavior,
particularly a person's perception, learning experiences, and self-image.

2. It is important for marketers to understand cultural values. Culture
refers to a people's shared customs, beliefs, values, and artifacts that
are transmitted from generation to generation. Values are an important
aspect of culture because they help shape not only what Americans will
buy but also determine the potential success of marketing activities
worldwide. Cultural differences and language variations can be found
within every individual country. Subcultures are segments of a population
with distinctive life-styles, values, norms, and beliefs. Marketers must
recognize that knowledge of subcultural differences can be important in
identifying possible target markets.

3. Marketers realize that every society has a social structure that can
influence behavior. Besides the family, the social groups of greatest
interest to marketers are social classes, reference groups, and opinion
leaders and innovators. Social class refers to a group distinguished by
characteristics such as occupation, education, possessions, and values.
Of importance to the marketer is that social values can change rapidly,
whereas cultural values do not. Marketers should get a sense of a target
market's social class and attempt to understand the impact that social
class has in not only determining why an item is purchased but also what
is purchased, where, and how the transaction is completed.

4. Reference groups are groups that serve as a model for an individual's
behavior and as a frame of reference for decision making. A reference
group can refer to the people to whom an individual identifies with to
the extent that one's values, norms, or behaviors are affected in the
development of an attitude or standards of behavior towards particular
topics. Individuals often establish different reference groups for different purposes. A reference group may influence a decision to buy by
being a member of a membership group, by reason of wanting to belong

called an _aspirational group_, or by reason of not wanting to buy called a _dissociative group_.

5. _Opinion leaders_ are those individuals who are capable of influencing others in a group. Opinion leaders often set a precedence by purchasing a particular range of products that tend to have impact on others. Opinion leaders tend to be experts in a particular category, trusted, and long-standing members of the community. Since the actions, information, and advice of opinion leaders affect others, marketers should try to develop appropriate strategies specifically directed toward them. An _innovator_ refers to a person who is first to find out about and use a new product. The two-step flow of communication occurs when ads or salespeople supply information first to opinion leaders, who then pass it on to followers.

6. The family is one of the marketer's favorite social groups. Family members are often close in values, have similar goals, and communicate amongst themselves. Marketers are interested in the behavior of various family members at each stage of the decision-making process. The way a family divides its roles can be affected by the way one is raised, one's cultural background, reference group values, and the interest family members express in decision making. This in turn can affect a marketer's decision as to the development of the appropriate marketing mix components needed to reach the family member. Marketers must modify their plans to reflect upon the changing role and influence of the family. As more and more women enter the labor force, products formerly marketed towards men are now being geared towards women. With more women working in the United States than ever before, women have been able to achieve greater independence and economic freedom. Purchases previously postponed because of the women's dependence on the husband for financial support can now be acquired. The role of children in the purchase decision is also important to the marketer. At various age levels children can exert tremendous influence upon the family in terms of what is purchased. Marketers must realize that buying responsibility and influence vary greatly. They must be able to understand the roles of family members and plan the appropriate strategy in order to reach the particular family member or family unit. The _family life cycle_ refers to the stages of traditional family formation and change. It starts with the unmarried state, continues through the rearing of children, and ends with the loss of a spouse. Using this concept, the marketer can combine family characteristics, such as marital status, the age of family members, the size of family, and work status of the head of household, in developing marketing strategy. Marketers should also be knowledgeable about roles. A _role_ refers to a kind of specialization of task. Roles are associated with a position in a social setting. Family roles include those concerning decisions that may be wife-dominated, husband-dominated, or autonomous. Marketers are also interested in how the population breaks down by age. Different age groups tend to purchase different products, thus marketers need to know and study age demographics.

7. Knowing how consumers react to stimuli is an important aspect to an effective understanding of consumer behavior. Marketers use many concepts borrowed from psychology to explain what goes on in the consumer's mind during the buying decision process. Motivation and perception, attitudes, personality, and learning are often used in explaining consumer behavior. Motivation is an inner state that activates or moves people toward goals. Abraham Maslow was the first to suggest a need hierarchy, or order, in which human needs arise. Maslow proposed five basic levels of motivating needs and believed that when one need is at least partially satisfied, the need at the next highest level arises. Maslow's hierarchy of need theory consists of physiological needs, safety needs, social needs, esteem needs and self-actualization needs. The more information marketers have on individual needs, the more marketers can develop the necessary goods and services that will satisfy one's needs. Although not everyone agreed with Maslow's theory, it nevertheless represented one of the first attempts to define and develop needs and explore their implications on one's behavior. Perception is the process by which an individual becomes aware of the environment and interprets it so that it fits into his or her frame of reference. Selective exposure is a process that people use to filter out information that they are not interested in. Selective perception occurs when people filter out information that conflicts with their ideas and beliefs. Selective retention occurs whe people have a selective memory filter that causes them to remember mainly information that supports their ideas and beliefs. It is a means of filtering conflicting information from our memory. An attitude is a state that includes a person's beliefs about and feelings toward some object, coupled with a tendency to behave in a certain way with respect to that object. An attitude can be positive or negative, pro or con, favorable or unfavorable. Marketers are very concerned about consumer attitudes toward their products, since favorable attitudes often lead to higher usage rates and unfavorable ones are difficult to change. Marketers often use several techniques to measure attitude. An attitude scale is a technique whereby consumers are asked to indicate the intensity of their agreement or disagreement with certain statements posed by the researcher. Personality is the sum of characteristics that make the person what he or she is and distinguishes each individual from every other individual. Marketers are interested in the connection between an individual's personality and product or store choice. Learning is any change in an individual's response or behavior resulting from practice, experience, or mental association. Learning usually involves drives, cues, and response. The theory of conditioned learning holds that learning takes place by association. The theory of instrumental learning works with the response rather than the stimulus. The theory maintains that people learn to act in a certain way when some of their responses are rewarded or reinforced, and others are punished. Over the years, principles of learning and practical applications have been developed. They include the belief that learning cannot be conditioned or reinforced in the

absence of a felt need, learning is fastest and most complete when people are actively involved, and people learn to generalize more easily than they learn to discriminate.

8. Marketers are interested in life-styles because consumers tend to buy goods and services that are compatible with or appeal to their life-styles. The Stanford Research Institute's Value and Life-Styles Program classified American adults as being integrated, achievers, emulators, belongers, societally conscious, experientials, I-am-me's, and need-driven. According to the studies, each group behaves differently in the marketplace and thus provides marketers with the opportunity to tailor a product, advertising campaign, or distribution system to reach a certain segment of the population.

9. Researchers have attempted to show how concepts from the social sciences fit together to describe consumer behavior. Buying often involves input, processing, and output. Input consists of all those factors not in the consumer's control that may affect his or her decision to buy. Problem awareness is the result of inputs or stimuli and often requires some form of fulfillment. Consumers seek to reduce feelings of uncertainty. In the processing stage, we begin an active search for alternative solutions and information. The information is evaluated and alternatives are chosen. Output consists of the purchase decision, the buyer makes a purchase choice, and the mechanics of the purchase decision are then worked out. In postpurchase evaluation, the buyer is concerned with the evaluation of the purchase decision and the degree of product satisfaction or dissatisfaction.

LEARNING GOALS

After reading this chapter, you should be able to:

1. Describe the scope of buying behavior, including contributions of the social sciences and the users, and uses of consumer behavior data.
2. Discuss how cultures and subcultures influence consumer behavior.
3. Describe social influences on consumer behavior, including the importance of social class, reference groups, opinion leaders and innovators, the family group, and age mix changes.
4. Discuss psychological influences on consumer behavior, including the importance of motivation, perception, attitudes, personality, and learning.
5. Describe the stages of the buying process, including the significance of input, processing, and output.

KEY CONCEPTS

From the list of lettered terms, select the one that best fits in the blank of the numbered statements that follow. Write the letter of that choice in the space provided.

(Answers to the key concepts appear at the end of the chapter.)

a. Social class
b. A culture
c. A reference group
d. An opinion leader
e. Selective retention
f. A membership group
g. A subculture
h. Learning
i. The theory of conditioned learning
j. Selective perception
k. Perception
l. Selective exposure
m. Input
n. Personality
o. Need hierarchy
p. The family life cycle
q. An attitude scale
r. The theory of instrumental learning
s. An innovator
t. Output
u. Motivation
v. An aspirational group
w. Buyer behavior
x. A role
y. An attitude
z. A dissociative group

1. _____ is the study that provides marketing managers with an understanding of what is behind the decision to spend money, time, and effort on consumption-related items.

2. _____ reflects facts not in a consumer's control that may affect decisions to buy.

3. _____ is any change in an individual's response or behavior resulting from practice, experience, or mental association.

4. _____ is a technique for measuring consumer attitudes that poses statements about which respondents are asked to indicate the intensity of their agreement or disagreement.

80

5. _____ is a member of a group who is capable of influencing others in it.

6. _____ is the theory of Abraham Maslow that there is an order in which human needs arise. When one need is at least partially satisfied, the need at the next highest level arises.

7. _____ reflects actual purchase and postpurchase evaluation by a consumer.

8. _____ is a process of filtering out or modifying information that conflicts with one's ideas or beliefs.

9. _____ reflects a people's shared customs, beliefs, values, and artifacts that are transmitted from generation to generation.

10. _____ is a process by which an individual becomes aware of the environment and interprets it so that it fits into his or her frame of reference.

11. _____ is a reference group to which a person may belong, such as family, friends, and neighbors.

12. _____ views that people learn to act in a certain way when some responses are rewarded (or reinforced) and others are punished.

13. _____ is a state that includes a person's beliefs about and feelings toward some object, combined with a tendency to behave in a certain way with respect to that object.

14. _____ is a person who is first to find out about and use a new product.

15. _____ is a group that serves as model for an individual's behavior and frame of reference for decision making.

16. _____ reflects a group distinguished by characteristics such as occupation, education, possessions, and values.

17. _____ is an inner state that activates or moves people toward goals.

18. _____ is a view holding that learning takes place by association.

19. _____ is the sum of characteristics that makes a person what he or she is and distinguishes each individual from every other individual.

20. _____ in sociology is a kind of specialization of task. Family roles include those concerning decisions that may be wife-dominated, husband-dominated, or autonomous (either spouse may decide).

21. _____ is a reference group from which a person may want to dissociate himself or herself.

22. _____ reflects a process of filtering out information that is not of interest.

23. _____ reflects a reference group with which a person may want to be identified.

24. _____ refers to the traditional stages through which families pass--from the unmarried state through child rearing, empty nest, and loss of a spouse.

25. _____ refers to memory of only what supports one's ideas or beliefs.

26. _____ is a subgroup within a larger culture that has distinctive life-styles, values, norms, and beliefs.

PROGRAMMED REVIEW

The following self-teaching exercises consist of short statements that require you to make a response by filling in the blank (or blanks) provided. You will find the correct response printed in the margin to the left of the question.

subcultures

1. Within the U.S. population there are certain segments with distinctive life-styles, values, norms, and beliefs known as _____.

a. by reason of being a member of a membership group
b. by reason of wanting to belong--aspirational group
c. by reason of not wanting to belong--dissociative group

2. What are the three ways that a reference group may influence a decision to buy?

a. _____
_____
_____

b. _____
_____
_____

c. _____
_____
_____

Occupation

3. _____ is the most important basis for determining a person's social class.

a. marital status
b. age of family members
c. size of family
d. work status of the
   head of household

characteristics
distinguishes

groups

inner state

a. drive
b. cues
c. response

influencing

4. What are the four factors that influence
    buyer behavior as they relate to the
    family life cycle?

    a. _____

    b. _____

    c. _____

    d. _____

    _____

5. Personality is the sum of _____
    that make the person what he or she is
    and _____ each indi-
    vidual from every other individual.

6. Sociology is the study of human behavior
    as it is influenced by _____
    such as the family and social class.

7. Motivation is an _____
    that activates or moves people toward
    goals.

8. What are the three basic steps that
    learning usually involves?

    a. _____

    b. _____

    c. _____

9. Opinion leaders are those individuals
    who are capable of _____
    others in a group.

a. Learning cannot be conditioned or reinforced in the absence of a felt need.
b. Learning is fastest and most complete when people are actively involved.
c. People learn to generalize more easily than they learn to discriminate.

environment
interprets

a. integrated
b. achievers
c. emulators
d. belongers
e. societally conscious
f. experientials
g. I-am-me's
h. need-driven

human mind
individual

10. Over the years, a large body of data about conditioned and instrumental learning has developed. What are three principles of practical value to marketers?

a. _____
_____
_____

b. _____
_____
_____

c. _____
_____
_____

11. Perception is the process by which an individual becomes aware of the _____ and _____ it so that it fits into a frame of reference.

12. A major scheme for classifying according to life-style is the Stanford Research Institute's Value and Life-Styles. In what way does this system classify adults?

a. _____
b. _____
c. _____
d. _____
e. _____
f. _____
g. _____
h. _____

13. Psychology is the study of the _____ and _____ behavior, particularly a person's perceptions, learning experiences, personality, attitudes, and self-image.

84

practice
experience
mental association

a. more interested and
    better read in the
    area they influence.
b. more self-confident
    and sociable.
c. slightly higher in
    social status.
d. slightly more
    innovative.

psychology

family life cycle

a. whether to buy the
    product at all
b. what brand to buy

Culture

role

Motivation

14. Learning is any change in an individ-
     ual's behavior resulting from
     _____, _____,
     or _____.

15. Opinion leaders have been found to be

     a. _____
         _____
         _____

     b. _____
         _____

     c. _____
         _____

     d. _____
         _____

16. Marketers use many concepts borrowed
     from _____ to
     explain what goes on in a consumer's
     mind during the buying-decision process.

17. The stages of traditional family forma-
     tion and change constitutes the
     _____.

18. What twofold decisions does purchasing
     usually involve?

     a. _____
         _____

     b. _____

19. _____ refers to a
     people's shared customs, beliefs,
     values, and artifacts that are trans-
     mitted from generation to generation.

20. A _____ refers to a kind of
     specialization task.

21. _____ is an inner
     state that activates or moves people
     toward goals.

85

a. physiological needs
b. safety needs
c. social needs
d. esteem needs
e. self-actualization
   needs

22. What were the five levels of motivating needs that Abraham Maslow suggested in his need hierarchy?

a. _____

b. _____

c. _____

d. _____

e. _____

Perception

23. _____ is the process by which an individual becomes aware of the environment and interprets it so that it fits into a frame of reference.

selective retention

24. The filtering of conflicting information from our memory is called _____ _____.

awareness
forgetfulness

25. Repeating messages has been found to work both in increasing _____ and in reducing _____.

MARKETING RIDDLE

The purpose of this exercise is to find the missing word that solves the riddle. Each of the statements requires you to make a response by filling in the blank (or blanks) for the appropriate missing word. Each statement contains a key letter which, when combined with the other key letters, will provide you with the solution to the riddle. Correct solutions to the riddle questions can lead to valuable prizes. See instructions for more information.

The ability to create a product or service and persuade the target market to buy these offerings over other competitors' offerings depends upon ___ ___ ___ ___ ___ ___ ___ into the consumer purchase
               1 2 3 4 5 6 7
process.

1. Marketers often use the attitude scale to measure attitudes. In this technique consumers are asked to indicate the ___ ___ ___ ___ ___ ___ ☐ ___ ___ of their agreement or disagreement with certain statements posed by the researcher.

2. A type of household that is gaining a larger share of the population is the ___ ___ ☐ ___ ___ ___ ___ ___ ___ household.

3. Although population can be segmented in a variety of ways, not all segments are of equal __ ☐ __ to marketers.

4. The first two levels of Maslow's need theory are __ __ __ __ ☐ __ __ __ in nature.

5. The family life cycle concept has been used in __ __ __ __ __ __ __ __ __ ☐ markets and targeting product and promotional appeals for more than 20 years.

6. The study of opinion leaders has shown marketers how important __ __ __ __ __ __ __ __ __ __ ☐ can be in spreading product information.

7. Anthropology studies the __ __ __ ☐ __ __ __ of a society or part of a society.

EXPERIENTIAL EXERCISE

The basic determinants of consumer behavior include the individual's needs, motives, perceptions, and attitudes. The interaction of these factors within an environment causes the consumer to act. Decision making is a process that brings together memory, thinking, information processing, and judgment evaluations.

The purpose of this exercise is to provide you with a decision-making situation whereby the decision-making process was used.

Reflect upon a recent purchase that you made. By means of the decision-making process, describe what basic flow of events and the effects of personal and nonpersonal variables caused you to make that purchase.

1. Identify and define the problem

_____
_____
_____
_____
_____

2. The search for alternative solutions and information

_____
_____
_____
_____
_____

3. The evaluation of alternatives

_____
_____
_____
_____
_____

4. Selecting a solution and reaching a decision

_____
_____
_____
_____
_____

5. Implementing the decision and follow-up with a postpurchase evaluation

_____
_____
_____
_____
_____

SELF-QUIZ

Multiple Choice

_____ 1. People over fifty make up _____ percent of the population but
have nearly 50 percent of the nation's disposable income.
a. 10
b. 25
c. 40
d. 60

_____ 2. When people use a selective memory filter that causes them to remember mainly information that supports their ideas and beliefs, it is
called
a. selective perception.
b. selective exposure.
c. selective recall.
d. selective retention.

_____ 3. In distinguishing social classes, the largest of the groups was the
   a. upper-upper and lower-middle class.
   b. upper-lower and lower-lower class.
   c. upper-lower and lower-middle class.
   d. lower-middle and lower-lower class.

_____ 4. The study of human behavior as it is influenced by groups such as the family and social classes is known as
   a. anthropology.
   b. sociology.
   c. demography.
   d. psychology.

_____ 5. An internal energizing force that moves an individual toward a goal is a(n)
   a. motive.
   b. personality.
   c. attitude.
   d. learning experience.

_____ 6. When introducing a new product or service, it is essential for marketers to identify and appeal to
   a. innovators.
   b. inner-directed people.
   c. other-directed people.
   d. the family life cycle.

_____ 7. Marketers use many concepts borrowed from _____ to explain what goes on in a consumer's mind during the buying decision process.
   a. sociology
   b. psychology
   c. anthropology
   d. demography

_____ 8. A change in an individual's response of behavior resulting from practice, experience, or mental association is known as
   a. learning.
   b. motivation.
   c. attitude.
   d. personality.

_____ 9. Consumer decision making involves more than just a conditioned or rewarded reflex. Buying is a form of problem solving. Recognition of a need, the search for information, and the evaluation of alternatives is known as
   a. input.
   b. output.
   c. processing.
   d. storage.

_____ 10. To be accepted into a reference group, an individual must be
   a. of the same age as other group members.
   b. of the same ethnic background.
   c. of the same cultural background.
   d. able to conform with the norms of the group.

True-False

_____ 11. Opinion leaders are those who are the first to find out about the use of new products.

_____ 12. An attitude is a state that includes a person's beliefs about and feelings toward some object, coupled with a tendency to behave in a certain way with respect to that object.

_____ 13. The theory of conditioned learning works with the response rather than the stimulus.

_____ 14. Processing inputs will have no effect unless the consumer chooses to act on them.

_____ 15. Cultural values are generally stable and do not respond to change in response to pressure both within and ouside a society.

_____ 16. Selective exposure occurs when people filter out information that conflicts with their ideas and beliefs.

_____ 17. Subcultures are certain segments within our population with distinctive life-styles, values, norms, and beliefs.

_____ 18. In determining the importance of social classes, income should be the only criteria.

_____ 19. A significant demographic change for marketers is the aging of the baby boomers.

_____ 20. Demography uses statistics to analyze various population characteristics such as residence, age, education, occupation, and income.

CHAPTER SOLUTIONS

Key Concepts

1.	w	6.	o	11.	f	16.	a	21.	z
2.	m	7.	t	12.	r	17.	u	22.	l
3.	h	8.	j	13.	y	18.	i	23.	v
4.	q	9.	b	14.	s	19.	n	24.	p
5.	d	10.	k	15.	c	20.	x	25.	e
								26.	g

Self-Quiz

1.	b	5.	a	9.	c	13.	F	17.	T
2.	d	6.	a	10.	d	14.	T	18.	F
3.	c	7.	b	11.	F	15.	F	19.	T
4.	b	8.	a	12.	T	16.	F	20.	T

CHAPTER 7
ORGANIZATIONAL BUYING BEHAVIOR

CHAPTER SUMMARY

1. The industrial market is composed of businesses, governments, and organizations that buy products and services for resale or for use in producing other products and services. The industrial market is much larger than the consumer market but the demand for industrial goods varies, as do selling and buying practices. Although there are similarities between the consumer and industrial markets, there are some very important differences between them. The industrial market has fewer buyers, is more concentrated geographically, and the demand for its products is derived.

2. Another major difference between consumer and industrial markets rests in the kinds of products that each buys and how the goods are acquired. Industrial products are divided into six major classes based on the way in which they are used. Raw materials are natural resources such as crude oil, iron ore, and other minerals, or cultivated products such as wheat, cotton, and timber. Buying procedures depend upon the current and anticipated supply, price, and the percentage of the finished product's total production cost that is due to the raw material. Often long-term contracts are negotiated and many suppliers used. Manufactured parts or materials are goods that have in some way been shaped or finished and are incorporated into another product. Spark plugs and batteries are examples. The buyer is interested in quality, price, and the seller's delivery performance since out-of-stock situations might require plant closings. Installations are large expensive goods necessary for the production of final products, although they do not become a part of those goods. Land, plants, and buildings are examples. Installations are capital goods that last for many years and, except for land, depreciate over time. Accessory equipment also does not become part of the final product, though it is necessary to the final product's manufacture. The equipment is similar to some of the smaller, standardized major equipment; however, it has a shorter, useful life, is less expensive, usually is smaller in size, and is bought with less executive influence when compared to installations. Examples include typewriters and operating tools. Supplies are those products needed for the maintenance or repair of equipment or for the operation of a business. Maintenance supplies are used to preserve the plant and equipment in operating condition. Examples include brooms, mops, light bulbs, pencils, and pens. Supplies are bought when needed and are considered expense items. Business services refer to those specialists outside the firm who are called upon to perform specific functions. Business services are expense items that are often contracted for when an organization believes that the service from outside specialists is less costly than having company employees perform it. Examples include maintenance and repair or advisory support.

3. There are a number of characteristics that, in general, distinguish the industrial market from the consumer market. Derived demand depends ultimately on how much consumers are willing to buy. Fluctuating demand is demand that varies in response to changing economic conditions or to changing consumer tastes. Joint demand is a market condition in which demand for one product will be affected by the availability of another product with which it is used. Inelastic demand occurs when demand remains relatively constant despite price changes.

4. The primary aim of industrial marketers is to satisfy their market's needs. This necessitates the ability to determine who amongst the participants has the final say and what that person values most. Industrial buying behavior is guided by both economic considerations and emotional factors. Industrial marketers must do everything possible to satisfy the needs of their customers. They must help a company's purchasing agent to make successful buying decisions to keep that customer's future business. Because industrial sales may take a long time to negotiate, marketers need to establish effective, personal contact with their customers. The industrial marketer must use its sales force to keep buyers aware of its products, even though sales may be infrequent. Reciprocity occurs when the buyer-seller arrangement, rather than economic or performance factors, influences the purchase decision.

5. Industrial buyers generally take a more formalized approach to buying than ultimate consumers do. Industrial buying can be divided into a straight rebuy, modified rebuy, and new task. A straight rebuy involves reordering something without any modifications. Competitive suppliers have a difficult time taking business from such a secure supplier. A modified rebuy is a repurchase in which the buyers want to modify product specifications, prices, terms, or suppliers. Competitive suppliers who can offer products that much better match the buyer's needs can take business from the present supplier. A new task involves buying a product or service for the first time. New task buying is common when a firm starts production of a new product. Often the reputations of potential suppliers are highly regarded in supplier selection. New task buying requires more time and people in the selection process.

6. The buying center refers to the group of people who are involved in purchasing for an industrial market. There are five principal roles in industrial buying. Users are those in the organization who work with the products purchased. Buyers are individuals, often called "purchasing agents," with the formal responsibility of placing orders. Influencers are those individuals who can affect the decision process by assisting in evaluating alternate products. Deciders are managers with the authority to make the final choice. Gatekeepers are organizational members who control the flow of information into the buying center.

7. Industrial buyers often have to decide whether to buy or lease products. Computers, trucks, and automobiles are often leased rather than purchased outright. A number of leasing advantages may include the elimination of

the need to borrow funds to purchase the equipment, lessee can replace leased equipment with more modern equipment, tax advantages including a deductible business expense, the maintenance and repair service usually included in leasing fees, and, unlike purchased equipment, leasing can provide equipment only when needed.

LEARNING GOALS

After reading this chapter, you should be able to:

1. Define an industrial market.
2. Describe the importance of the industrial market to the United States economy.
3. Differentiate between consumer and industrial markets.
4. Differentiate between the six major classes of industrial products and describe how the goods are used.
5. Describe the nature of demand in the industrial sector and differentiate between derived, fluctuating, joint, and inelastic demand.
6. Describe the characteristics of buyer behavior in the industrial market.
7. Differentiate between the three types of buying decisions.
8. Describe the five principal roles in industrial buying situations.
9. Discuss the importance of leasing as opposed to the buying of industrial goods.

KEY CONCEPTS

From the list of lettered terms, select the one that best fits in the blank of the numbered statements that follow. Write the letter of that choice in the space provided.

(Answers to the key concepts appear at the end of the chapter.)

a. A modified rebuy
b. Raw material
c. Accessory equipment
d. Inelastic demand
e. A gatekeeper
f. Supplies
g. An industrial distributor
h. A decider
i. Derived demand
j. Manufactured materials or parts
k. A new task

l. A buying center
m. An influencer
n. An industrial market
o. A straight rebuy
p. Joint demand
q. A buyer
r. An installation
s. Reciprocity
t. Fluctuating demand
u. A user

1. _____ consists of natural resources such as crude oil or a cultivated product such as wheat used in the production of finished products.

2. _____ is an organization member who controls the flow of information into the buying center.

3. _____ is a person, often called purchasing agent, with the formal responsibility of placing orders.

4. _____ are industrial goods that have in some way been shaped or finished and are incorporated into another product.

5. _____ consists of businesses, governments, and organizations that buy goods and services for resale or for use in producing other goods and services.

6. _____ consists of demand in the industrial sector that may vary widely in response to changing economic conditions or changes in consumer tastes.

7. _____ refers to the group involved in purchasing for an industrial market.

8. _____ is a wholesaler who sells to the industrial market.

9. _____ is a repurchase in which the buyer wants to modify product specifications, prices, terms, or suppliers.

10. _____ is a repurchase without any modifications to the product, terms, or suppliers.

11. _____ is a manager with authority to make the final choice.

12. _____ is a large, expensive, industrial product necessary for the production of final products but not a part of those goods--for example, industrial parts and major equipment.

13. _____ consists of less expensive industrial products necessary to the final product's manufacture though not part of it--for example, hand tools and office equipment.

14. _____ is the purchase of a good or service for the first time.

15. _____ is a market condition when demand for one product will be affected by the availability of another product with which it is used.

16. _____ occurs when demand remains relatively constant despite price changes.

17. _____ is one who can affect the decision process by assisting in evaluating alternative products.

18. _____ occurs when demand by industrial users depends on consumer demand for the finished product.

19. _____ are industrial products needed for the maintenance or repair of equipment or for the operation of a business.

20. _____ is a member of a buying center who works with the products purchased.

21. _____ in industrial marketing refers to the relationship between buyer and seller that influences purchasing decisions rather than economic or performance factors.

PROGRAMMED REVIEW

The following self-teaching exercises consist of short statements that require you to make a response by filling in the blank (or blanks) provided. You will find the correct response printed in the margin to the left of the question.

sales
long

1. The purchase of installations is a major decision. Consequently, _____ negotiations take place over _____ periods of time.

a. raw materials
b. manufactured materials and parts
c. installations
d. accessory equipment
e. supplies
f. business services

2. What are the 6 major classes of industrial products?

   a. _____

   b. _____

   c. _____

   d. _____

   e. _____

   f. _____

buyer-seller

3. A relationship involves reciprocity when the _____ arrangement, rather than economic or performance factors, influences the purchase decision.

buy

4. The demand for industrial products is considered derived demand. It depends ultimately on how much consumers are willing to _____.

96

modifications

a. economic considerations
b. emotional factors

a. straight rebuy
b. modified rebuy
c. new task

relationships

purchasing agents

a. derived
b. fluctuating
c. joint
d. inelastic

buying center

shaped
finished

5. A straight rebuy involves reordering
    something without any _____.

6. In the industrial market, what are two
    ways in which buyer demand is influ-
    enced?

    a. _____

    b. _____

7. Industrial buyers make decisions dif-
    ferently, depending on whether the pur-
    chase is routine or complex. What are
    the three types of buying decisions?

    a. _____

    b. _____

    c. _____

8. Unlike consumer markets, buyers and
    sellers in the industrial sector often
    build _____
    that span years.

9. Buyers are individuals, often called
    _____, with
    the formal responsibility of placing
    orders.

10. In the industrial sector, what are the
    four ways in which the nature of demand
    is described?

    a. _____

    b. _____

    c. _____

    d. _____

11. Gatekeepers are organizational members
    who control the flow of information into
    the _____.

12. Goods that have in some way been
    _____ or _____
    and incorporated into another product
    are known as manufactured materials or
    manufactured parts.

a. users
b. buyers
c. influencers
d. deciders
e. gatekeepers

13. According to one system of classification, what are the five principal roles in an industrial buying situation?

a. _____

b. _____

c. _____

d. _____

e. _____

natural
cultivated

14. Raw materials are _____ resources such as crude oil, iron ore, and other minerals, or _____ products such as wheat, cotton, and timber.

a. fewer buyers
b. geographic concentration
c. nature of demand

15. What are three important differences between the industrial market and consumer markets?

a. _____

b. _____

c. _____

installations

16. Large, expensive goods necessary for the production of final products, although they do not become a part of those products, are known as

_____ .

a. businesses
b. governments
c. organizations

17. What are the three groups that the industrial market is composed of?

a. _____

b. _____

c. _____

money
service

18. Among the benefits of leasing rather than buying are that the user has _____ free for other uses, and that lessors often _____ the products they lease.

industrial distributors

19. Companies that manufacture accessory equipment may depend upon _____ _____, or wholesalers, that sell to the industrial market to sell their products.

a. price
b. quality
c. features
d. service

20. Because businesses are motivated by profit considerations, and governments and institutions must be accountable for their budgeting expenses, what four economic considerations are often the primary considerations of industrial buyers?

a. _____

b. _____

c. _____

d. _____

tax advantages

21. Companies that lease goods may also enjoy _____, including deductibility of rental expense.

roles

22. Distinguishing the persons in a buying center and the _____ they play is crucial to making a sale.

authority

23. Deciders are managers with the _____ to make the final choice.

anticompetitive

24. The Justice Department and the Federal Trade Commission frown on reciprocal agreements that are _____ _____, but such arrangements are legal as long as they do not involve coercion or seriously limit the competition in that industry.

first time

25. A new task involves buying a product or service for the _____.

MARKETING RIDDLE

The purpose of this exercise is to find the missing word that solves the riddle. Each of the statements requires you to make a response by filling in

99

the blank (or blanks) for the appropriate missing word. Each statement contains a key letter which, when combined with the other key letters, will provide you with the solution to the riddle. Correct solutions to the riddle questions can lead to valuable prizes. See instructions for more information.

Because of inflation, recession, and rising costs, institutional or nonprofit organizations are approaching the purchasing function more as business firms do. They want to maximize efficiency to __ __ __ __ __ __ __ their increasingly scarce funds.
　　　　　1　2　3　4　5　6　7

1. Because demand in the industrial ☐ __ __ __ __ __ is derived from consumer preferences, it may fluctuate widely in response to changing economic conditions or when consumer tastes change.

2. Many firms find that an efficient way to generate high-quality sales leads is to attend ☐ __ __ __ __ shows of the business they serve.

3. Many firms conduct extensive marketing research to identify buyer roles. The research guides them in __ __ __ __ __ ☐ __ __ __ a sales message that addresses the concerns of each participant.

4. For companies that use equipment only part of the year, __ ☐ __ __ __ __ __ can be particularly more attractive than buying.

5. A major difference between consumer and industrial markets rests in the kinds of __ __ __ __ __ __ ☐ __ that each buys.

6. The purchase of installations is a major __ __ ☐ __ __ __ __ __, and sales negotiations usually take place over long periods of time.

7. Industrial marketing accounts for well over ☐ __ __ __ the economic activity in the United States and Canada.

EXPERIENTIAL EXERCISE

The industrial market, as well as the consumer market, requires careful analysis and evaluation. Unlike the consumer market, the industrial market requires a more rational and systematic attempt at generating sales.

Assuming you are a manufacturer of light bulbs, describe how you would approach the sale of light bulbs to a medium-size supermarket chain and to a large manufacturer for use as manufactured materials and parts.

	Sales to Supermarket Chain	Sales to Large Manufacturer
Describe the Users		
Describe the Buyers		
Describe the Influencers		
Describe the Deciders		
Describe the Gatekeepers		

Multiple Choice

_____ 1. Manufacturing industries in eight states accounted for _____ of total U.S. shipments in 1985.
   a. one-quarter
   b. one-half
   c. one-third
   d. two-thirds

_____ 2. Which of the following groups does not directly participate in industrial marketing?
   a. the consumer
   b. the government
   c. trade associations
   d. service organizations

_____ 3. The type of demand that depends ultimately on how much consumers are willing to buy is called
   a. joint demand.
   b. derived demand.
   c. fluctuating demand.
   d. inelastic demand.

_____ 4. Which of the following types of agreements does the Justice Department and the Federal Trade Commission often frown upon?
   a. price discounts
   b. credit allowances
   c. reciprocal
   d. advertising allowances

_____ 5. Managers with the authority to make the final choice are known as
   a. users.
   b. influencers.
   c. gatekeepers.
   d. deciders.

_____ 6. Large, expensive goods necessary for the production of final products, though they do not become a part of those products, are known as
   a. installations.
   b. raw materials.
   c. supplies.
   d. manufactured materials and parts.

_____ 7. The organizational members who control the flow of information into the buying center are known as
a. gatekeepers.
b. buyers.
c. users.
d. deciders.

_____ 8. The type of buying decision in which the buyer wants to alter product specifications, prices, terms, or suppliers is called a
a. straight rebuy.
b. modified rebuy.
c. change order.
d. new task.

_____ 9. The industrial product classification that includes the need to use the services of specialists to perform specific functions is known as
a. installations.
b. accessory equipment.
c. supplies.
d. business services.

_____ 10. The type of demand that occurs when the demand of one product will be affected by the availability of another product with which it is used is known as
a. inelastic demand.
b. fluctuating demand.
c. joint demand.
d. derived demand.

True-False

_____ 11. Accessory equipment does not become part of the final product.

_____ 12. In the industrial market, advertising is much more important than personal selling.

_____ 13. Trade show selling is less expensive than paying visits to buyers and often requires fewer follow-up calls.

_____ 14. A growing pattern in industrial buying behavior is to buy products instead of leasing them.

_____ 15. While the scope of industrial buying is vast, it is startling to realize how few buyers actually account for such enormous sums.

_____ 16. The purchase of installations is a minor decision. Consequently, sales negotiations take place over a short period of time.

_____ 17. Supplies are those products that are needed for the maintenance or repair of equipment or for the operation of a business.

_____ 18. Goods that have in some way been shaped or finished and are not incorporated into another product are known as manufactured materials or parts.

_____ 19. Joint demand occurs when the demand for one product is affected by the availability of another product with which it is used.

_____ 20. Influencers are those who affect the buying decision process by assisting in evaluating alternative products.

CHAPTER SOLUTIONS

Key Concepts

1.	b	5.	n	9.	a	13.	c	17.	m
2.	e	6.	t	10.	o	14.	k	18.	i
3.	q	7.	l	11.	h	15.	p	19.	f
4.	j	8.	g	12.	r	16.	d	20.	u
								21.	s

Self-Quiz

1.	b	5.	d	9.	d	13.	T	17.	T
2.	a	6.	a	10.	c	14.	F	18.	F
3.	b	7.	a	11.	T	15.	T	19.	T
4.	c	8.	b	12.	F	16.	F	20.	T

CHAPTER 8
PRODUCT AND SERVICE CONCEPTS

CHAPTER SUMMARY

1. The key element in any marketing program is an organization's product.
    Before making decisions about pricing, promotion, and placement, a firm
    has to determine what product it will present to the public. A product
    is anything that can be offered to a market for attention, acquisition,
    use, or consumption and that satisfies a want or need. It includes
    physical objects, services, persons, places, organizations, and ideas.
    When buyers purchase a product, they are buying the benefits and satis-
    faction they believe the product will provide. In today's competitive
    marketplace, developing new products is a difficult and expensive under-
    taking. If organizations do not change their product mix to meet the
    changing needs of the target market, they'll fail in the long run. Most
    initially successful products eventually decline in sales and profits
    and are removed from the market. Therefore, new products are constantly
    needed to fill the gap.

2. A product is like an apple. It has several layers, each of which con-
    tributes to the total product image. At the core is the basic benefit
    of the product or service, which answers the question, "What problem does
    this product solve?" Another layer, or dimension of the product, is
    the development of the physical or functional features. These consist of
    physical characteristics such as packaging, product features, and dis-
    tinctive styling. Additional benefits and services added to a product
    make up the outer layer of the apple. These may include such things as
    a warranty on a new car, installation, credit, or delivery. Products
    may be thought of as having three dimensions. They include a basic bene-
    fit, physical or functional features, and additional benefits or services.

3. Products can be grouped into categories according to the markets they
    serve. Consumer products are those goods sold to individuals or house-
    holds for their personal use. Consumer products are usually grouped
    according to the manner in which consumers buy them. Marketers often
    group consumer products as either convenience, shopping, or specialty
    goods. Convenience goods are products that individuals buy quickly and
    often. Examples include candy, drug products, food snacks, and ciga-
    rettes. Convenience goods could be further divided into staple items,
    which are bought through habit; impulse items, which are bought on the
    spur of the moment; or emergency items, which are bought when an unex-
    pected need arises. Convenience goods are low priced, are purchased
    regularly, and require the manufacturer to make them as convenient as

possible because consumers are unwilling to make much effort in purchasing them. Convenience goods are the fastest-growing category of consumer goods. Shopping goods are products that individuals buy only after making comparisons in competing stores. Examples include clothing, furniture, and appliances. Homogeneous shopping goods are those products that are purchased when the basis of comparison is price. Heterogeneous shopping goods are those goods purchased when the basis of comparison is quality or style. Shopping goods are usually more expensive than convenience goods and consumers are willing to make an effort to purchase them. Specialty goods are so named because consumers are willing to make a special effort to obtain them. Examples include Porsche sports cars and Gucci handbags. Specialty goods are high priced, and consumers will seek them out, accepting no substitutes. Specialty goods are a growing category of products because many Americans are becoming more affluent and have more leisure time. To a marketer, determining whether a product is a convenience, shopping, or specialty good depends upon the buying habits of the shopper. To one shopper, a good may be a convenience item. To another shopper, it could be a shopping item or a specialty item. A marketer must consider how the majority of buyers view the company's product. Industrial products are those goods purchased by an organization's purchasing agent, or by middlemen, to make other goods, to resell them, or to carry on some other exchange-related activity. The five major classes of industrial products are installations, accessory equipment, raw materials, component parts and materials, and supplies.

4. To a marketer, a successful brand name can have a tremendous impact on market share, competition, and profits. A brand is a name, term, sign, symbol, design, or some combination used to identify the products of one firm and to differentiate them from competitors' products. A brand name is that part of the brand that can be spoken, including letters, words, and numbers. A brand mark is that part of the brand which can be recognized but cannot be spoken. It may consist of symbols, designs, or distinctive lettering or colors. A trademark is the part of the brand that has been given legal protection.

5. A world without brands would be hard to imagine. On an average, consumers see 1500 different brands each day. If goods were packaged in a plain white wrapper, life would be less colorful and competition would decrease. Companies would have little incentive to put out better goods or services because consumers would be unable to readily distinguish one firm's product from those of another. Licensing is a process by which designer or character names or identities are leased to businesses for use on their products in exchange for royalties. Branding permits a business to distinguish its products from those of others. Branding also lends value to other products the company produces and guarantees consistent quality. The halo effect is the transfer of goodwill from one product in a company's line to another. Although consumer groups complain that establishing a brand name involves heavy advertising costs that are inevitably passed on to consumers, effective branding can provide

guaranteed consistent quality, allows for comparison shopping, and gives status or prestige to their owners.

6. Marketers generally distinguish two types of brands. A <u>family brand</u> covers many products under one name. Family branding is most effective for specialized firms or those companies with specialized product lines. It also enables companies to capitalize on a uniform image and promote the same name continually. <u>Individual brands</u> give each of the company's products a distinct name. Separate brands are used for each item or product category manufactured by the company. With individual branding not only does each product have distinct images and appeals, but each must be marketed differently. <u>Multiple brand strategy</u> occurs when some companies actually promote individual brands that compete with one another.

7. Different types of products require different types of names. Marketers have established basic criteria for choosing a brand name. The name should be easy to pronounce, recognize, and remember. The name should have impact, be relevant and suggest positive images to the consumer, be appropriate to the product category, and the name should be available for use. Today many companies are using computers to help them select product names. By combining various letters of the alphabet, computers can provide millions of potential product names. Unfortunately, most of the names are not pronounceable. In some cases companies select product names without necessarily having a product. The names are then put on reserve until appropriate products are developed. <u>National brands</u> are those branded items distributed by national manufacturers. <u>Private, or distributor brands</u>, are products sold under the name of a retailer or wholesale middlemen. <u>Generic products</u> are unbranded, slightly lower-grade goods that receive no advertising. They are usually sold in plain white packages with black lettering and are often referred to as "no frills" goods. Their low cost is due mostly to the absence of advertising and other forms of promotion.

8. In 1986 U.S. consumers spent over 2 trillion dollars on services including such things as life insurance, air travel, college tuition, medical care, and financial advice. Today the service industry represents one of the largest and growing segments of the U.S. economy. Services are product offerings in which a buyer receives no tangible good. Company offerings can be arranged on a continuum with regard to how much of an offer consists of a tangible product and how much consists of a service. The four categories of offerings include a pure tangible good, a tangible good with accompanying services, a major service with accompanying minor goods and services, and a pure service. The four characteristics that are unique to services and influence the way they are marketed include intangibility, perishability, simultaneous consumption and production, and lack of control. A good image is important in selling a service because there are few standards for measuring service quality. Products can be compared on the basis of weight, size, color, and so on, but services must often be judged subjectively. Not only are services usually

completed before their quality can be evaluated, but inferior services cannot be returned. Marketers must carefully plan and develop the product mix in order to reach the appropriate target market with the appropriate service. To achieve success, a marketer must analyze the market, the competition, and the tangible elements surrounding the service.

LEARNING GOALS

After reading this chapter, you should be able to:

1. Define a product and describe the problems associated with new product development.
2. Describe how a basic benefit, physical or functional features, and additional benefits or services can be called the three dimensions of products.
3. Define consumer products and differentiate between convenience, shopping, and specialty goods.
4. Define industrial products and differentiate between installations, accessory equipment, raw materials, component parts and materials, supplies, and business services.
5. Discuss the importance of branding as well as its problems.
6. Differentiate between a brand, a brand name, a brand mark, and a trademark.
7. Describe the importance of planning as it relates to branding.
8. Differentiate between a family brand and individual brands.
9. Describe the factor that a company must keep in mind when choosing a brand name.
10. Differentiate between national brands and private or distributor brands.
11. Define and describe the importance of generic products.
12. Discuss the importance of marketing services and distinguish them from tangible goods.
13. Describe the four major categories of a product continuum.
14. Differentiate between intangibility, perishability, simultaneous consumption and production, and lack of control as characteristics of services.
15. Describe marketing strategy decisions as they relate to services.

KEY CONCEPTS

From the list of lettered terms, select the one that best fits in the blank of the numbered statements that follow. Write the letter of that choice in the space provided.

(Answers to the key concepts appear at the end of the chapter.)

a. A private (distributor) brand
b. Homogeneous shopping goods
c. A product
d. Shopping goods
e. A family brand
f. A multiple brand strategy
g. Convenience goods
h. The halo effect
i. A generic product

j. Emergency items
k. Heterogeneous shopping goods
l. Consumer products
m. Licensing
n. A national brand
o. An individual brand
p. Impulse items
q. Speciality goods

1. __C__ is anything that can be offered to a market for attention, acquisition, use, or consumption that might satisfy a want or need.

2. __P__ are products bought on the spur of the moment.

3. __G__ are products that individuals buy quickly and often.

4. __K__ are products that a consumer will buy only after making a comparison of the style or quality of brands--for example, a dress or suit.

5. __m__ refers to the process by which designer or character names or identities are leased to businesses for use on their products in exchange for royalties.

6. __a__ refers to a product sold under the name of a retailer or wholesale middleman.

7. __i__ is a product that is unbranded and marketed with minimal advertising.

8. _____ refers to a distinct name given to each product a company produces.

9. __e__ refers to a brand that covers many products under one brand name.

10. __q__ are products that a consumer is willing to make a special effort to obtain.

11. __b__ are goods sold to individuals or households for their personal use.

12. __d__ are products that a consumer buys only after making comparisons among competing stores.

13. __n__ refers to a branded item distributed by national manufacturers.

14. _____ are products bought when an unexpected need arises.

15. _____ refers to the corporate practice of promoting individual brands that compete with one another.

16. _____ are products that a consumer buys only after making price comparisons among sellers--consumers see them as essentially the same.

17. _____ is the transfer of goodwill from one product in a company's line
to another.

PROGRAMMED REVIEW

The following self-teaching exercises consist of short statements that
require you to make a response by filling in the blank (or blanks) provided.
You will find the correct response printed in the margin to the left of the
question.

a. It must be easy to
    pronounce, recognize,
    and remember.
b. It should have impact.
c. It should be relevant
    and suggest product
    benefits.
d. It should suggest posi-
    tive images to the con-
    sumer.
e. It should be appro-
    priate to the product
    category.
f. It should be available
    for use.

1. What are the general rules that marketers
    have established in the search for a
    good brand name?

    a. _____
        _____
    b. _____
        _____
    c. _____
        _____
    d. _____
        _____
    e. _____

    f. _____
        _____

comparisons

2. Shopping goods are products that individ-
    uals buy only after making _____
    in competing stores.

legal protection

3. A trademark is that part of the brand
    that has been given _____
    _____.

standardize

4. The quality of service delivered is hard
    to control. Marketers of services try
    to compensate by controlling where they
    can. Some companies go to great lengths
    to _____ their services.

110

a. convenience goods
b. shopping goods
c. specialty goods

letters
words
numbers

a. a pure tangible good
b. a tangible good with
   accompanying services
c. a major service with
   accompanying minor
   goods and services
d. a pure service

special effort

distinguish

a. staple items
b. impulse items
c. emergency items

spoken

5. What are the three ways in which consumer goods are classified?

   a. _____

   b. _____

   c. _____

6. The brand name refers to that part of
   the brand that can be spoken, including
   _____ , _____ ,
   and _____ .

7. What are the four categories of offerings
   in the goods-service continuum?

   a. _____
      _____

   b. _____
      _____

   c. _____
      _____

   d. _____
      _____

8. Specialty goods are so named because
   consumers are willing to make a
   _____ to obtain
   them.

9. Companies favor branding because it
   permits a company to _____
   its products from those of others.

10. Into what three categories can conven-
    ience goods be divided?

    a. _____

    b. _____

    c. _____

11. The brand mark refers to that part of
    the brand that can be recognized but
    not _____ .

111

price

national
private

goodwill

leased
royalties

a. It permits a company
    to distinguish its
    products from those
    of others.
b. The brand name is the
    value it creates and
    lends to other prod-
    ucts the company
    produces.

anticipate
respond

substitutes

12. Although generics command only a small
    share of the grocery business, many
    stores claim they will continue to carry
    them in order to offer consumers a
    three-tier _____ choice.

13. A family brand covers many products
    under _____ brand name.

14. The "battle of the brands" refers to
    the competition that exists between
    owners of _____ and
    _____ brands to win
    retail outlet shelf space and consumer
    loyalty.

15. The halo effect refers to the transfer
    of _____ from one
    product in a company's line to another.

16. Licensing is a process by which a
    designer or character names or identi-
    ties are _____ to
    businesses for use on their products in
    exchange for _____.

17. What are two advantages of branding?

    a. _____
        _____
        _____

    b. _____
        _____
        _____

18. Because services require no inventory,
    it is especially important for service
    providers to _____ and
    _____ to changing levels
    of demand.

19. Specialty-goods buyers differ from
    shopping-goods buyers in that the former
    know what they are looking for and have
    a particular brand in mind. They are
    unwilling to settle for _____.

a. intangibility
b. perishability
c. simultaneous con-
   sumption and produc-
   tion
d. lack of control

20. What four characteristics unique to services influence the way in which they are marketed?

   a. _____

   b. _____

   c. _____

       _____

   d. _____

name
term
sign
symbol
design

21. A brand is a _____,
_____, _____,
_____, _____, or
some combination used to identify the products of one firm and to differentiate them from competitors' products.

same time
customers

22. Services are used at the _____
_____ that they are produced. This typically puts the supplier of services into close contact with
_____.

a. basic benefit
b. physical or functional features
c. additional benefits or services

23. What are the three dimensions of products?

   a. _____

   b. _____

       _____

   c. _____

       _____

image

24. In developing services, special attention should be paid to creating advertising and promotion that gives the service a concrete _____ in the public's mind.

a. homogeneous goods
b. heterogeneous goods

25. Into what two categories can shopping goods be divided?

   a. _____

   b. _____

MARKETING RIDDLE

The purpose of this exercise is to find the missing word that solves the
riddle. Each of the statements requires you to make a response by filling in
the blank (or blanks) for the appropriate missing word. Each statement contains a key letter which, when combined with the other key letters, will provide you with the solution to the riddle. Correct solutions to the riddle
questions can lead to valuable prizes. See instructions for more information.

> Companies can only protect their brands if they register their
> trademarks with the U.S. patent office. Many companies have lost
> their trademark rights because the trademark fell into the public
> __ __ __ __ __ __ and began to be used to identify a generic
> 1 2 3 4 5 6
> product class.

1. An important reason for using a brand name is the value it creates and
    __ __ __ ☐ __ to other products the company produces.

2. Consumer products are usually __ __ ☐ __ __ __ __ according to the man-
    ner in which consumers buy them.

3. Consumers of services tend to perceive relatively greater risk when they
    are shopping for a service. They rely more heavily on the
    __ __ __ __ ☐ __ __ __ __ __ __ __ __ __ of others.

4. Once the basic benefit offered by the product or service is defined, a
    product planner can begin developing __ __ __ __ __ __ ☐ __ or functional
    features of a product.

5. If a company's product is __ __ ☐ __ __ __, and it has the resources to
    promote the product, the advantages of branding far outweigh the dis-
    advantages.

6. Service industries must keep consumers' __ __ __ __ __ ☐ __ in mind
    when designing a marketing strategy.

EXPERIENTIAL EXERCISE

Consumer products are usually grouped according to the manner in which consumers buy them. The products are often classified as being either a convenience, shopping, or specialty good. Select a product that you recently
purchased from each classification and describe why you purchased the product
and why you classified it in that category.

1. Convenience Good

    _____

    _____

    _____

    _____

    _____

    _____

2. Shopping Good

    _____

    _____

    _____

    _____

    _____

3. Specialty Good

    _____

    _____

    _____

    _____

    _____

SELF-QUIZ

Multiple Choice

_C_ 1. The part of the brand which can be recognized but cannot be spoken
        and consists of symbols, designs, or distinctive lettering or colors
        is known as
        a. a brand.
        b. a brand name.
        c. a brand mark.
        d. a trademark.

_b_ 2. Goods purchased on the spur of the moment are known as
        a. staple items.
        b. impulse items.
        c. demand items.
        d. emergency items.

_a_ 3. A brand that covers many products under one brand name is known
   as
   a. a family brand.
   b. an individual brand.
   c. a multiple brand.
   d. a brand type.

_____ 4. It has been estimated that the average retail grocery store contains between _____ different items.
   a. 1,000 and 3,000
   b. 5,000 and 7,000
   c. 7,000 and 10,000
   d. 10,000 and 13,000

_b_ 5. A process by which designer or character names or identities are
   leased to businesses for use on their products in exchange for
   royalties is known as
   a. a halo effect.
   b. licensing.
   c. a generic product.
   d. a warranty.

_c_ 6. A product that individuals buy quickly and often is known as
   a. a shopping good.
   b. a specialty good.
   c. a convenience good.
   d. a soft good.

_a_ 7. A part of the brand that has been given legal protection is known
   as
   a. a trademark.
   b. a brand mark.
   c. a legal mark.
   d. a brand.

_____ 8. The service sector accounts for _____ of the U.S.
   gross national product.
   a. one-fifth
   b. one-half
   c. two-thirds
   d. seven-eighths

_____ 9. In recent years new product introductions have increased to the
   rate of nearly _____ per month.
   a. 50
   b. 100
   c. 125
   d. 150

a 10. Products such as Budweiser beer, Coca Cola, Tide soap, and Bic pens are known as
   a. national brands.
   b. distributor brands.
   c. generic brands.
   d. private brands.

True-False

F 11. Heterogeneous shopping goods are those products that consumers purchase only after price has been compared.

F 12. Emergency items are those goods that are purchased through habit.

T 13. Specialty goods are so named because consumers are willing to make a special effort to obtain them.

F 14. A trademark is that part of the brand that can be spoken, including letters, words, and numbers.

T 15. The transfer of goodwill from one product in a company's line to another is known as the halo effect.

____ 16. A family brand gives each of the company's products a distinct name.

F 17. Products sold under the name of a retailer or wholesale middlemen are called national brands.

T 18. A brand is a name, term, sign, symbol, design, or some combination used to identify the products of one firm and to differentiate them from competitors' products.

T 19. "The battle of the brands" refers to the competition that exists between owners of national and private brands to win retail outlet shelf space and consumer loyalty.

F 20. A staple item is generally bought on the spur of the moment.

CHAPTER SOLUTIONS

Key Concepts

1. c	5. m	9. e	13. n	17. h
2. p	6. a	10. q	14. j	
3. g	7. i	11. l	15. f	
4. k	8. o	12. d	16. b	

1.	c	5.	b	9.	d	13.	T	17.	F
2.	b	6.	c	10.	a	14.	F	18.	T
3.	a	7.	a	11.	F	15.	T	19.	T
4.	c	8.	c	12.	F	16.	F	20.	F

CHAPTER SUMMARY

1. Organizations must realize that behind most successful products lies a vast amount of time, effort, and money. Intrapreneurship is the entre- preneurial activity within an organization. Developing a good product requires an ongoing evaluation of the marketplace to determine consumer wants and needs. A new product is a good or service new to the company producing it. A new product could also be one in which the company has made major or minor revisions, an improvement on an existing product, or a major change in the product itself. To maintain a competitive edge, the creation of new products and the improvements of old products are necessary to the survival of a firm.

2. Products often pass through a series of phases from the time they are introduced to the time they are no longer marketed. The product life cycle reflects the five phases through which most products pass. In the incubation phase, a company conceives, develops, and tests a product before bringing it to the marketplace. In the introductory phase, a com- pany brings the new product to the national marketplace. In the growth stage, both product availability and marketing efforts expand, and sales and profits surge upward. In the maturity phase, the number of buyers continues to grow, but more slowly, until a leveling-off arises. In the decline phase, products start losing a significant number of customers without replacing them. The product life cycle is an important tool for planning and developing marketing strategy. The successful management of a product is enhanced when management understands the process by which products are adopted, the factors that cause changes in consumer tastes, competition, and channel support.

3. Some products have a very long life cycle. However, for most types of products marketers have found that product lives are shorter than pre- viously. A fad has an extremely short life cycle, usually no more than two years. The lifespan of most products falls somewhere between that of fads and basic innovative products. To manage a product effectively, one should plan for each stage of a product's life. The product life cycle informs management that sooner or later a product will die and tells management that a firm's products must compete with the products of other companies for consumer attention. Unfortunately, it is some- times difficult to determine exactly where one phase ends and the other one begins.

4. In the incubation phase, new product ideas are proposed, and the better ones screened out and produced. During the conception stage, companies usually derive their new product ideas from their work force, customers, or competitors. During the development stage, companies sift through the

ideas that flow in, gear up for production, and conceive a workable marketing program for the new product. Many companies delegate responsibility for new product decisions to various groups rather than to an individual. The new product committee is composed of top-level executives and representatives of several departments. The new product department is a permanent committee that works on new product ideas on a day-to-day basis. The new product venture team usually assumes total responsibility for a new product from its conception through its decline. During the developmental process, screening, business analysis, and planning occur. Screening refers to the first attempt to separate those ideas worth pursuing from those that are not. The business analysis involves estimating the future sales and profit potential of the new product. Careful planning often necessitates the use of test marketing, which provides companies with the opportunity to test their products by marketing them through retail outlets in selected cities under controlled conditions. Test marketing, however, provides no guarantee of product success. Effective product positioning can bring the product to the consumers' attention and keep attention focused on it. A product's position is the image that product has in consumers' minds, especially in relation to competing products. Product positioning refers to the decisions marketers make to create or maintain a certain product concept in consumers' minds. Products can be positioned in two ways. Marketers may choose to position their product in head-to-head competition with the industry leader or they may wish to position a new product so that it does not erode sales, or cannibalize, those of earlier brands. Product positioning enables a firm to plan its product offerings in terms of consumer perceptions, desires, competition, other company products, and environmental conditions.

5. The marketing mix strategy should change as products move from the incubation phase until their decline and removal from the market. In the introductory phase, managers may set high or low prices, seek out as many distributors as possible, and spend heavily on promotion to acquaint the public with the product. The marketing manager's aims during this phase are to make the general public aware of the product's benefits and to recover some of the costs incurred during the incubation phase.

6. In the growth phase, marketers begin improving and expanding on the product and use promotion to build brand recognition and preference. Firms must begin to increase the desirability of its product to counteract competition. Often the marketer may introduce minor product modifications that would strengthen its position or broaden its appeal. The most common types of minor modifications are the addition of new sizes, the introduction of new packages, and the addition of new product features and models. Marketers may lower an initial high price which may discourage potential competitors. Expenditures for promotion are likely to remain high, but the content of the messages changes. As demand increases, marketers may continue to expand the market of distribution outlets.

7. In the maturity phase, marketers focus on winning market share by making major product improvements and by increasing promotion and distribution channels. Often a company can increase a product's share of the market by capturing a larger share of the market by luring customers away from competitors. This can be achieved by finding new uses for the product, discovering new users, adding flanker, or related, products to the company line, and making major product modifications. Flanker products are items related to an already established product and bearing the same brand name. Because of intense competitive pressures, marketing managers often lower the price of their products. Instead of competing directly with other companies on the basis of price, most marketing managers prefer to compete indirectly through new promotional programs such as the use of comparative advertising. Also firms compete indirectly by trying to place products in more outlets than competitors.

8. In a product's decline phase, marketers reduce the number of styles and models of a product, eliminate distributors, cut prices, and may even demarket the product. Demarketing is an attempt by a company to persuade the public that there are valid economic reasons for withdrawing the product. In this stage a product's price usually reaches a low point so that a company can liquidate its stock as quickly as possible. Often we find that a firm may cut back on the number of middlemen who handle the product. The decision to lower prices, eliminate distributors, and promote the idea of the product's elimination should be made only after careful analysis of the product's future in the marketplace.

LEARNING GOALS

After reading this chapter, you should be able to:

1. Define intrapreneurship and discuss its importance within an organization.
2. Define a new product.
3. Define the product life cycle and describe its phases and importance.
4. Describe what takes place in the incubation phase including the importance of conception, development, organizational arrangements, test marketing, and product positioning.
5. Discuss the marketing mix strategy that takes place in the intorductory, growth, maturity, and decline phases of the product life cycle.

KEY CONCEPTS

From the list of lettered terms, select the one that best fits in the blank of the numbered statements that follow. Write the letter of that choice in the space provided.

(Answers to the key concepts appear at the end of the chapter.)

a. A new product committee
b. A product life cycle
c. Demarketing
d. The introductory phase
e. Intrapreneurship
f. The growth phase
g. A new product venture team
h. Flanker products
i. The maturity phase
j. Cannibalization

k. The incubation phase
l. The new product department
m. A business analysis
n. The decline phase
o. A product position
p. A fad
q. A new product
r. Product positioning
s. Screening
t. Test marketing

1. __B__ refers to the five phases through which a product passes. They include incubation, introduction, growth, maturity, and decline.

2. __j__ refers to the process by which a company's new product takes sales away from existing products in the same company's line.

3. __f__ is the stage of product life cycle during which product availability and marketing efforts expand and sales and profits surge upward.

4. __Q__ refers to a product or service new to the company producing it.

5. __m__ is the process of estimating future sales and profit potential of a new product.

6. __h__ are items related to an already established product and bearing the same brand name.

7. __t__ is the testing of products by marketing them through retail outlets under controlled conditions in selected cities.

8. __O__ is the image that a product has in consumers' minds, especially in relation to competing products.

9. __K__ is the stage of product life cycle during which a product is conceived, developed, and tested.

10. __P__ is a product with a short life cycle, usually no more than two years.

11. __A__ refers to a group of top-level executives and representatives of several departments that meets regularly to consider new products.

12. __r__ refers to the decisions marketers make to create or maintain a certain product concept in consumers' minds.

13. __C__ refers to promotion aimed at persuading the public that there are valid economic reasons for withdrawing a product.

14. __n__ is the stage of product life cycle during which products start losing a significant number of customers without replacing them.

15. __S__ is the first attempt to separate ideas worth pursuing from those that are not.

16. __G__ refers to a group that usually assumes total responsibility for a new product from conception through decline.

17. __i__ is the stage of product life cycle during which the number of buyers continues to grow, but more slowly, until sales level off.

18. __e__ refers to entrepreneurial activity within an organization.

19. __L__ is a permanent committee that works on new product ideas on a day-to-day basis.

20. __d__ is the stage of product life cycle during which a company brings a new product to the marketplace.

PROGRAMMED REVIEW

The following self-teaching exercises consist of short statements that require you to make a response by filling in the blank (or blanks) provided. You will find the correct response printed in the margin to the left of the question.

a. incubation
b. introduction
c. growth
d. maturity
e. decline

1. What are the five phases which make up the product life cycle?

a. _____
b. _____
c. _____
d. _____
e. _____

short
two

2. Fads have extremely _____ life cycles, usually no more than _____ years.

a. new product committees
b. new product departments
c. new product venture teams

conception
decline

a. head-to-head
   competition
b. avoid cannibalizing
   of earlier brands

acceptance

a. find new uses
b. discover new users
c. add flanker or
   related products
d. make major product
   modifications

estimating

3. What are the three groups to whom many companies now delegate responsibility for new product decisions?

a. _____

b. _____

c. _____

4. Venture teams usually assume total responsibility for a new product from its _____ through its _____ .

5. Product positioning is a natural out-growth of market segmentation. What two ways can products typically be positioned?

a. _____
   _____

b. _____
   _____

6. The growth phase is sometimes referred to as the market _____ phase.

7. What are the four ways in which managers can increase a product's market share by reworking its image?

a. _____

b. _____

c. _____
   _____

d. _____
   _____

8. The business analysis involves _____ the future sales and profit potential of the new product.

laboratory

9. A serious drawback to test marketing is
    that it sometimes produces what is
    referred to as the _____
    effect.

top-level
several

10. A new product committee is composed of
    _____ executives
    and representatives from _____
    departments.

decline

11. When products start losing a signifi-
    cant number of customers without
    replacing them, they enter the
    _____ phase.

a. their work force
b. customers
c. competitors

12. What are the three ways that companies
    usually derive new product ideas from?

    a. _____

    b. _____

    c. _____

existing

13. More commonly, a new product is an
    improvement on an _____
    product.

improper timing

14. A product priced correctly, promoted
    heavily, and distributed widely can
    still fail because of _____
    _____.

a. A product idea is
    conceived.
b. A product idea is
    developed.
c. A product is
    tested.

15. In the incubation of a product, what
    are the three important steps?

    a. _____

        _____

    b. _____

        _____

    c. _____

        _____

replaced
advertising

16. A declining product may have to be
    _____; a mature product
    may simply need more _____.

a. cheaper than any
possible compet-
itor's product.
b. totally nonreusable.
c. guaranteed to be
habit forming.

17. According to one marketing wit, the
"perfect product" is one that is

a. _____
_____
b. _____
c. _____
_____

reinforce

18. Once a positioning strategy has been
determined, marketers use the various
elements of the marketing mix to
_____ that product's image
in customers' minds.

a. to make the general
public aware of the
product's benefits
b. to recover some of
the costs incurred
during the incubation
phase

19. Risks are higher during the introduction
phase of a product's life cycle, when
a product first becomes available
nationally. What are the marketing
manager's aims during this phase?

a. _____
_____
_____
b. _____
_____
_____

inevitable
permanent

20. The problem with a don't-rock-the-boat
approach to product improvement is that
changes in the market are
_____, and the pen-
alty for being second with an innovation
is a _____ loss
of customers.

126

a. the addition of new
   sizes
b. the introduction of
   new packages
c. the addition of new
   product features

21. Radical product changes in the growth
    phase would be unwise because they would
    confuse the public. What are the most
    common types of minor modifications?

    a. _____

       _____

    b. _____

       _____

    c. _____

       _____

image

22. While production managers work out the
    physical dimensions of the product,
    marketing managers develop the
    _____ of the product.

a. drop-errors
b. go-errors

23. Screening refers to the first attempt
    to separate those ideas worth pursuing
    from those that are not. What are the
    two types of errors that often occur
    in the screening process?

    a. _____
    b. _____

withdrawing

24. Demarketing is a special type of promo-
    tion that attempts to persuade the
    public that there are valid economic
    reasons for _____
    the product.

a. screening
b. business analysis
c. planning for pro-
   duction and marketing

25. What are the three important functions
    during the developmental process?

    a. _____
    b. _____
    c. _____

       _____

MARKETING RIDDLE

The purpose of this exercise is to find the missing word that solves the riddle. Each of the statements requires you to make a response by filling in the blank (or blanks) for the appropriate missing word. Each statement contains a key letter which, when combined with the other key letters, will provide you with the solution to the riddle. Correct solutions to the riddle questions can lead to valuable prizes. See instructions for more information.

To consumers, the lure of new products offers an
___ ___ ___ ___ ___ ___ from the routine.
   1 2 3 4 5 6

1. As buyer interest ☐ ___ ___ ___ ___ ___ ___, a product moves into its growth phase.

2. A business analysis involves ___ ☐ ___ ___ ___ ___ ___ ___ ___ ___ the future sales and profit potential of the new product.

3. A product priced correctly, promoted heavily, and distributed widely can still fail because of improper timing. Timing is ☐ ___ ___ ___ ___ ___ ___ in the introductory phase.

4. ___ ___ ___ ___ ___ ☐ ___ ___ from customers is an important source of new product ideas.

5. The new product department is a ☐ ___ ___ ___ ___ ___ ___ ___ ___ committee that works on new product ideas on a day-to-day basis.

6. Marketers may choose to position products in
___ ___ ___ ___   ___ ___   ___ ☐ ___ ___ competition with the industry leader.

EXPERIENTIAL EXERCISE

Like humans, products pass through a series of phases. Marketers have many reasons for using the product life cycle as a means of managing their businesses.

Select a specific product in each of the five stages of the product life cycle. Describe why you believe the product is at this stage. What environmental changes do you believe may affect the product's movement within the cycle? (see Chapter 3)

	Product	Environmental Changes
Incubation Phase		
Introduction Phase		
Growth Phase		
Maturity Phase		
Decline Phase		

129

Multiple Choice

B 1. Items related to an already established product and bearing the same brand name are termed
   a. test market products.
   b. flanker products.
   c. demarketing products.
   d. developmental products.

A 2. The process that involves estimating the future sales and profit potential of proposed new products is known as
   a. a business analysis.
   b. screening.
   c. test marketing.
   d. product positioning.

D 3. The group that usually assumes total responsibility for a new product from its conception through its decline is known as
   a. the new product committee.
   b. the new product department.
   c. the new product staff.
   d. the new product venture team.

D 4. A recent study showed that new products would account for _____ of U.S. companies' profits in the 1980s.
   a. one-fifth
   b. one-third
   c. one-half
   d. two-thirds

C 5. Marketers estimate what percentage of the new consumer products that enter the marketplace fail?
   a. 30 percent
   b. 50 percent
   c. 70 percent
   d. 80 percent

d 6. In what phase of the product life cycle do we find the highest risk?
   a. decline phase
   b. maturity phase
   c. incubation phase
   d. introductory phase

_C_ 7. In what phase do we find marketers reducing the number of styles and models of a product, eliminating distributors, cutting prices, and even demarketing the product?
   a. incubation phase
   b. introductory phase
   c. decline phase
   d. maturity phase

_a_ 8. The process that refers to the first attempt to separate those ideas worth pursuing from those that are not is known as
   a. screening.
   b. test marketing.
   c. business analysis.
   d. product positioning.

_b_ 9. The method used by marketers to persuade the public that there are valid economic reasons for withdrawing the product is known as
   a. cannibalizing.
   b. demarketing.
   c. product positioning.
   d. test marketing.

_a_ 10. A fad usually lasts no more than _____ years.
   a. two
   b. three
   c. four
   d. five

True-False

_F_ 11. Test marketing always provides a guarantee of product success.

_T_ 12. Product positioning refers to the decisions marketers make to create or maintain a certain product concept in consumers' minds.

_F_ 13. Each phase of the product life cycle requires the same marketing strategy.

_F_ 14. Demarketing is an attempt to persuade the public that there are valid economic reasons for keeping the product on the market.

_T_ 15. The growth phase of the product life cycle is also sometimes referred to as the market acceptance phase.

_T_ 16. Cannibalizing is a process by which a company's new product takes sales away from existing products in the same company's line.

_F_ 17. A flanker product is an item that is not related to an already established product.

F 18. Intrapreneurship is an activity outside of an organization.

T 19. More commonly, a new product is an improvement on an existing product.

F 20. In a holistic approach, product development is the responsibility of the new product department.

CHAPTER SOLUTIONS

Key Concepts

1. b	5. m	9. k	13. c	17. i
2. j	6. h	10. p	14. n	18. e
3. f	7. t	11. a	15. s	19. l
4. q	8. o	12. r	16. g	20. d

Self-Quiz

1. b	5. c	9. b	13. F	17. F
2. a	6. d	10. a	14. F	18. F
3. d	7. c	11. F	15. T	19. T
4. b	8. a	12. T	16. T	20. F

CHAPTER 10
PRICING CONCEPTS AND PRACTICES

CHAPTER SUMMARY

1. Pricing is considered by many businesspeople to be the most important activity in the free-enterprise system. Price in a monetary or nonmonetary form is a key component of an exchange. It appears in every marketing transaction. Price represents profit--what is left over after expenses are deducted from revenue. Even though pricing of a product or service in the early stages may be such that profit is little or nonexistent, pricing decisions should include an anticipation of sufficient future profits to make up for losses in the early stages of a product's introduction. In setting prices, firms must consider buyer demand, supply and costs, competition, government regulations, and other elements of the marketing mix.

2. In setting prices, top management makes the major decisions, but lower-level people carry out, or administer, the prices. Top management has the responsibility of stating the company's pricing objectives and policies and translating these goals into specific prices.

3. The first step in setting prices is to set pricing objectives. Pricing objectives are the long-range goals that managers wish to pursue in their pricing decisions. Marketers often define their objectives in terms of target rate of return, sales-related goals, status quo, or social issues.

4. The second step in setting prices is to estimate buyer demand. The law of demand states that, in general, more goods are sold at a lower price than at a higher one. In addition, marketing managers are concerned with elasticity of demand which determines how fast demand changes in response to price changes. Demand is inelastic if an increase in price also increases total revenue or a decrease in price decreases total revenue. Elastic demand means that a decrease in price will increase the seller's revenues, while a price increase will decrease revenues. The type of demand that exists is based upon the availability of substitutes and the urgency of need.

5. The third step in setting prices is to calculate costs. Fixed costs are those that do not vary with a firm's output. Also referred to as "overhead," these costs include all contractual payments such as interest, rents, associated property taxes, and executive and clerical wages. Variable costs are costs that increase or decrease with the amount of output. Examples include direct labor costs and the costs of materials and utilities used in the production of goods and services. During the past decade, costs have greatly increased and have caused companies to pass along increases to consumers, modify products and services, and discontinue some offerings.

133

6. The fourth step in setting prices is to analyze competitors' prices. Ideally, prices are set by the interaction of supply and demand. A company is in a better position to establish prices when it is aware of the prices charged for competing brands. Being aware of the competitors' prices is not an easy task. It requires input from the market research department as well as from recognized marketing services.

7. The fifth step in setting prices is to select a pricing policy. <u>Pricing policies</u> are more specific than objectives and deal with situations in the foreseeable future that generally recur. Pricing policies can establish the basic long-term framework for the good or service and is a logical extension of pricing objectives. An effective pricing policy can define the initial price and provide for direction for price changes over the life of the product. Three important policy-making issues are: (1) whether to offer a product at a single price or many different prices; (2) whether to price at, above, or below the market; and (3) how to price a new product. In addition, government regulations must be considered. A <u>one-price policy</u> offers goods purchased at the same time and in the same quantity at a single price to all. A <u>variable-price policy</u> allows special prices for different customers. The government has been particularly active in enforcing pricing laws. The government has looked into <u>price collusion</u>, or the joint fixing of prices by competitors. It has strengthened antitrust laws by making price collusion a criminal violation, extending the definition of price collusion, and allowing states to sue corporations for damages. In addition, the government watches for cases of price deception and price discrimination. <u>Bait pricing</u> is an illegal practice of a seller advertising a "special" but with no intention of selling it. <u>Price discrimination</u> occurs when price cuts are made that are not offered equally to every buyer. In devising a pricing policy a company can meet competitors' prices, undercut the going rate, or price at a higher level. A <u>price leader</u> is a dominant member of an industry that sets a price that the other companies match. In establishing a price on a new good or service, a firm may engage in price skimming or penetration pricing. <u>Skimming</u> is a pricing policy under which new products are often priced high, and their price is gradually lowered as they mature. Price skimming is often used to maximize short-term profits or to recover product investment and research costs. <u>Penetration pricing</u> is a policy of setting initial price for a new product very low to achieve the largest possible market share quickly. Penetration pricing discourages competitors from entering a market and builds brand loyalty.

8. The sixth step in setting price is to determine price-setting methods. Often objectives and policies are used as the framework for determining prices. Firms that use <u>cost-plus pricing</u> set prices by totaling their costs and adding a margin of profit. This method is used by contractors, public utilities, and most service businesses. Cost-plus pricing is used most often when it is difficult to estimate the costs of producing a product, when a company has the desire for a fair rate of return, and when price competition plays a role. Often a company may find the rate of

inflation high and unpredictable, thus the difficulty in determining costs. Contribution, or incremental, pricing is a special type of cost-plus pricing that allows companies to produce unprofitable items in order to cover variable costs. Airlines use this method of arriving at prices when they offer half-price fares at off-peak hours. Markup is the difference between the cost of an item and its selling price. In modern merchandising, firms generally express this difference in terms of the markup percentage. Markup pricing is used extensively by wholesalers and retailers in determining their pricing methods. Some businesses use an average markup, in which the same markup percentage is used for each item in a given product line. Turnover reflects the number of times average inventory is sold during a given period. Generally, the slower the item moves off the shelf, the higher is the markup. A loss leader is an item that is priced below cost to attract customers. The main reason for setting prices on the basis of costs is that the method is convenient and easy to apply. The breakeven analysis is a way for price setters to determine what will happen to profits at various price levels. It is the point at which the costs of producing a product equal the revenue made from selling the product. This is the point at which neither profit nor loss is being made on the product. The breakeven analysis allows marketers to examine the relationship among costs, revenues, and profits.

9. The seventh step in setting prices is to decide on a final price. Pricing policies and methods should help provide the guidance necessary in the selection of the final price. A list price reflects the selling price quoted to buyers. This price is often negotiable. A discount is a reduction made from the list price and offered to wholesalers and retailers and occurs in many forms. A trade discount is a reduction from list price to middlemen for services performed. A cash discount is a reduction from list price made for early payment. A quantity discount is a reduction in list price to middlemen for buying in large volume. There are two types of quantity discounts. Noncumulative discounts are one-time reductions for larger-than-usual orders. Cumulative discounts permit a customer to total consecutive orders to qualify for the discount. A seasonal discount provides cash savings for buying out of season. These purchases often receive forward dating so that the customer does not pay for goods until after the order is received. The benefits to the manufacturer are lower storage costs, minimal risks, and a more stabilized production schedule. When determining discounts, a company must be sure that the discounts are fairly available to all competing channel members in order to avoid any government legal hassle.

10. Many companies sell their goods to customers over wide geographic areas. The cost of distribution can be a very large part of the total price paid by the customer. Geographic adjustments necessitate reductions for transportation costs or other costs associated with the physical distance between the buyer and the seller. Geographic pricing describes

the responsibility for transportation changes. F.O.B. pricing (free on board) is the practice of having the buyer choose and pay for transportation and take title to the goods from the time they are loaded on board a carrier. F.O.B. destination occurs when the manufacturer pays freight to the destination. Title and responsibility for shipment do not pass until the merchandise reaches the buyer. F.O.B. origin occurs when the buyer pays for transportation and takes title to the goods from the time they are loaded on board a carrier. If the goods are damaged in transit, the buyer must file a claim against the carrier. Uniform-delivery pricing works by averaging the transportation charges of all buyers and adding that figure to the selling price. This provides a fixed average cost of transportation. A variation of uniform-delivery is zone-delivery pricing which allows manufacturers to divide the country or their market into two or more zones, charging the same rate within a zone but different rates between zones. Base-point pricing is a geographic pricing policy that allows for calculating freight charges not from the factory, but from a city or cities designated by members of the industry.

11. Prices must often be modified to meet consumer expectations. Price lining provides for the grouping of merchandise into classes by means of price. A company can set a limited number of prices for selected groups or lines of goods. Customary pricing is pricing some types of products, usually small-valued items such as candy bars, gum balls, and newspapers, at a certain level or consumer demand drops off rapidly. Very often a company may have to consider tradition in selecting an appropriate price. Odd pricing is a retail practice of adjusting prices to end with an odd number or just under a round number. Consumers often believe that odd pricing represents price reduction because a firm thinks carefully about its prices and sets them as low as possible.

LEARNING GOALS

After reading this chapter, you should be able to:

1. Describe the basic considerations in price setting, including such items as buyer demand, supply and costs, consumption, government regulations, and other elements of the marketing mix.
2. Discuss who sets prices and describe the specialists who participate in setting prices.
3. Describe the price-setting process, including the broad outlines that are the responsibility of top management.
4. Explain the reason behind the setting of price objectives, including the differences between a target rate of return, sales-related goals, status quo objectives, and social objectives.

5. Describe the importance of estimating buyer demand including the importance of the law of demand.
6. Describe the importance of calculating costs, that is, how much money producers need to pay out to supply goods or services.
7. Analyze the role of competitors' prices in the process of price setting.
8. Describe the techniques used in selecting a pricing policy, including deciding on one price or many; the importance of government regulations; pricing at, above, or below the market; and the pricing of new products.
9. Explain the price-setting methods, including cost-plus pricing, markup pricing, evaluation of cost-plus and markup pricing, and breakeven plus demand pricing.
10. Describe the importance of deciding on a final price. Areas of concern include discounts, geographical adjustments, and consumer-related price adjustments.

KEY CONCEPTS

From the list of lettered terms, select the one that best fits in the blank of the numbered statements that follow. Write the letter of that choice in the space provided.

(Answers to the key concepts appear at the end of the chapter.)

a. A markup
b. A cash discount
c. Pricing objectives
d. Base-point pricing
e. Skimming
f. A variable-price policy
g. Fixed costs
h. The law of demand
i. Contribution (incremental pricing)
j. Profit
k. A seasonal discount
l. Uniform-delivery pricing
m. A loss leader
n. The breakeven analysis
o. A cumulative discount
p. A noncumulative discount
q. Elastic demand
r. A price leader
s. Zone-delivery pricing
t. Variable costs
u. A one-price policy

v. Price lining
w. Markup percentage
x. A discount
y. Pricing policies
z. Customary pricing
aa. Price discrimination
bb. F.O.B. pricing
cc. Penetration pricing
dd. Cost-plus pricing
ee. A target rate of return
ff. Average markup
gg. Price collusion
hh. Turnover
ii. Utility
jj. Inelastic demand
kk. A trade discount
ll. Odd pricing
mm. A quantity discount
nn. A list price
oo. Elasticity of demand
pp. Bait pricing

1. _aa_ refers to price cuts that are not offered equally to every buyer.

2. _____ is a way for price setters to determine what will happen to profits at various price levels.

3. _g_ are costs that do not vary with a firm's output; also called overhead.

4. _____ refers to the policy under which sellers divide the country or market into two or more zones, charging the same rate within a zone but different rates between zones.

5. _____ is a special price for buying out of season.

6. _____ refers to the policy of setting prices by totaling costs and adding a margin of profit.

7. _____ is a deduction made from the list price and offered to wholesalers and retailers.

8. _____ refers to the policy of calculating freight charges not from their factories but from a city or cities designated by members of an industry.

9. _____ refers to the relationship that holds between price and revenue if total revenue increases with price rises or declines with price cuts.

10. _____ are long-range goals that managers wish to pursue in their pricing decisions.

11. _____ is an illegal practice of advertising a "special" at a cut-rate price with no intention to sell at the price advertised.

12. _____ refers to the number of times average inventory is sold during a given period.

13. _____ is a one-time reduction for a larger-than-usual order.

14. _____ is the practice of grouping merchandise into classes by means of price.

15. _____ refers to the special type of cost-plus pricing that allows companies to produce unprofitable items to cover variable costs.

16. _____ is reduction in list price to middlemen for buying in large volume.

17. _____ is the want-satisfying power of goods or services.

18. _____ is the relationship that holds between price and revenue if total revenue increases with a price drop or decreases with a price rise.

19. _____ refers to the single percentage used to determine the selling price of each item in a given product line.

20. _____ is a reduction from list price made for early payment.

21. _____ is the practice of having the buyer choose and pay for transportation from the time goods are loaded on a carrier ("free on board"). The buyer takes title at that time.

22. _____ refers to the rate at which demand changes in response to price changes.

23. _____ is the practice of quoting a single price to all sellers regardless of location, reached by averaging the transportation charges of all buyers and adding that figure to the selling price.

24. _____ is the goal stated as a certain percentage of return of sales or investment.

25. _____ refers to the policy that allows special prices for different customers.

26. _____ are pricing plans for dealing with situations in the future that generally recur.

27. _____ refers to the policy that permits a customer to total up consecutive orders to qualify for the discount.

28. _____ are costs that increase or decrease with the amount of output.

29. _____ refers to a reduction to "the trade" (wholesalers and retailers) from list price.

30. _____ is an economic rule that generally states more goods are sold at a lower price than at a higher one.

31. _____ refers to joint fixing of prices by competitors.

32. _____ is the selling price quoted to buyers.

33. _____ refers to a pricing policy under which new products are often priced high, and their price is gradually lowered as they mature.

34. _____ refers to the difference between the cost of an item and its selling price.

35. _____ is a dominant member of an industry that announces pricing policies other companies often follow.

36. _____ refers to the pricing of some types of products--usually small-value items--at a certain level to avert consumer resistance at higher levels.

37. _____ refers to what is left over after expenses are deducted from revenue (income).

38. _____ refers to the policy of offering goods purchased at the same time and in the same quantity at a single price to all.

39. _____ is an item priced below cost to attract customers.

40. _____ is the retail practice of adjusting prices to end with an odd number or just under a round number.

41. _____ refers to the markup expressed as a percentage.

42. _____ is a policy of setting initial price for a new product very low in order to achieve the largest possible market share quickly.

PROGRAMMED REVIEW

The following self-teaching exercises consist of short statements that require you to make a response by filling in the blank (or blanks) provided. You will find the correct response printed in the margin to the left of the question.

a. set pricing objectives
b. estimate buyer demand
c. calculate costs
d. analyze competitors' prices
e. select a pricing policy
f. determine price-setting methods
g. decide on a final price

1. What are the factors that most marketers weigh when determining a price?

a. _____
_____

b. _____
_____

c. _____
_____

d. _____
_____

e. _____
_____

f. _____
_____

g. _____
_____

supply
demand

2. Ideally, prices are set by the interaction of _____ and _____.

a. making price collusion a criminal violation.
b. extending the definition of price collusion.
c. allowing states to sue corporations for damages.

3. The government has been particularly active recently in enforcing laws against price collusion. In the government's view, price collusion lessens competition and harms consumers. It has therefore strengthened antitrust laws by

a. _____
_____

b. _____
_____

c. _____
_____

special

4. Bait pricing is the practice whereby a seller advertises a _____ at a cut-rate price with no intention to sell at the price advertised.

141

a. state the company's
   pricing objectives.
b. translate these goals
   into specific prices.

5. The process of setting a price requires
   the understanding of broad outlines
   which are the responsibility of top managers. Their tasks are to

   a. _____
      _____
      _____

   b. _____
      _____
      _____

a. buyer demand
b. supply and costs
c. competition
d. government regulations
e. other elements of the
   marketing mix

6. What five factors should be considered
   in setting prices?

   a. _____
   b. _____
   c. _____
   d. _____
   e. _____
      _____

cost
selling

7. Markup has traditionally been defined as
   the difference between the _____
   of an item and its _____
   price.

a. It allows a firm to
   recover its initial
   investment quickly.
b. It gives the company
   a chance to work out
   flaws in production
   before having to meet
   maximum demand.
c. By establishing an
   initial high quality
   image, skimming leaves
   consumers with the
   impression that they
   are getting a good buy
   when prices go down.

8. What are the three advantages of price
   skimming?

   a. _____
      _____
      _____

   b. _____
      _____
      _____

   c. _____
      _____
      _____
      _____

group

within
between

profit

a. target rate of return
b. sales-related goals
c. status quo objectives
d. social objectives

perceive

a. whether to offer a
    product at a single
    price or many dif-
    ferent prices
b. whether to price at,
    above, or below the
    market
c. how to price a new
    product

demand

9. Price lining is a practice used by com-
    panies to _____ merchan-
    dise into classes by means of price.

10. Zone-delivery pricing is a pricing
    policy whereby manufacturers divide the
    country or their market into two or
    more zones, charging the same rate
    _____ a zone but differ-
    ent rates _____ zones.

11. Businesspeople see prices from a dif-
    ferent perspective. They cannot ignore
    the want-satisfying dimension, espe-
    cially if they belong to a market-
    oriented firm. But for them, price
    represents _____.

12. What are the four categories in which
    most pricing objectives can be
    grouped?

    a. _____

    b. _____

    c. _____

    d. _____

13. While there is some evidence that high
    prices do not correspond to high qual-
    ity, customers do tend to _____
    such a relationship.

14. Three important policy-making issues are:

    a. _____
       _____
       _____
    b. _____
       _____
       _____
    c. _____
       _____

15. The price a firm may charge for a prod-
    uct depends to a large extent on
    _____.

143

decrease
increase

bankruptcy

a. Cost figures are
    relatively easy to
    secure.
b. The business seeks a
    fair rate of return,
    rather than maximum
    profits.
c. Price competition
    within the industry
    may not be very
    keen.

inventory

profits
price

a. It must cover all the
    expenses of the item.
b. It must contain an
    allowance for planned
    profit.

list

16. Elastic demand means that a _____
    in price will _____ the
    seller's revenue, while a price increase
    will decrease revenue.

17. In the long run, businesses must cover
    all their costs in setting prices or
    face _____.

18. In cost-plus pricing, what three condi-
    tions prevail?

    a. _____
        _____
    b. _____
        _____
    c. _____
        _____
        _____

19. Turnover refers to the number of times
    average _____ is
    sold during a given period.

20. The breakeven analysis is a way for
    price setters to determine what will
    happen to _____ at
    various _____ levels.

21. What are the two purposes of markup
    percentage?

    a. _____
        _____
    b. _____
        _____

22. Discounts are deductions made from the
    _____ price, are offered to
    wholesalers and retailers, and come in
    many forms.

144

a. fixed
b. variable

23. What two types of costs must sellers cover?

a. _____

b. _____

averaging
selling

24. Uniform-delivery pricing works by _____ the transportation charges of all buyers and adding that figure to the _____ price.

a. cost-plus pricing
b. markup pricing
c. breakeven plus demand pricing

25. What three methods do companies use to set prices?

a. _____

b. _____

c. _____
_____

MARKETING RIDDLE

The purpose of this exercise is to find the missing word that solves the riddle. Each of the statements requires you to make a response by filling in the blank (or blanks) for the appropriate missing word. Each statement contains a key letter which, when combined with the other key letters, will provide you with the solution to the riddle. Correct solutions to the riddle questions can lead to valuable prizes. See instructions for more information.

Price represents the value the company places on its products and services. In addition, price often conveys an image of the company and its products to the potential buyers. For an exchange to take place, both the buyer and seller must believe that the price of a product or service provides an

__ __ __ __ __ __ __ __ __   value.
1 2 3 4 5 6 7 8 9

1. The price a firm may charge for a product depends to a large extent on __ ☐ __ __ __ __.

2. Many customers associate high price with ☐ __ __ __ __ __ __ __ , although the relationship does not always exist.

3. Variable costs, as the name implies, are costs that increase or decrease with the amount of __ __ __ __ __ ☐ __.

145

4. Discounts are deductions made from the __ ☐ __ __ price, are offered to wholesalers and retailers, and come in many forms.

5. Discounts to the wholesaler and retailer vary according to the __ __ __ __ ☐ __ __ __ they perform and their profit needs.

6. Turnover reflects the number of times ☐ __ __ __ __ __ __ inventory is sold during a given period.

7. When an item is priced ☐ __ __ __ __ cost to attract customers, it is called a loss leader.

8. Cost-plus pricing may be a poor method when rapid __ __ __ ☐ __ __ __ __ __ is expected.

9. The major advantage of variable pricing is its __ __ ☐ __ __ __ __ __ __ __ __.

EXPERIENTIAL EXERCISE

A pricing policy is more specific than objectives and may not be stated explicitly. It is generally known throughout the organization.

Select a product currently on the market and describe whether the firm, in your opinion, engaged in a one price or many pricing policy at, above, or below the market; price skimming; or price penetration. Explain why you believe each company followed its policy.

1. One Price or Many Pricing Policy

_____
_____
_____
_____
_____
_____

2. At, Above, or Below the Market

_____
_____
_____
_____
_____
_____

3. Price Skimming

    _____
    _____
    _____
    _____
    _____
    _____

4. Price Penetration

    _____
    _____
    _____
    _____
    _____
    _____

Multiple Choice

_____ 1. When a company establishes an initial price for a new product that
           will be very low in order to achieve the largest possible market
           share quickly, it is engaging in
           a. price skimming
           b. cost-plus pricing.
           c. penetration pricing.
           d. price lining.

_____ 2. The practice manufacturers use to calculate freight charges not
           from their factories, but from a city or cities designated by mem-
           bers of their industry, is known as
           a. base-point pricing.
           b. price lining.
           c. zone-delivery pricing.
           d. F.O.B. pricing.

_____ 3. If an increase in price also increases total revenue or a decrease
           in price decreases total revenue, demand is therefore said to be
           a. elastic.
           b. indifferent.
           c. inelastic.
           d. less.

_____ 4. A price policy that allows special prices for different customers is known as a
a. one-price policy.
b. price policy.
c. variable-price policy.
d. customer price policy.

_____ 5. When a firm rejects profit maximization and establishes a pricing objective which is designed to achieve a certain fair percentage return, it is expressed as
a. a method to prevent competition.
b. profit stabilization.
c. market share.
d. a target rate of return.

_____ 6. The practice of grouping merchandise into classes by means of price is known as
a. price lining.
b. customary pricing.
c. odd pricing.
d. zone pricing.

_____ 7. The joint fixing of prices by competitors is known as
a. price penetration.
b. price skimming.
c. cost-plus pricing.
d. price collusion.

_____ 8. The practice of permitting a customer to total up consecutive orders to qualify for the discount is known as
a. quantity discounts.
b. cumulative discounts.
c. noncumulative discounts.
d. seasonal discounts.

_____ 9. The method often used by price setters to determine what will happen to profits at various price levels is referred to as
a. list pricing.
b. markup pricing.
c. cost-plus.
d. breakeven analysis.

_____ 10. The term used to describe a seller advertising a "special" but having no intention of selling the item is called
a. price discrimination.
b. bait pricing.
c. price leader.
d. variable pricing.

True-False

_____ 11. In penetration pricing, new products are often priced high, and their price is gradually lowered as they mature.

_____ 12. Cumulative discounts are one-time reductions for larger than usual orders.

_____ 13. In setting prices, top management makes the major decisions; but lower-level people carry out, or administer, the prices.

_____ 14. The law of demand states that, in general, fewer goods are sold at a lower price than at a higher one.

_____ 15. Variable costs are expenses that increase or decrease with the amount of output.

_____ 16. Today most firms operate in markets where imperfect competition is the rule. In some cases, monopolies exist in which one seller has absolute control over the price.

_____ 17. In general, the more substitutes for a product the more inelastic is the demand, and vice versa.

_____ 18. Fixed costs are those that do not vary with a firm's output.

_____ 19. Unlike objectives, pricing policies may be stated explicitly.

_____ 20. Markup has traditionally been defined as the difference between the variable cost of an item and its selling price.

CHAPTER SOLUTIONS

Key Concepts

1. aa	9. jj	17. ii	25. f	34. a
2. n	10. c	18. a	26. y	35. r
3. g	11. pp	19. ff	27. o	36. z
4. s	12. hh	20. b	28. t	37. j
5. k	13. p	21. bb	29. kk	38. u
6. dd	14. v	22. oo	30. h	39. m
7. x	15. i	23. l	31. gg	40. ll
8. d	16. mm	24. ee	32. nn	41. w
			33. e	42. cc

1.	c	5.	d	9.	d	13.	T	17.	F
2.	a	6.	a	10.	b	14.	F	18.	T
3.	c	7.	d	11.	F	15.	T	19.	F
4.	c	8.	b	12.	F	16.	T	20.	F

CHAPTER 11
CHANNELS AND WHOLESALING

CHAPTER SUMMARY

1. Marketing is concerned with not only determining what goods and services
    consumers want, but also getting the goods into those locations where con-
    sumers will purchase the merchandise as needed. Be it complex or simple,
    every product must follow some path from the producer to the consumer.
    A marketing (distribution) channel refers to the people and organizations
    involved in making a product available to a user. A marketing channel
    requires at minimum a seller and a buyer. The buyer may be a consumer or
    an industrial user. In addition, a marketing channel may include various
    middlemen. Retailers sell directly to consumers. Wholesaling middlemen
    do most of their selling to retailers, other wholesaling middlemen, or
    industrial users rather than consumers. Although channel decisions need
    not precede other marketing decisions, they do have a great influence on
    the other components in the marketing mix. There are various levels of
    intermediaries used by producers in order to get their products to the
    ultimate user.

2. Obtaining adequate distribution requires a careful analysis of distribu-
    tion costs and at the same time the desire to provide a good or service
    where the consumer wants and expects to buy it. Middlemen, particularly
    retailers, serve consumers by bringing together a wide assortment of
    goods, locating that assortment in a convenient spot, providing credit,
    offering money-saving services, and giving consumers the desired product
    in the desired quantity. Middlemen also serve producers. Wholesaling
    middlemen and retailers help simplify contacts between producers and
    consumers. Middlemen also help producers financially. Middlemen who
    take title to goods relieve manufacturers of some of the financial risk
    they might suffer if their goods did not sell. In addition, middlemen
    are able to communicate marketing information to producers, thus providing
    them with knowledge concerning marketing trends.

3. The transfer principle states that all of the functions of the marketing
    channel are vital and, when not performed by one channel member, they
    must be taken over by another. The major tasks facing marketers special-
    izing in distribution are to design marketing channels so that goods
    reach a market efficiently and to manage problems that arise within a
    channel. The four principal decisions that must be made concerning chan-
    nels are channel length, number, member types, and width.

4. Channel length concerns itself with the decision whether to use whole-
    saling middlemen, retailers, or some combination. There are important
    differences between the channels of distribution for consumer and indus-
    trial products. Most consumer goods go through a four-link channel,
    employing both wholesale and retail middlemen. Consumer products can
    also go through a five-link, three-link, or even a two-link channel.

    A two-link channel describes the direct movement of goods from the
manufacturer directly to the consumer with no intermediaries. An example
of this channel is a farmer who grows crops and then proceeds to sell the
goods at a roadside stand to consumers. This channel represents the
least used method of distribution.

    A three-link channel describes the movement of goods from the manu-
facturer to the retailer then to the consumer. The J. C. Penney Company
can purchase merchandise in bulk, proceed to have the goods delivered
to its stores, and subsequently sold to the consumer. This channel
appears to be growing in popularity amongst those large retailers who
have many store locations, financial resources, and management expertise to expediate the movement of goods themselves.

    A four-link channel describes the movement of goods from the manu-
facturer to the wholesaler, to the retailer, then to the ultimate consumer. This channel represents the traditional and most widely used
channel in the distribution process. This channel is used by small companies with limited financial resources and by those companies that sell
convenience goods. The Phillip Morris Company, a large organization,
distributes its various brands of tobacco products directly to wholesalers who in turn sell to retailers, and they in turn sell to the ultimate consumers. In some instances, manufacturers can also use sales representatives to call on retailers to supplement the wholesaler's sales
force in selling goods to retailers.

    A five-link channel describes the movement of goods from the manu-
facturer to the agent or broker, who in turn distributes the goods to
the wholesaler, who in turn distributes the goods to the retailer, then
on to the ultimate consumer. The Marks Candy Company distributes candy
to agents or brokers who then proceed to distribute candy to wholesalers,
whose job is to find wholesale buyers for the products. The wholesalers,
in turn, distribute the candy to retailers and others who deal in the
distribution of the product to the ultimate consumer.

    Most industrial goods go through fewer channels than consumer goods.
Direct selling is by far the most common channel in industrial marketing.
A two-link channel for industrial goods represents a direct movement of
goods from the manufacturer to the industrial user. This channel is much
more important to the industrial goods market than it is to the consumer
market. Most major installations, accessory equipment, and component
parts and materials are marketed in this fashion. IBM often uses its own

sales force to sell large computers directly to buyers. Because most of the goods sold are already in finished form and often can be large and bulky, there may be no need to use a middleman.

A three-link channel represents the occasion to use the agent or broker to distribute the good. This method often occurs when a manufacturer needs to have the goods sold and does not want to hire a sales force. With the use of this channel, the agent, in essence, becomes the company's sales force. In addition, when transportation accounts for a small percentage of the total cost, this method can effectively be used. Another example of a three-link channel describes a channel often used by a manufacturer to purchase operating supplies such as pencils and pens, mops and brooms, and screwdrivers and hammers. Because the purchase price of operating supplies is generally not as high as when accessory equipment is desired, a company may prefer to purchase locally from a wholesaler who is in a position to provide various supplies as needed.

A four-link channel describes a channel in which the manufacturer distributes goods to brokers and agents who in turn distribute to wholesalers. The wholesalers in turn sell to the industrial users. Often export agents from foreign countries use this channel to distribute merchandise to manufacturers in the United States.

In seeking out the most efficient channel length, a manufacturer has to consider the characteristics of the product, the market, the company, and the environment. Market characteristics should be one of the first things that a manufacturer has to consider in developing a channel of distribution. Of primary concern to the manufacturer will be the determination of the individuals most likely to buy the good or service. A manufacturer that wants to distribute goods nationwide cannot thoroughly canvas the country. He must rely on wholesalers who are located locally to deliver the goods. On the other hand, a manufacturer that wants to distribute goods locally can use his own sales force. Often the product and its particular characteristics are used in selecting channels of distribution. For example, perishable products such as fruits and vegetables would require a short channel with minimal number of intermediaries. On the other hand, men's shorts or T-shirts could command a longer channel in that their demand and acceptance do not require immediate distribution. A manufacturer should also consider the complexity of the product. Many products because of their technical features often require a need for direct communication between seller and buyer. With such wide geographically dispersed targets, marketers realize that intermediaries are needed in order to adequately move goods. Thus, in selecting channels, marketers include a retailer as the last step in reaching the consumers. In addition, consumer buying preferences may affect the channel selected. Today, more and more consumers are purchasing goods through mail-order catalogs. In planning channel selections, companies may have to consider this trend. Ten years ago many women purchased nylons by patronizing specialty nylon retail stores. When companies began to distribute and consumers purchased nylons in retail stores

153

from supermarkets to drug stores, the use of specialty nylon stores began to fade. Thus consumers, by their preferred methods of purchase, helped to determine the appropriate channel for nylons. Industrial buyers are concentrated in a few regions with only a small number of potential buyers. This provides the marketer with the potential to engage in direct selling and thus avoid the need for retailers. The marketing manager needs to know who is most likely to buy the product, what are their life-style characteristics, and whether they are heavy or light users of the product.

A manufacturer has to determine whether it wishes to give up some control over how and to whom the products are sold. Once goods are sold to a middleman, it is very difficult for a manufacturer to determine who has purchased the good, in what locations, and at what price. Control may be very important when companies are concerned with promotional activities and new product introductions. Manufacturers have to determine whether they have the financial and managerial abilities to undertake distribution themselves. In addition, with proper financing adequate warehousing can be established. The Ford Motor Company uses thousands of independent dealers to sell its automobiles. It would be very difficult for Ford to purchase its dealers outright. Other companies are so production oriented that intermediaries, with their superior managerial abilities, are used in making goods widely available and accessible to target markets. The experience, exposure, and degree of specialization offer an organization more than it can accomplish on its own.

Companies that have a variety of products often market their products themselves since it becomes advantageous to have your own sales force. The Pepsi Cola Company manufactures a variety of soda products which include Pepsi, Pepsi Light, and Pepsi Free. The company has its own fleet of trucks and drivers who sell Pepsi Cola products directly to retailers. Often economic conditions may cause some companies to use low-cost distributors rather than a high-cost company sales force. There are many laws and regulations that can affect channel selection. For example, there are laws that can restrict the sale of products. Liquor must be sold in authorized stores to qualified individuals. In addition, there are state restrictions as to the days of the week and hours within each day that liquor can be sold. With the large number of products on the market, manufacturers often find that wholesale middlemen are overburdened with a large number of goods and are not interested in handling new products. Other environmental factors can include geographic and promotional considerations. Because of climatic conditions and topography, marketers have to be knowledgeable of geography. During extensive cold periods, merchandise may have to be transported by air to Alaska. On other occasions, merchandise may be shipped by vessel.

Often companies believe that intermediaries do not adequately promote products. This belief often causes a marketer to select an appropriate channel that can provide for a more efficient means of promotion.

5. Channel number concerns itself with the decision of how many different marketing channels to employ. There are four basic reasons why companies might use more than one marketing channel. They may be selling to entirely different markets, different market segments, different geographic regions, and different-size buyers.

6. Channel member types concerns itself with what kinds of wholesaling middlemen and retailers to bring in. Merchant wholesalers are independents who buy goods from manufacturers, take physical possession of the goods, and sell them to other middlemen. Agents merely arrange for the buying and selling of goods, but never actually take title or physical possession of goods. Wholly owned wholesalers, often called manufacturers' sales branches and offices, are the distribution arm of manufacturers who set them up. Choosing the right wholesale middlemen from among the various types can be the key decision in establishing an effective distribution system.

7. Merchant wholesalers represent the largest category of wholesalers. Merchant wholesalers can be classified as full-service or limited-function wholesalers. The full-service wholesaler assembles goods from manufacturers, stores and delivers them, finances retailer purchases, and provides marketing information for both manufacturers and retailers. There are three types of full-service wholesalers. They are wholesale merchants, industrial distributors, and rack jobbers. The wholesale merchants supply mainly retailers and some institutions. The industrial distributors are the counterparts of wholesale merchants in the industrial market. They are often best suited to companies that have a large base of potential customers, have a product line that is relatively easy to stock, sell in small quantities, and sell to customers at a low level in their organization. Rack jobbers supply grocery and other retail stores with nonfood items such as housewares, toys, and health and beauty aids. The goods are owned by the rack jobber who displays the goods and sells them on a consignment basis.

8. The second type of merchant wholesaler is the limited-function merchant wholesaler who provides only a few services for his customers. The four principal types are the cash-and-carry wholesalers, drop shippers, truck wholesalers, and mail-order wholesalers. The cash-and-carry wholesaler does not give credit. Most buyers pick up their goods at the wholesaler's place of business. The drop shippers neither maintain warehouses nor carry inventories. They do, however, take title to the goods and are responsible for billing a customer and collecting payment. Truck wholesalers perform all the functions of full-service organizations except financing. They maintain a warehouse, but they operate by selling and making deliveries directly from a truck. Mail-order wholesalers do not engage in any personal selling. Instead, they send catalogs to retail firms or other wholesalers with instructions on how to order goods.

9. An <u>agent</u> is a wholesale middleman who merely arranges for the buying and selling of goods but never actually acquires ownership or possession of goods. The various types of agents can include selling agents, manufacturers' agents, commission merchants, brokers, and auction companies. <u>Selling agents</u> handle the entire output of small manufacturers. <u>Manufacturers' agents</u> usually take over the selling functions in the areas that it does not pay the manufacturer to cover with his or her own sales force. <u>Commission merchants</u> may store the goods they handle until enough are gathered for a sale, though they do not take title to the goods. They are often used in selling the output of small farmers. <u>Brokers</u> are common in fields like real estate and agriculture where there are mainly buyers and sellers and no central marketplace for exchange. They bring buyers and sellers together, acting on behalf of one or the other. <u>Auction companies</u> consist of those fast-talking auctioneers who sell tobacco, flowers, or other farm products at a frantic pace. In addition, artwork, antiques, and other products that vary widely in quality, and thus must be sold individually, are also handled by them. The auctioneer works for a commission and may often store goods but does not take title.

10. <u>Wholly owned wholesalers</u> provide either sales offices or sales branches. They are the distribution arm of the manufacturer that sets it up. A <u>sales office</u> acts as a headquarters away from a company's manufacturing plants for the sales force. As a general rule, they do not carry stock. A <u>sales branch</u> differs in that in most cases they do carry stock and, more importantly, they act as servicing centers.

11. <u>Channel width</u> concerns itself with how many outlets or individual firms to employ at each level of the channel. Marketers have to decide on the number of intermediaries within each channel level. This necessitates the need to determine what degree of market exposure that a product or service should have. <u>Intensive distribution</u> occurs when the producer decides that goods and services are to be sold through almost all available wholesale or retail outlets. In the consumer market, almost all branded convenience items require intensive distribution in order to provide the consumer with the opportunity to purchase the product with the minimum of effort. Out-of-stock conditions may cause the consumer to seek out substitute products. In the industrial market, office supplies and other standardized, low-cost products purchased in quantity are sold this way. Intensive distribution can result in mass promotional coverage, a large volume of sales, low unit prices, and the use of wholesalers for distribution. <u>Exclusive distribution</u> occurs when the producer decides to sell a product or service through only one wholesaler or retailer in a given area. Well-known expensive consumer items are sold through a few stores. Market coverage may not be as thorough or intensive; however, greater cooperation can be developed between manufacturers and retailers. This may result in reduced marketing costs, higher profits, and improved product image. Companies that engage in exclusive distribution must be aware that our government does not look favorably on agreements that grant exclusive geographic rights

because they often violate antitrust laws. Industrial marketers might use it in distributing expensive installations or special parts. Selective distribution occurs when the producer involves the use of more than one but less than all the firms that might carry a product. Many durable goods such as appliances and liquor may be distributed selectively. Such products are more expensive than convenience goods and require the marketer to select those stores that properly convey the image, quality, and price that the goods project. Most consumers will purchase goods only after comparing price, quality, service, and style. Industrial goods are often sold on a selective basis in order to maintain control over sales. Very often cooperative advertising may exist between the manufacturer and retailer. Manufacturers often use selective distribution when it costs less than intensive distribution due to the fact that there are fewer clients to call on, it lessens the possibility of price cutting because competition is less intense, and it promotes close cooperation between the selected channel members who feel that they have an important stake in selling the product.

12. Often one company or individual in the channel of distribution is able to exercise power and control conflict. The channel captain emerges when one strong member in the channel has either the power or the leadership ability to set policy and resolve conflict. Conflict can occur because of communication difficulties or because of a disagreement about goals. The channel captain has the power to establish, enforce, and coerce policy. His position in channel strategy can constitute a dominant force in the controlling of conflict. In the past, the channel captains had been the wholesale middlemen and the manufacturers. It now appears that the channel captain may well be the retailer.

13. A vertical marketing system (VMS) is one in which one channel member owns, controls, or coordinates the operations of other channel members. The fast-food restaurant industry is an example of how the VMS is used. The vertical marketing system was developed when it appeared that there was a need to manage the functions of intermediaries at various levels of the distribution channel. The VMS combines various channel stages from production to the ultimate user stage under one ownership or management. The three types of vertical marketing systems include administered, corporate, and contractual. The administered system occurs when such things as what a product will sell for, how it will be displayed, and how much money will be spent on its advertising are included in a detailed plan that the channel leader submits to other members. In an administered system, authority still remains with individual channel members. Sears, by virtue of its importance and strong reputation in retailing, is able to employ a VMS in administering its operations. A corporate system develops when one channel member owns, or at least partially owns, the business operations of two or more channel levels. He is able to develop interorganizational relationships through contracts or other legal means. The channel member can own the business operations of two or more channel levels or the members can agree by contract to cooperate with each other. The contractual system involves a formal legal agreement (or contract) between channel

157

members to cooperate on such matters as buying, advertising, accounting practices, and other such functions. The theory behind the contractual system is that if all parties live up to their sides of the contract, the system will work well. It is anticipated that the contractual system, and in general all vertical marketing systems, are to continue to grow in the future.

LEARNING GOALS

After reading this chapter, you should be able to:

1. Define a marketing or distribution channel.
2. Describe the nature and importance of wholesale and retail middlemen, describe how middlemen serve consumers and producers, and explain the importance of the transfer principle.
3. Describe typical channels of distribution for consumer goods and industrial goods.
4. Describe the factors to consider in designing marketing channels, including the importance of channel length, number, member types, and width.
5. Explain the importance of managing channels, including problems, solutions, and the role of the channel captain; and describe how coercion and cooperation exist within the channels.
6. Define a vertical marketing system, including the importance of administered, corporate, and contractual systems.

KEY CONCEPTS

From the list of lettered terms, select the one that best fits in the blank of the numbered statements that follow. Write the letter of that choice in the space provided.

(Answers to the key concepts appear at the end of the chapter.)

a. An auction company
b. A channel number
c. A wholly owned wholesaler
d. Channel width
e. The transfer principle
f. A cash-and-carry wholesaler
g. A sales office
h. A mail-order wholesaler
i. Distribution
j. A merchant wholesaler
k. Selective distribution
l. A channel member type
m. A wholesale middleman
n. A broker

o. A limited-function merchant wholesaler
p. A drop shipper
q. A corporate system
r. A truck wholesaler
s. A commission merchant
t. A sales branch
u. Intensive distribution
v. A vertical marketing system (VMS)
w. A selling agent
x. A wholesale merchant
y. Channel length
z. A retailer
aa. A contractual system
bb. A manufacturers' agent
cc. A marketing (distribution) channel
dd. A full-service merchant wholesaler
ee. An industrial distributor
ff. An agent
gg. A channel captain
hh. An exclusive distribution
ii. A rack jobber
jj. An administered system

1. _aa_ is a vertical marketing system based on a formal agreement among channel members to cooperate on such matters as buying, advertising, accounting practices, and other functions. Forms are franchises, retail-sponsored cooperatives, and wholesale-sponsored voluntaries.

2. _r_ is a limited-function merchant wholesaler who performs all the functions of full-service organizations except financing; operates by selling and making deliveries directly from a truck.

3. _v_ refers to a system in which one channel member owns, controls, or coordinates the operations of other channel members.

4. _ff_ is a wholesale middleman who merely arranges for the buying and selling of goods but never actually acquires ownership or possession of the goods.

5. _t_ is the headquarters for a sales force away from a company's plant.

6. _x_ is the link that sells to retailers, other wholesaling middlemen, or industrial users.

7. _u_ refers to the distribution arm of the manufacturer that sets it up. It can be manufacturers' sales branches or sales offices.

8. _____ is a merchant wholesaler who provides only a few services for customers.

9. _____ is a full-service merchant wholesaler who supplies mainly retailers or institutions.

10. _____ is the principle that all functions of the marketing channel are vital and when not performed by one channel member must be taken over by another.

11. _____ is a full-service merchant wholesaler who supplies grocery and other retail stores with nonfood items on display racks and who owns the goods and racks.

12. _____ refers to the people and organizations involved in making a product available to a user.

13. _____ is a manufacturing firm's service center and stock storehouse.

14. _____ refers to the kind of wholesaling middlemen and retailers in a marketing channel.

15. _____ is an independent who buys goods from manufacturers, takes physical possession of them, and sells them to other middlemen.

16. _____ is a wholesale middleman who performs a wide variety of distribution tasks such as assembly, storage and delivery, and financing, and may provide market information.

17. _____ refers to the selling of a product through only one wholesaler or retailer in a given area.

18. _____ is a limited-function merchant wholesaler who neither maintains a warehouse nor carries inventories but who takes title to goods and is responsible for billing and collecting.

19. _____ is a limited-function merchant wholesaler who does not engage in personal selling; sales catalogs are sent to retail firms or other wholesalers.

20. _____ is an agent wholesaler who handles marketing for the entire output of small manufacturers.

21. _____ refers to a vertical marketing system in which one member secures agreement from other members of a channel on certain plans concerning price, display, and advertising.

22. _____ is an agent wholesaler who markets the output of small farmers for a commission; may store goods but does not take title.

23. _____ refers to the use of more than one but less than all firms that might carry a product.

24. _____ refers to the number of links (middlemen types) in a particular marketing chain.

25. _____ is a limited-function merchant wholesaler who does not give credit.

26. _____ is a middleman who sells directly to consumers.

27. _____ is a wholesaler who sells to the industrial market.

28. _____ is an agent wholesaler who brings buyers and sellers together, acting on behalf of one or the other, and used on a one-time basis.

29. _____ is an agent wholesaler who handles marketing in areas a manufacturer chooses not to cover with the manufacturer's own sales force.

30. _____ refers to a vertical marketing system in which one channel member fully or partially owns the business operations of two or more channel levels.

31. _____ refers to the quantity of different marketing channels to use in order to reach buyers.

32. _____ refers to the selling of a product through almost all available wholesale or retail outlets.

33. _____ refers to a member of a marketing channel with power or ability to set and enforce policy.

34. _____ refers to the activity directed toward placing goods and services where they are needed and when they are wanted.

35. _____ refers to the number of outlets or individual firms to employ at each level in a channel.

36. _____ is an agent wholesaler that works for a commission; may store goods but does not take title.

PROGRAMMED REVIEW

The following self-teaching exercises consist of short statements that require you to make a response by filling in the blank (or blanks) provided. You will find the correct response printed in the margin to the left of the question.

a. bringing together a
   wide assortment of goods
b. placing that assortment
   in a convenient
   location
c. providing credit
d. offering money-saving
   services
e. giving consumers the
   desired product in the
   desired quantity

1. What are the five ways that market intermediaries, particularly retailers, serve
   consumers?

   a. _____
      _____
   b. _____
      _____
   c. _____
      _____
   d. _____
      _____
   e. _____
      _____

all

2. Intensive distribution is a strategy of
   selling goods and services through almost _____ available wholesale
   or retail outlets.

seller
buyer

3. A marketing channel requires at minimum
   a _____ and a
   _____.

a. wholesale merchants
b. industrial distrib-
   utors
c. rack jobbers

4. What are the three types of full-service
   wholesalers?

   a. _____
   b. _____
   c. _____

a. full-service whole-
   saler
b. limited-function
   wholesaler

5. What are the two categories that merchant wholesalers are classified as?

   a. _____
   b. _____

independents
physical possession
sell

6. Merchant wholesalers are _____
   who buy goods from manufacturers, take
   _____ of
   them, and _____ them to other
   middlemen.

162

a. administered
b. corporate
c. contractual

7. A vertical marketing system (VMS) is one in which one channel member owns, controls, or coordinates the operations of other channel members. What are the three types of vertical marketing systems?

   a. _____

   b. _____

   c. _____

conflicts
voluntary cooperation

8. Channel captains help to minimize _____ by encouraging _____ among the various members of the channel.

a. channel length
b. channel number
c. channel member types
d. channel width

9. What are the four principle decisions that must be made concerning channels?

   a. _____

   b. _____

   c. _____

   d. _____

retailers
other wholesaling middlemen
industrial users

10. Wholesaling middlemen do most of their selling to _____, _____, or _____ rather than to consumers.

a. intensive distribution
b. exclusive distribution
c. selective distribution

11. In determining channel width, what are the three choices that a firm may select from in determining the type of market exposure that a product should have?

   a. _____

   b. _____

   c. _____

163

a. characteristics of the
   product
b. the market
c. the company
d. the environment

12. What are the four factors that can
    influence the decision of channel
    length?

    a. _____

    _____

    b. _____

    c. _____

    d. _____

retailers
institutions

13. Wholesale merchants supply mainly
    _____ and some
    _____ .

one

14. Exclusive distribution occurs when a
    firm sells a product through only
    _____ wholesaler or retailer in
    a given area.

a. cash-and-carry
   wholesalers
b. drop shippers
c. truck wholesalers
d. mail-order whole-
   salers

15. The limited-function merchant whole-
    salers provide only a few services for
    their customers. What are the four
    principal types?

    a. _____

    b. _____

    c. _____

    d. _____

every step

16. The first step in effectively control-
    ling distribution costs is to evaluate
    _____ in the
    distribution process.

contacts

17. Wholesaling middlemen and retailers
    help simplify _____
    between producers and consumers.

a. They may be selling to entirely different markets.
b. They may be selling to different market segments.
c. Different geographic regions may require different channels.
d. Different-size buyers may be reached through different channels.

18. What are the four basic reasons why companies might use more than one marketing channel?

a. _____
   _____
   _____

b. _____
   _____
   _____

c. _____
   _____
   _____

d. _____
   _____
   _____

administered
corporate

19. Contractual systems are really a middle ground between _____ and _____ systems.

a. selling agents
b. manufacturers' agents
c. commission merchants
d. brokers
e. auction companies

20. What are five commonly used categories of agents?

a. _____
b. _____
c. _____
d. _____
e. _____

wholesale
retail

21. Consumer goods commonly go through a four-link channel employing both _____ and _____ middlemen.

a. It costs less than intensive distribution because there are fewer clients to call on.
b. It lessens the possibility of price cutting because competition is less intense.
c. It promotes close cooperation between the selling channel members.

22. What are three advantages that manufacturers see in the use of selective distribution?

a. _____
_____
_____
_____

b. _____
_____
_____
_____

c. _____
_____
_____
_____

a. sales offices
b. sales branches

23. What are two examples of wholly owned wholesaler's outlets?

a. _____
b. _____

vital
taken over

24. The transfer principle states that all of the functions of the marketing channel are _____ and, when not performed by one channel member, they must be _____ by another.

a. assembling goods from manufacturers
b. storing and delivering goods
c. financing retailer purchases
d. providing marketing information for both manufacturers and retailers

25. What are the four distribution tasks that a full-service wholesaler performs?

a. _____
_____

b. _____
_____

c. _____
_____

d. _____
_____

MARKETING RIDDLE

The purpose of this exercise is to find the missing word that solves the
riddle. Each of the statements requires you to make a response by filling in
the blank (or blanks) for the appropriate missing word. Each statement contains a key letter which, when combined with the other key letters, will provide you with the solution to the riddle. Correct solutions to the riddle
questions can lead to valuable prizes. See instructions for more information.

> After the marketing manager has determined his target market,
> he should specify channel objectives. As with marketing objectives,
> these should be specific, realistic, and
>
> __ __ __ __ __ __ __ __ __ __ .
> 1 2 3 4 5 6 7 8 9 10

1. A channel captain, whether a manufacturer or a retailer, can force its
    will on other channel members or use ☐ __ __ __ __ __ __ to win their
    voluntary cooperation.

2. Channel width is concerned with how many __ __ __ __ ☐ __ __ or individ-
    ual firms to employ at each level of the channel.

3. Exclusive distribution gives middlemen some incentive to build sales in
    their assigned territory because they ☐ __ __ __ __ will profit.

4. Besides communication difficulties, conflict between a manufacturer and
    its distributors can arise because of a genuine disagreement about
    __ __ __ __ ☐ .

5. From the retailers' point of view, the major advantages of an integrated
    corporate system are a lower cost for goods purchased and guaranteed
    access to __ ☐ __ __ __ __ __ __ .

6. Most industrial goods go through __ __ __ __ ☐ channels than consumer
    goods.

7. A corporate system can develop when one channel member owns or at least
    partially owns the business __ __ __ __ ☐ __ __ __ __ __ of two or more
    channel levels.

8. The use of one or more intermediaries allows the channel
    ☐ __ __ __ __ __ __ to be shared by more parties.

9. Limited-function merchant wholesalers became popular mainly because
    __ __ ☐ __ - __ __ __ __ __ __ __ wholesalers are expensive, and some
    manufacturers do not need the full range of services.

10. In general, all high-volume transactions between large suppliers and large buyers are __ __ __ ☐ __ __.

EXPERIENTIAL EXERCISE

The selection of appropriate marketing channels is very important in the distribution of goods and services. As a manufacturer of a single line of frozen foods, describe what criteria you would take into account in selecting appropriate channels of distribution.

1. Manufacturer Considerations

_____
_____
_____
_____
_____
_____

2. Product Considerations

_____
_____
_____
_____
_____
_____

3. Buyer Considerations

_____
_____
_____
_____
_____
_____

4. Environmental Considerations

_____

_____

_____

_____

_____

_____

SELF-QUIZ

Multiple Choice

_a_ 1. The specific characteristics of the product, the market, the company, and the environment help to determine the selection of a
channel. This group of characteristics is concerned with the
proper selection of
   a. channel length.
   b. channel number.
   c. channel member types.
   d. channel width.

_c_ 2. What type of system do we find when such things as what a product
will sell for, how it will be displayed, and how much money will
be spent on its advertising are included in a detailed plan that
the channel leader submits to other members?
   a. contractual
   b. corporate
   c. administered
   d. cooperative

_c_ 3. Almost all convenience goods come through a _____ channel
employing both wholesale and retail middlemen.
   a. two-link
   b. three-link
   c. four-link
   d. five-link

_a_ 4. The wholesaler who takes title and provides the greatest number of
functions is known as the
   a. full-service merchant wholesaler.
   b. limited-function wholesale merchant.
   c. agent.
   d. wholly owned wholesaler.

_b_ 5. The distribution practice of using more than one but less than
       all the firms that might carry a product is known as
       a. exclusive distribution.
       b. selective distribution.
       c. constructive distribution.
       d. intensive distribution.

_d_ 6. The group that is common in the fields such as real estate and
       agriculture where there are mainly buyers and sellers and no
       central marketplace for exchange is known as
       a. auction companies.
       b. manufacturers' agents.
       c. selling agents.
       d. brokers.

_d_ 7. The group that usually takes over the marketing functions in areas
       that it does not pay the manufacturer to cover with his or her
       own sales force is known as
       a. agents.
       b. commission merchants.
       c. selling agents.
       d. manufacturers' agents.

_b_ 8. The distribution area of manufacturers is known as
       a. agents.
       b. wholly owned wholesalers.
       c. full-service wholesalers.
       d. merchant wholesalers.

_b_ 9. A wholesaler who neither maintains a warehouse nor carries inven-
       tories but takes title to the goods and is responsible for billing
       a customer and collecting payment is known as
       a. a cash-and-carry wholesaler.
       b. a drop shipper.
       c. a mail-order wholesaler.
       d. a truck wholesaler.

_a_ 10. What type of system do we find when one channel member owns, con-
       trols, or coordinates the operations of other channel members?
       a. a vertical marketing system (VMS)
       b. an administered system
       c. the transfer system
       d. a corporate system

True-False

_T_ 11. Agents merely arrange for the buying and selling of goods but
       never actually take title or physical possession of goods.

F 12. Middlemen perform valuable functions for only the producers.

F 13. Conflict among channel members rarely occurs.

T 14. Distribution is concerned with placing goods and services where they are needed and when they are wanted.

F 15. Rack jobbers are merchant wholesalers who provide only a few services for their customers.

T 16. Merchant wholesalers are independents who buy goods from manufacturers, take physical possession of them, and sell them to other middlemen.

F 17. Marketing scholars now recognize that excluding services from the study of channels is correct.

T 18. Truck wholesalers perform all the functions of full-service organizations except financing.

F 19. A marketing channel requires either a buyer or a seller to be successful.

F 20. Channel length is concerned with how much market exposure a product should have.

CHAPTER SOLUTIONS

Key Concepts

1. aa	8. o	15. j	22. s	29. bb
2. r	9. x	16. dd	23. k	30. q
3. v	10. e	17. hh	24. y	31. b
4. ff	11. ii	18. p	25. f	32. u
5. g	12. cc	19. h	26. z	33. gg
6. m	13. t	20. w	27. ee	34. i
7. c	14. l	21. jj	28. n	35. d
				36. a

Self-Quiz

1. a	5. b	9. b	13. F	17. F
2. c	6. d	10. a	14. T	18. T
3. c	7. d	11. T	15. F	19. F
4. a	8. b	12. F	16. T	20. F

CHAPTER 12
RETAIL MARKETING: STRUCTURE AND MANAGEMENT

CHAPTER SUMMARY

1. Retailing offers a great opportunity for individuals interested in cater-
    ing to the needs of individuals. Nearly half of all American businesses,
    or about two million establishments, are engaged in retailing. In
    addition, retailing is one of America's largest employers providing
    purchasing power for millions of individuals. Retailers provide an
    assortment of goods and services and need to develop the proper shopping
    environment to attract and stimulate consumer interest. When we shop for
    groceries, shoes, clothing, legal advice, magazines, and many other prod-
    ucts, we are patronizing retail organizations. Retailing includes all
    the activities involved in selling goods or services directly to final
    consumers for their personal, nonbusiness use.

2. Retailing is diversified not only in the way it is organized, but in the
    types of institutions that sell to consumers. Scrambled merchandising
    refers to retailers who previously specialized in a particular line but
    now sell many nontraditional lines as well. Although most retailers are
    quite small, the field is dominated by a few organizations. The many
    goods and services provided by retailers reflect the life-styles and
    other needs of our society.

3. It is becoming difficult to classify stores because of the trend toward
    scrambled merchandising. Nevertheless, retailers are often classified
    according to product mix, price, and by unique distribution approaches.
    Retail businesses classified by product mix can be best described by the
    kind of merchandise they offer for sale. A specialty store concentrates
    on selling a large selection of only one line of merchandise. Examples
    of specialty stores can include those that sell children's clothing,
    toys, sporting goods, and pet supplies. A specialty store provides a
    larger selection of merchandise than a department store, provides more
    knowledgeable customer and sales personnel, and is predominately independ-
    ently owned. A superstore is a large store that carries a broad selection
    of one type of product at low prices. Examples of superstores can in-
    clude those that sell garden supplies, televisions, and books. A depart-
    ment store is an establishment that brings together a number of product
    lines under one roof. A department store is organized by departments
    which usually sell a wide variety of merchandise that can include house-
    hold lines, dry goods, family apparel, televisions, furniture, and appli-
    ances. Today a major challenge to department stores is in the low prices
    offered by discount houses and off-price retailers. A supermarket is a
    food store divided into areas carrying dry goods, dairy products, and
    fresh produce and allows customers to make their own selection. Profits
    are derived mainly from high volumes and low margins. Supermarkets are
    now responding to the challenge of higher costs and lower profits by

providing scrambled merchandise to market many nonfood items such as clothing, small appliances, toiletries, books, and magazines. Convenience stores are small retail outlets providing snacks and staple goods quickly and conveniently. Their convenience includes short lines, parking close by, long hours, and locations near busy streets and intersections. They generally provide consumers with fill-in merchandise such as bread, milk, butter, eggs, and newspapers. Convenience stores are generally small and serve surrounding neighborhoods. A combination store is what results when a drug store is crossed with a supermarket. Combo stores profit by exposing food shoppers to general merchandise. A hypermarket is a large mass merchandiser that offers a broad selection of hard and soft goods and grocery items at discount prices on a self-serve basis. A hypermarket resembles a warehouse, concentrates on volume sales, and spends a low amount of money on labor. Many retailers, in addition to selling goods, are now expanding into the sale of services which may include legal, financial, and tax assistance.

4. A second way to look at the retail business is to emphasize price. A discount store sells fast-moving branded merchandise at cut-rate prices. In addition, a discount store carries a relatively broad selection of merchandise, is in a low-rent location, is self-service, and has most merchandise displayed on the selling floor. A warehouse store is a no-frills operation that sacrifices atmosphere and customer services to offer consumers the lowest possible prices. Home improvement centers are really large-scale hardware stores for do-it-yourself consumers. Their prices may be somewhat lower than traditional hardware stores, but their main attraction is one-stop shopping for around-the-house needs. A catalog showroom combines the low prices of discount stores with the advertising value of a catalog. The merchandise in the showroom shows a limited selection of the items in the catalog. Customers choose what they want, place their orders, and receive their goods from an adjacent warehouse.

5. A third way to look at the retail business is to emphasize location as a form of distribution approach. There are two major areas in which stores now locate. They are the central business district and shopping centers. The central business district is the downtown shopping area of most cities, and it consists of large department stores and specialty stores. This location is typically the point at which public transportation systems converge, and the place where stores attract customers from the entire metropolitan area and even from nonresidents. With the popularity of shopping centers, many retailers in the central business district declined in number and importance. Recently we have seen a rebirth of the central business district due to such activities as the rehabilitation of downtown districts and the return of households back to the city from suburban areas. A shopping center is a group of stores planned, owned, and managed as a unit. It has ample parking facilities and is usually located in a suburban area. There are three types of shopping centers. The neighborhood shopping center serves up to 20,000

customers and has between 5 and 15 stores. A community shopping center is larger--15 to 35 stores. A regional shopping center is the largest of all, with many diverse stores. As with the central business district, a regional center is attempting to lure shoppers into town again by turning decaying slums or waterfront warehouse districts into fashionable shopping centers. This is the essence of the center city marketplace. Off-price and factory outlet shopping centers are now being formed by having several of these businesses deciding to bank together into shopping centers.

6. Although most retail transactions occur in stores, nonstore retailing is important for many products. Door-to-door selling is one of the oldest methods of selling. It takes place without consumers visiting a store and provides maximum consumer convenience and personal attention. The problems of door-to-door sales include their high sales costs, legal restrictions, and consumer mistrust. To offset many of these problems, party-plan selling is becoming very popular. Another form of nonstore retailing is direct marketing. A mail order firm provides customers with a wide variety of goods ordered from catalogs and shipped by mail. Examples of goods purchased by mail order include ready-to-wear clothing, magazines, insurance, and kitchen gadgets. This form of retailing offers convenience for customers, low operating costs, the opportunity to secure new market segments over a wide geographic area, and the availability of a large selection of items to choose from. The problems facing the mail-order business include the increase in competition due to the surge in catalog selling, the large expenditure needed with start-up costs, and the high number of returns. Other forms of direct marketing include news-paper inserts, direct-response ads in magazines, 800-number advertising on radio and television, and telephone selling. Telemarketing is the form of telephone selling in which salespeople phone potential customers. Vending machines dispense goods automatically after money is inserted. They are very often used in locations where it would be unprofitable to operate a store or employ a salesperson, and they allow for around-the-clock sales and the need to place a machine outside rather than inside a store. Cigarettes, candy, and beverages are the three most popular items that are sold through vending machines. The problems associated with vending machines include their high cost, the need for intensive servic-ing because of breakdowns, out-of-stock items, and vandalism. With the increase in communication technology and changing consumer life-styles, there appears to be a very large growth potential in nonstore retailing. Marketers must be constantly aware of new developments and attempt to capitalize on them.

7. There are two distinct forms of retail store organization. A chain store consists of a group of stores, centrally owned and managed, that sells similar goods. An independent store is usually a one-unit operation owned and managed by a single person, partnership, or corporation. Most retail establishments are independents. They are relatively easy to set up and require little capital or formal education. Consumers patronize independents because they provide convenience in shopping, service extras,

174

and timely goods. Chain stores are characterized by centralized buying and centralized management. In addition to buying goods, the main office sets price and creates advertising that stores run locally. Also, store layout is standardized. A disadvantage of chain stores is offering timely goods. Centralized buying requires ordering in advance and in massive quantities. Often this procedure does not take into account the changing wants and needs of consumers. Among independents, the trend today is to take advantage of some of the benefits of group membership without giving up freedom and flexibility. An ownership group consists of stores owned by a corporation in which management functions are performed centrally and some centralized buying for nonfashion goods may be practiced. However, stores keep their separate names and do most of their buying and planning independently. An ownership group is quite common among department stores.

8. In a franchising arrangement, an independent businessperson agrees to sell the products or services of a parent company and use its policies in exchange for an exclusive territory. It provides the franchisee with a method of owning a business quickly for a specific dollar amount, often a proven record of success, buying capabilities, the image of a large multiunit retailer, and the opportunity to receive management training. Among the common complaints are that franchising fees drain profits, national programs ignore local needs, and companies sometimes arbitrarily cancel a franchise. Merchandising conglomerates are retail empires that combine several, often unrelated, business units under central management. Conglomerates practice centralized buying, warehousing, and transportation, which lead to cost savings.

9. Retailers have to be very concerned with store image. Just as individuals have images, so do retail stores. Customers often judge a retail store by its external and internal appearance. The store design and subsequent layout have to be developed according to the type of store and the merchandise sold within the store. Atmospherics is the marketing task of creating certain effects in buyers by designing store environments. Marketers must be aware of how customers perceive the store environment. Often such factors as type and density of employees, merchandise, fixtures, sound, odor, prices, and advertising can affect one's perception of a store.

10. Two explanations have been forwarded in an attempt to find patterns in retail change and the causes of change. According to Malcolm McNair's wheel of retailing, changes in retailing are cyclical. At first, a new store challenges an existing institution by providing few services and low-cost goods. Once the store is established, it starts trading up its merchandise. The store then suffers the fate of its old competitor as a new store type develops, using cost-cutting tactics. The life cycle hypothesis states that retail stores, like products, have retail life cycles that consist of the innovation, accelerated development, maturity, and the decline phases. The movement to a new phase is brought about by competitive pressures. The retail life cycle necessitates the

need for retailers to be flexible so that they can adapt to various life cycle stages, carefully analyze the risks and profits of each life cycle stage, and develop ways to extend the maturity stage of the product life cycle.

11. There have been many changes in retailing during the past 30 years. Retailers are predicting additional changes that may have profound effects not only in the types of goods sold but also in the way the goods will be sold. A number of changes will reflect demographics, competition, deregulation, two-income affluent households, psychological wants, the nontraditional household, and one-stop shopping habits caused by time parameters.

LEARNING GOALS

After reading this chapter, you should be able to:

1. Define retailing and describe its scope.
2. Describe the development of retailing institutions.
3. Understand and be able to explain the types of retailers that emphasize product mix. You should also be able to differentiate between specialty stores, superstores, department stores, supermarkets, convenience stores, combination stores, and hypermarkets.
4. Understand and be able to explain the types of retailers that emphasize price. You should also be able to differentiate between discount stores, warehouse stores, home improvement centers, and catalog showrooms.
5. Understand and be able to explain why some retailers emphasize location, including the importance of store site location. Describe a central business district, shopping center, center city marketplace, and off-price and factory outlet shopping centers.
6. Describe the nonstore retailer, including door-to-door selling, direct marketing, and automatic vending machines.
7. Explain the organization of retailing, including independents, chains, associations of independents, and merchandise conglomerates.
8. Describe the importance of a store image, including store design and the marketing mix factors.
9. Explain retail changes, including the wheel of retailing and the retail life cycle hypothesis.

KEY CONCEPTS

From the list of lettered terms, select the one that best fits in the blank of the numbered statements that follow. Write the letter of that choice in the space provided.

(Answers to the key concepts appear at the end of the chapter.)

a. A hypermarket
b. A retail life cycle
c. A department store
d. Scrambled merchandising
e. A chain store
f. A catalog showroom
g. A shopping center
h. A superstore
i. A convenience store
j. A combination store
k. A vending machine
l. A home improvement center

m. A mail-order firm
n. A warehouse store
o. A merchandising conglomerate
p. An independent store
q. Atmospherics
r. Telemarketing
s. Retailing
t. A supermarket
u. The wheel of retailing
v. A central business district
w. A discount store
x. A specialty store

1. _____ refers to a company that provides a wide range of goods ordered by customers from catalogs and shipped directly to them by mail.

2. _____ refers to a group of stores planned, owned, and managed as a unit and with ample parking, usually in a suburban area.

3. _____ refers to all the activities involved in selling goods or services directly to final consumers for their personal, nonbusiness use.

4. _____ is a marketing task of creating certain effects in buyers by designing store environments.

5. _____ is the practice, by previously specialized retailers, of selling many unrelated lines of goods.

6. _____ is a combination of a supermarket and a drug store under a single roof.

7. _____ refers to a view that retail stores, like products, have life cycles that consist of phases: innovation, accelerated development, maturity, and decline.

8. _____ is a retail organization combining several, often unrelated, business units under central management.

9. _____ is a retail discount business based on catalog promotion and showrooms that display a limited selection of the items in the catalog. Customers receive goods from an adjacent warehouse.

10. _____ is a giant mass merchandiser that offers a broad selection of hard and soft goods and grocery items at discount prices on a self-serve basis.

11. _____ is a theory that all retail innovators start as low-cost, low-price stores; improve services and raise prices at maturity; and decline when new types of low-cost stores challenge them.

177

12. _____ is a large-scale hardware store that offers one-stop shopping for around-the-house needs at prices that may be somewhat lower than those at smaller hardware stores.

13. _____ is a store that brings together a number of items under one roof.

14. _____ refers to the downtown shopping area of most cities, consisting of large department stores and specialty stores.

15. _____ is a no-frills store that emphasizes lower prices over atmosphere and customer service.

16. _____ is a large store that carries a broad selection of one type of product at low prices--sometimes called "category killers."

17. _____ is a group of stores centrally owned and managed that sell similar goods.

18. _____ describes the practice of direct selling in which salespeople telephone potential customers.

19. _____ is a retail food store that carries dry groceries, dairy products, and fresh produce and allows customers to make their own selection.

20. _____ is a store owned and managed by a single person, partnership, or corporation, usually a one-unit operation.

21. _____ is a store that concentrates on selling a selection of only one line of merchandise.

22. _____ is a device that dispenses products automatically after money is inserted.

23. _____ is a store that sells fast-moving branded merchandise at cut-rate prices.

24. _____ is a small retail outlet that provides snacks and staple groceries quickly and conveniently.

PROGRAMMED REVIEW

The following self-teaching exercises consist of short statements that require you to make a response by filling in the blank (or blanks) provided. You will find the correct response printed in the margin to the left of the question.

a. Stores are owned by a corporation.
b. Some management functions are performed centrally.
c. Some centralized buying for nonfashion goods may be practiced.

1. Among department stores, the ownership group is quite common. What are three characteristics associated with the ownership group?

   a. _____
   _____

   b. _____
   _____

   c. _____
   _____
   _____

cyclical

2. According to Malcolm McNair, changes in retailing are _____ .

a. door-to-door selling
b. direct marketing
c. automated vending machines

3. Nonstore retailing includes what three categories?

   a. _____
   b. _____
   c. _____

product lines

4. A department store is an establishment that brings together a number of _____ under one roof.

a. the central business district
b. shopping centers

5. What are the two major areas in which stores now locate?

   a. _____
   b. _____

drug
supermarket

6. A combination store is what results when you cross a _____ store and a _____ .

a. convenience in shopping
b. service extras
c. timely goods

7. What are three important benefits that consumers may derive from patronizing independent stores?

   a. _____
   b. _____
   c. _____

image

a. Franchise fees drain
   profits.
b. National programs
   ignore local needs.
c. Companies sometimes
   arbitrarily cancel a
   franchise.

branded
cut-rate

a. specialty stores
b. department stores
c. supermarkets

layout

a. independents
b. chains
c. associations of
   independents
d. merchandise con-
   glomerates

change

8. Once retail proprietors have decided
   on a product line, pricing strategy,
   location, and ownership, they must consider the type of _____
   they want their stores to project.

9. What are three common complaints that
   franchise owners have against the
   franchisor?

   a. _____
      _____
   b. _____
      _____
   c. _____
      _____
      _____

10. Discount stores sell fast-moving
    _____ merchandise at
    _____ prices.

11. What are the three kinds of retailers
    that emphasize product mix?

    a. _____
    b. _____
    c. _____

12. The first task any store designer faces
    is _____.

13. What are four ways of organizing retail
    establishments?

    a. _____
    b. _____
    c. _____
    d. _____

14. It has been said that the only thing
    that is constant in life is _____.

a. discount stores
b. warehouse stores
c. home improvement
   centers
d. catalog showrooms

15. What are the four types of retail estab-
    lishments that specialize in offering
    low prices?

    a. _____

    b. _____

    c. _____

    d. _____

atmosphere
services
prices

16. Warehouse stores provide no-frills
    operations that sacrifice _____
    and customer _____ in
    order to offer consumers the lowest
    possible _____.

a. innovation
b. accelerated develop-
   ment
c. maturity
d. decline

17. What are the four phases of the retail
    life cycle?

    a. _____

    b. _____

    c. _____

    d. _____

one

18. Specialty stores concentrate on selling
    a large selection of only _____
    line of merchandise.

a. short lines
b. parking close by
c. long hours
d. locations near busy
   streets and inter-
   sections

19. What are four reasons why today's con-
    sumers are attracted to convenience
    stores?

    a. _____

    b. _____

    c. _____

    d. _____

    _____

scrambled merchandising
expanding
automating

20. Supermarkets are responding to the
    challenge of higher costs and lower
    profits by instituting _____
    _____. In addi-
    tion, stores are _____
    to achieve even greater savings through
    volume sales, and many are _____
    the checkout stand.

a. the neighborhood shopping center
b. the community shopping center
c. the regional shopping center

discount
catalog

a. newspaper inserts
b. direct-response ads in magazines
c. 800-number advertising on radio and television
d. telephone selling

hardware
do-it-yourself

catalogs
mail

21. What are the three types of shopping centers which are distinguished by size and types of stores?

    a. _____

    b. _____

    c. _____

22. Catalog showrooms combine the low prices of _____ stores with _____ promotion.

23. Along with direct-mail marketing, what four forms of direct marketing are growing in importance?

    a. _____

    b. _____

    _____

    c. _____

    _____

    d. _____

24. Home improvement centers are really large-scale _____ stores for _____ customers.

25. The mail-order firm provides customers with a wide variety of goods ordered from _____ and shipped by _____.

MARKETING RIDDLE

The purpose of this exercise is to find the missing word that solves the riddle. Each of the statements requires you to make a response by filling in the blank (or blanks) for the appropriate missing word. Each statement contains a key letter which, when combined with the other key letters, will provide you with the solution to the riddle. Correct solutions to the riddle questions can lead to valuable prizes. See instructions for more information.

Retailing is one of America's largest industries employing millions of people. Retailers are often positioned within the industry according to their levels of service and price and the
$\overline{}$ of assortment.
 1 2 3 4 5

1. Off-price retailers, who sell brand names at discount prices, have launched a flurry of __ __ ☐ __ __ __ __ __ against established department stores, charging them with price fixing and attempting to intimidate manufacturers.

2. Combination stores profit by __ __ __ __ __ ☐ __ __ food shoppers to general merchandise.

3. Marketers have taken note of the interest in mail-order shopping, and the number of catalogs produced has __ __ __ __ __ ☐.

4. Door-to-door salespeople have been experiencing some serious problems. As a result, __ __ __ ☐ __-__ __ __ __ selling now does best in close-knit working class and ethnic areas.

5. Today __ ☐ __ __ __ stores account for most of the sales of department stores.

EXPERIENTIAL EXERCISE

Retailing includes all the activities involved in selling goods or services directly to final consumers for their personal, nonbusiness use.

The purpose of this exercise is to provide you with an opportunity to discuss with a store manager the operation of his retail store. Visit a specialty store and discuss with the manager the retail functions he performs and obtain the answers to the following questions.

1. What type of ownership is the specialty store?

_____

_____

2. What types of goods are sold in the store?

_____

_____

_____

_____

3. What types of customers does the store attempt to reach?

_____

_____

_____

_____

4. What services does the store provide?

_____

_____

_____

5. From what sources does the retailer receive his merchandise?

_____

_____

_____

_____

6. Is the store manager pleased with the store's performance and progress?

_____

_____

_____

_____

7. What does the store manager anticipate as possible future trends for the specialty retailer?

_____

_____

_____

_____

Multiple Choice

_d_ 1. The type of small retailer that provides snacks and staple goods quickly and conveniently and includes short lines, parking close by, long hours, and locations near busy streets and intersections is called a
a. combination store.
b. superstore.
c. specialty store.
d. convenience store.

_____ 2. The Direct Marketing Association predicts that by the year 2000 about _____ percent of consumer dollars will be spent on mail-order sales.
a. 15
b. 25
c. 35
d. 50

_c_ 3. A different way of viewing retail change is the hypothesis that retail stores, like products, have life cycles. What is the stage that occurs after innovation?
a. maturity
b. decline
c. accelerated development
d. acceptance

_b_ 4. Retailers who previously specialized in a particular line and now sell many nontraditional lines as well engage in selling
a. convenience goods.
b. scrambled merchandise.
c. specialty goods.
d. shopping goods.

_a_ 5. The store that brings together a number of product lines under one roof is known as a
a. department store.
b. supermarket.
c. discount store.
d. combination store.

_c_ 6. A large-scale hardware store for the do-it-yourself customer, whose prices may be somewhat lower than traditional hardware stores and whose main attraction is one-stop shopping for around-the-house needs, is called a
a. catalog showroom.
b. warehouse store.
c. home improvement center.
d. department store.

_b_ 7. The store that is a no-frills operation that sacrificed atmosphere and customer services in order to offer consumers the lowest possible prices is known as a
   a. home improvement center.
   b. warehouse store.
   c. catalog showroom.
   d. chain store.

_b_ 8. The store that sells fast-moving branded merchandise at cut-rate prices is known as a
   a. department store.
   b. discount store.
   c. superstore.
   d. hypermarket.

_d_ 9. The store that combines the low prices of discount stores with catalog promotion is known as a
   a. variety store.
   b. hypermarket.
   c. warehouse store.
   d. catalog showroom.

_a_ 10. The type of retail facility where we find a group of stores planned, owned, and managed as a unit and with ample parking facilities, usually located in suburban areas, is known as
   a. shopping centers.
   b. convenience centers.
   c. central business districts.
   d. hypermarkets.

True-False

_____ 11. The first task any store designer faces is layout.

_____ 12. Price does not affect a store's image.

_____ 13. Nearly half of all American businesses, or about two million establishments, are engaged in retailing.

_____ 14. Department stores have lasted for over 30 years because of their ability to provide low prices.

_____ 15. Superstores are large, 5,000-to-10,000 square-foot stores that offer shoppers a small variety of products and services.

_____ 16. The central business district is the downtown shopping area of most cities, and it consists of large department stores and specialty stores.

_____ 17. The main characteristics of chain stores are centralized buying and centralized management with the ability to sell similar goods.

_____ 18. Among independents, the trend today is to take advantage of some of the benefits of group membership without giving up their freedom and flexibility.

_____ 19. The business of selling services is a decreasing part of our economy and not growing as fast as product retailing.

_____ 20. Nonstore retailing is now on the rise, with many consumers shopping through catalogs or electronic means.

CHAPTER SOLUTIONS

Key Concepts

1.	m	6.	j	11.	u	16.	h	21.	x
2.	g	7.	b	12.	l	17.	e	22.	k
3.	s	8.	o	13.	c	18.	r	23.	w
4.	q	9.	f	14.	v	19.	t	24.	i
5.	d	10.	a	15.	n	20.	p		

Self-Quiz

1.	d	5.	a	9.	d	13.	T	17.	T
2.	b	6.	c	10.	a	14.	F	18.	T
3.	c	7.	b	11.	T	15.	F	19.	F
4.	b	8.	b	12.	F	16.	T	20.	T

CHAPTER 13
DISTRIBUTING GOODS

CHAPTER SUMMARY

1. Marketers must be concerned with the physical distribution of goods and
    services. They must be knowledgeable of the activities surrounding the
    physical handling and movement of goods from the manufacturer into the
    hands of the buyer or user. Physical distribution includes all those
    activities required to move finished goods along marketing channels,
    including storing the goods along the way. The three most important of
    these activities include warehousing, inventory control, and transpor-
    tation. The marketer's attitude toward physical distribution has changed
    since 1950. This change has been primarily the result of the adoption of
    the marketing concept, the focus of firms on consumer wants, and the
    increases in the number of products offered to consumers. Over the past
    decade, marketers have found that by increasing the efficiency of physical
    distribution, they can generate tremendous cost savings.

2. The total physical distribution concept states that all management func-
    tions related to moving products to buyers must be fully integrated. The
    physical distribution manager must be able to balance the need to minimize
    costs to the firm considered as a whole and the need to provide a satis-
    factory level of customer service. Visible costs, which show up on a
    profit and loss statement, include the direct expenses of running ware-
    houses and hiring transportation, as well as the indirect ones of insuring
    goods and paying property taxes. Hidden costs, which accountants cannot
    record, include losses that result from a customer failing to order or
    canceling an order. A cost trade-off is allowing costs to increase in
    one area to bring down costs in others. Cost trade-offs generally occur
    between transportation and storage costs, storage and manufacturing costs,
    as well as between packaging and other costs. New computer software,
    data transmission facilities, and coded product identification systems
    now enable physical distribution managers to update sales and inventory
    planning faster, accurately, and more frequently. Distribution changes
    that may lower costs should not be made if they result in a significant
    lessening of customer service. Firms must balance reasonable customer
    service with realistic cost outlays.

3. Warehousing, inventory control, and transportation account for most of
    the costs of physical distribution. A marketer must know about the vari-
    ous choices offered by the different types of storage facilities. Knowl-
    edge of warehousing can provide management with the information as to
    the type of warehouse to operate, whether to own or rent facilities, and
    where to locate them. The two main types of warehouses are the storage
    warehouse and the distribution center warehouse. A storage warehouse is
    a facility where goods are stored for weeks, months, or years until they
    are needed. Firms often use storage warehouses to stock goods that are

in demand only seasonally, to stock goods that generate year-round demand but can only be produced seasonally, and as a result of the ups and downs of the business cycle. Recently we have seen companies use an <u>automated warehouse</u> which is an advanced materials handling system under the control of a central computer. The <u>distribution center warehouse</u> is established primarily as a temporary way-station prior to the very rapid movement of goods to customers. The centers discharge goods usually within a week's time and tend to specialize in making bulk or breaking bulk. They also strive for rapid inventory turnover and not as a long-term storage facility. The distribution center appears to represent the future trend in warehousing.

4. Once the type of warehouse has been selected, a decision must be made whether to use a private or public facility. In a <u>private warehouse</u>, the building, equipment, and labor are company-owned or controlled. A firm must incur an initial fixed investment to purchase the warehouse or sign a long-term lease; however, a private warehouse can be designed to the firm's specific needs. A <u>public warehouse</u> is controlled by an independent, can be rented by anyone needing space for a short time, and is usually shared by a number of companies. A firm using a public warehouse has no initial investment and can rent only the space that it needs; however, the firm has no control over the design and the layout of the facility. In recent years, public warehouses have begun to offer a number of services besides physical handling and storage. These can include filing monthly inventory status reports, preparing transportation documents, weighing shipments, monitoring loss and damage from transportation, and assisting the company in filing claims for such losses.

5. The location of a warehouse is also an important distribution decision. A manager may position a warehouse near the company's factory, close to the market, or at an intermediate point between the two. A <u>factory-positioned warehouse</u> may store raw materials and fabricated parts until they are needed for manufacture. Or, they may serve as traditional warehouses or distribution centers for finished products. A <u>market-positioned warehouse</u> is designed to collect the products of one or more manufacturers in or near the market served before shipping the goods short distances to customers. An <u>intermediate-positioned warehouse</u> is usually chosen by manufacturers with several plants and widely scattered markets. The warehouses gather the products of the various plants and mix them for shipment. In choosing a specific site, management should consider the availability of transportation, quantity and quality of labor, cost of land, taxes, and services provided by the local government.

6. <u>Inventory control</u> represents a second major expense of physical distribution. Inventory decisions are very important to the success of manufacturing, wholesaling, and retailing organizations primarily because inventory represents a large portion of the firm's investment. Inventory reflects the amount of merchandise being stored. The inventory manager should provide an adequate level of customer service by avoiding out-of-stock situations and should minimize a company's investment in inventory.

An ABC analysis is a technique for identifying those items with the biggest sales payoffs. Inventory always involves some type of cost. Acquisition costs and carrying costs are two costs that are of particular concern to the inventory manager. Acquisition costs are expenses incurred in preparing for manufacturing or in buying the product to put in inventory. Carrying costs are the expenses involved in holding goods over a period of time. It is difficult to determine the correct inventory size. Often firms have to depend on sales forecasts in an attempt to estimate inventory. The economic order quantity (EOQ) is that amount of stock that costs the least to keep on hand in order to meet the average level of demand. It specifies only the stock needed to meet the average level of demand. Safety stock refers to the amount above the basic stock level to handle emergencies. It is also difficult to determine how fast stock is moving. A physical count involves analyzing products on hand at a specific time. Perpetual inventory is a list of all goods in stock and is updated frequently.

7. Transporting products represents the third and usually the largest single item in the overall cost of physical distribution. Failure to plan for transportation can result in late deliveries, excessive freight costs, and damaged merchandise. Physical distribution managers should know the means of transportation that can best deliver a product and the various government regulations that affect the shipment of goods. The five modes of transportation that link producers and consumers are railroads, motor carriers, water transportation, air transportation, and pipelines. Although railroads have lost a great deal of traffic to other modes of transportation, they still account for about one-third of the nation's freight. They can carry a wide variety of products, can serve almost every city in the United States, are the preferred means of transportation over long distances between cities, and provide reliability because weather rarely interrupts rail traffic schedules. In addition, the deregulation of transportation has increased competition and has meant an increase in single-line service. The limitations of railroads include the fact that they must be used with other modes of transportation to provide door-to-door service, their average rate of speed is very slow, and they are unable to reach all places. In order to capture a large percentage of rail traffic, the railroads have introduced piggyback which provides for transporting truck trailers on rail cars, unit trains which provide for trains that are loaded with one commodity, such as coal, and travel nonstop between two points, and a run-through train which avoids delays by bypassing intermediate terminals. Motor carriers rank very high in meeting the transportation needs of many manufacturers. Improved highways have enabled trucks to achieve a high rank in the frequency and dependability of their scheduling. In addition, they are often the fastest way of shipping goods over moderate distances, may provide door-to-door service, and the rates are more economical over the short haul. The limitations of motor carriers include their inability to carry bulk goods, their vulnerability to traffic tie-ups, inclement weather delays, breakdowns, and their high cost of transporting heavy goods. Water transportation provides the cheapest form of freight

transportation for bulky goods over a long distance; however, they are the slowest and their scheduled runs are less frequent. Another limitation includes the possibility that all buyers and sellers may not be located on a major waterway. This may necessitate another form of transportation to complete the transaction. Air transportation offers the fastest but the most expensive means of moving goods over long distances. Other limitations include the need for extra handling and the scattering of airports, thus their inaccessibility when compared to trucks and railroads. Generally air transportation is limited to merchandise of high value and certain perishable items. Since the 1950s, pipelines have greatly increased in popularity. They are dependable and provide low cost of operation. Pipeline transportation is limited to products that are in a liquid or gaseous state; their capacity is limited by the diameter of the pipe; and their routes are one-directional, with storage terminals required at the receiving end. In determining which transportation mode to use, a firm should consider cost, time, reliability, and accessibility, as well as theft and damage considerations.

8. There are four classifications of carriers, and each group operates with different functions. A common carrier includes all those transport companies that must serve the general public. The government requires them to publish their rates and charge the same fees to all persons requiring transportation service. A contract carrier is less regulated because it serves only a limited number of customers, not the general public. Exempt carriers include all those forms of transportation that are not subject to direct federal regulations. A private carrier includes all transportation owned by an individual company that is not primarily in the transportation business. There are many manufacturers who cannot afford to own or lease transportation. Freight forwarders collect small shipments from a number of companies, consolidate them for transport in full loads, and then see that the goods reach their final destination. Freight forwarders provide fast service since large shipments move more quickly than small shipments. Shippers' associations serve the same function except that they work on a nonprofit basis for members of the same industry.

9. A physical distribution manager should be familiar with recent trends in transportation. One trend seeks to combine various modes for more efficiency. Intermodal transportation refers to the coordinating of two or more transportation modes to minimize the disadvantages and maximize the strong points of each. Three common intermodal forms include piggyback, fishyback, and birdyback . Piggyback is a truck-railroad combination. Fishyback is a joining of truck and ship. Birdyback is a truck and air service. A second trend in transportation is the container, which is a large, standard-size metal box into which goods are placed for shipping and then sealed. A third trend is the formation of multimodal companies, which combine shipping modes and seek to offer shippers global door-to-door service.

LEARNING GOALS

After reading this chapter, you should be able to:

1. Define physical distribution.
2. Describe the changing ideas about physical distribution, including the total physical distribution concept, and the need to implement the concept by minimizing costs and providing satisfactory customer service.
3. Understand warehousing, including the types of operations, such as storage warehouses and distribution center warehouses, the types of ownership, and the importance of warehouse location.
4. Recognize the importance of inventory control and understand the goals of inventory management--determining inventory size and keeping track of inventory.
5. Describe the importance of transportation, including the five basic transportation modes (railroads, motor carriers, water transportation, air transportation, and pipelines), the transportation rate structure, savings in transportation, and recent trends in transportation.

KEY CONCEPTS

From the list of lettered terms, select the one that best fits in the blank of the numbered statements that follow. Write the letter of that choice in the space provided.

(Answers to the key concepts appear at the end of the chapter.)

a. A private warehouse
b. Intermodal transportation
c. A freight forwarder
d. Physical distribution
e. A common carrier
f. A storage warehouse
g. An economic order quantity (EOQ)
h. An exempt carrier
i. A public warehouse
j. Visible costs
k. A shippers' association
l. Carrying cost
m. A market-positioned warehouse
n. An intermediate-positioned warehouse
o. A multimodal shipping company
p. A contract carrier
q. An automated warehouse
r. A cost trade-off
s. A container
t. A private carrier
u. Hidden costs
v. A total physical distribution concept

w. A distribution center warehouse
x. Perpetual inventory
y. Safety stock
z. A physical count
aa. An acquisition cost
bb. A factory-positioned warehouse
cc. An ABC analysis

1. _____ is a facility in which goods are stored for weeks, months, or years until they are needed.

2. _____ refers to a means of transport that serves only a limited number of customers and may negotiate different rates for different customers.

3. _____ is a storage center controlled by an independent, available for rent for a short time, and usually shared by a number of companies.

4. _____ is an expense incurred in preparing for manufacturing or in buying the product for inventory.

5. _____ is a storage place designed to collect the products of one or more manufacturers in or near markets served before shipping goods short distances to customers.

6. _____ refer to the costs of doing business--for example, a cancelled order--that do not show up on a profit and loss statement.

7. _____ refers to a frequently updated list of all goods in stock.

8. _____ is the coordination of two or more transportation modes to minimize the disadvantages and maximize the strong points of each.

9. _____ refers to the amount of stock that costs the least to keep on hand in order to meet the average level of demand.

10. _____ refers to transportation owned by an individual company that is not primarily in the transportation business.

11. _____ refers to a storage place that serves manufacturers with several plants and widely scattered markets by gathering products of various plants and mixing them for shipment.

12. _____ is the practice of allowing costs to increase in one business area to bring down costs in another.

13. _____ is a storage center owned or controlled by the company that uses it.

14. _____ refers to organizations that serve the same function as freight forwarders, except that they work on a nonprofit basis for members of the same industry.

15. _____ is a large, standard-sized metal box into which goods are placed for shipping and then are sealed.

16. _____ refers to the amount above the basic stock level to handle emergencies.

17. _____ refers to the process of storing and moving products along marketing channels.

18. _____ is a facility used to store raw materials and fabricated parts until they are needed for manufacture or one that serves as a traditional warehouse or distribution center for finished products.

19. _____ is the principle that all management functions related to moving products to buyers must be fully integrated.

20. _____ is a form of transportation not subject to direct federal regulation.

21. _____ refers to a transport company that must serve the general public.

22. _____ is a firm that combines shipping modes.

23. _____ refers to a compnay that consolidates small shipments from a number of companies for transport in full loads.

24. _____ is a facility that serves primarily as a temporary way-station before the goods are rapidly moved to customers.

25. _____ is the inventory practice of totaling the number of items of each line on hand at a regular interval.

26. _____ is an inventory technique for identifying items with biggest sales payoffs by listing them by sales volume. Best sellers ("A" products) must be stocked at all times.

27. _____ are direct and indirect costs that show up on a profit and loss statement.

28. _____ is the expense of holding goods over a period of time.

29. _____ is a facility with advanced materials-handling systems under control of a central computer.

The following self-teaching exercises consist of short statements that require you to make a response by filling in the blank (or blanks) provided. You will find the correct response printed in the margin to the left of the question.

a. warehousing
b. inventory control
c. transportation

1. What are the three most important activ-
    ities of physical distribution?

    a. _____

    b. _____

    c. _____

on hand

2. A physical count involves analyzing
    products _____ at
    a specific time.

a. near the company's
    factory
b. close to the market
c. an intermediate point
    between the two

3. What are the three options that the
    physical distribution manager has in
    deciding where to locate a warehouse?

    a. _____

       _____

    b. _____

       _____

    c. _____

       _____

water

4. By far, _____ transportation
    provides the cheapest way of carrying
    bulky goods over a long distance.

a. availability of
   transportation
b. quantity and
   quality of labor
c. cost of land
d. taxes
e. services provided by
   the local government

5. Location decisions are complex. Once a general strategy for positioning a warehouse is decided upon, what five factors must be weighed in choosing a site?

   a. _____

   _____

   b. _____

   _____

   c. _____

   d. _____

   e. _____

   _____

a. minimize costs to the
   firm
b. provide a satisfactory
   level of customer service

6. What are two objectives that the physical distribution manager must balance?

   a. _____

   _____

   b. _____

   _____

general

7. Common carriers include all those transport companies that must serve the _____ public.

a. to provide an
   adequate level of
   customer service by
   avoiding out-of-stock
   situations
b. to minimize a company's
   investment in inventory

8. What two goals does the inventory manager pursue?

   a. _____

   _____

   _____

   _____

   b. _____

   _____

   _____

sales

9. A technique called ABC analysis identifies items with the biggest _____ payoffs.

196

a. acquisition costs
b. carrying costs

10. What two costs are of particular con-
    cern in inventory management?

    a. _____

    b. _____

Trucks

11. _____ are often the
    fastest way of shipping goods over mod-
    erate distances because they ship
    directly.

a. transportation
b. storage

12. In an attempt to keep total costs down,
    what are the two most frequently used
    cost trade-offs?

    a. _____

    b. _____

private
public

13. After physical distribution managers
    determine the type of warehouse that
    suits their needs, they must decide
    whether to use a _____ or
    _____ facility.

a. storage ware-
    houses
b. distribution cen-
    ter warehouses

14. Warehouses are distinguished mainly by
    the functions they perform. What are
    the two main types of warehouses?

    a. _____

    b. _____

integrated

15. The total physical distribution concept
    states that all management functions
    related to moving products to buyers
    must be fully _____ .

a. railroads
b. motor carriers
c. water transportation
d. air transportation
e. pipelines

16. What are the five modes of transporta-
    tion that link producers and consumers?

    a. _____

    b. _____

    c. _____

    d. _____

    e. _____

small
consolidate
destination

17. Freight forwarders collect _____ shipments from a number of companies, _____ them for transport in full loads, and then see that the goods reach their final _____.

a. piggyback
b. unit trains
c. run-through trains

18. Spurred by the prospect of capturing a larger percentage of traffic in manufactured and high-value products, what three services have the railroads introduced?

a. _____

b. _____

c. _____

costs
customer service

19. To manage inventory successfully, physical distribution managers must start with the company's goals for balancing _____ with _____ _____.

a. piggyback
b. fishyback
c. birdyback

20. What are the three most common modes that are used in intermodal transportation?

a. _____

b. _____

c. _____

temporary

21. A distribution center warehouse is established primarily as a _____ way-station prior to the very rapid movement of goods to customers.

a. store raw materials and fabricated parts until they are needed for manufacture
b. serve as traditional warehouses or distribution centers for finished products

22. What two purposes does a factory-positioned warehouse serve?

a. _____
   _____
   _____

b. _____
   _____
   _____

198

period of time

a. what type of ware-
   house to operate
b. whether to own or
   rent facilities
c. where to locate
   them

a. the means of trans-
   portation that can
   best deliver a
   product
b. regulations that
   affect the shipment
   of goods

23. Carrying costs are the expenses involved
    in holding goods over a _____
    _____.

24. Significant opportunities for savings,
    without lessening customer service,
    exist in the area of warehousing. What
    three matters in particular are of
    interest to management?

    a. _____
       _____

    b. _____
       _____

    c. _____
       _____

25. What are two areas of most concern to
    physical distribution managers?

    a. _____
       _____
       _____

    b. _____
       _____
       _____

MARKETING RIDDLE

The purpose of this exercise is to find the missing word that solves the
riddle. Each of the statements requires you to make a response by filling in
the blank (or blanks) for the appropriate missing word. Each statement contains a key letter which, when combined with the other key letters, will provide you with the solution to the riddle. Correct solutions to the riddle
questions can lead to valuable prizes. See instructions for more information.

      Physical distribution relates to overall channel strategy. A
      firm seeking extensive distribution needs many
      ‾‾ ‾‾ ‾‾ ‾‾ ‾‾ ‾‾ ‾‾ ‾‾ ‾‾ warehouses.
       1 2 3 4 5 6 7 8 9

1. Being out of stock of finished products can be very costly to a company.
    Customers easily become ☐ __ __ __ __ __ __ __ __ __ __ __ __ and turn to
    competitors.

199

2. If a company does not produce enough goods to keep a warehouse constantly stocked or cannot predict sales, using __ __ __ __ ☐ __ facilities may make better sense.

3. In finding ways to lower costs, marketers must weigh the effects of cost savings on customer ☐ __ __ __ __ __ __ .

4. With the deregulation of the rail industry in 1980, railroads have had to become more __ __ __ ☐ __ __ __ __ __ __ __ .

5. Safety stock refers to the amount __ __ __ __ ☐ the basic stock level to handle emergencies.

6. Carrying costs are the expenses involved in holding goods over a __ __ ☐ __ __ __ of time.

7. The run-through train avoids delays by __ __ __ __ ☐ __ __ __ __ __ intermediate terminals.

8. Physical distribution managers use sales forecasts to project the amount of inventory they need to order when it is time to __ __ __ __ ☐ __ __ __ stock.

9. Exempt carriers include all those forms of transportation that are not subject to ☐ __ __ __ __ __ federal regulation.

EXPERIENTIAL EXERCISE

In managing transportation, the physical distribution manager must be aware of new trends.

Describe the trends that you anticipate will occur in each of the following transportation modes.

1. <u>Railroads</u>

_____

_____

_____

_____

_____

2. Motor Carriers

_____
_____
_____
_____
_____

3. Water Transportation

_____
_____
_____
_____
_____

4. Air Transportation

_____
_____
_____
_____
_____

5. Pipelines

_____
_____
_____
_____
_____

SELF-QUIZ

Multiple Choice

_____ 1. The expenses incurred in preparing for manufacturing or in buying
the product to put in inventory are called
a. acquisition costs.
b. carrying costs.
c. inventory costs.
d. preparation costs.

_____ 2. By far the cheapest way of carrying bulky goods over a long distance is to use
   a. pipelines.
   b. motor carriers.
   c. water transportation.
   d. air transportation.

_____ 3. The list of all goods in stock which is updated frequently is known as
   a. a physical count.
   b. inventory.
   c. perpetual inventory.
   d. merchandise control.

_____ 4. The carrier that is less regulated because it serves only a limited number of customers, not the general public, is known as the
   a. contract carrier.
   b. common carrier.
   c. exempt carrier.
   d. private carrier.

_____ 5. The group that collects small shipments from a number of companies, consolidates them for transport in full loads, and then sees that the goods reach their final destination is known as
   a. private carriers.
   b. freight forwarders.
   c. exempt carriers.
   d. shippers' associations.

_____ 6. When companies increase costs in one area in order to bring down costs in others, it is known as
   a. cost reduction.
   b. visible costs.
   c. hidden costs.
   d. cost trade-off.

_____ 7. A well-known principle of inventory management is that usually about _____ percent of the products a company carries account for the majority of sales.
   a. 20
   b. 30
   c. 40
   d. 50

_____ 8. The warehouse that is established primarily as a temporary way-station prior to the very rapid movement of goods to customers is known as the
   a. private warehouse.
   b. distribution center warehouse.
   c. automated warehouse.
   d. storage warehouse.

_____ 9. When a warehouse is designed to collect the products of one or more manufacturers in or near the market served before shipping the goods short distances to customers, it is called a (an)
   a. intermediate-positioned warehouse.
   b. market-positioned warehouse.
   c. factory-positioned warehouse.
   d. control-positioned warehouse.

_____ 10. More than _____ of the nation's freight goes by rail.
   a. one-fifth
   b. one-quarter
   c. one-third
   d. one-half

True-False

_____ 11. The ABC analysis identifies items with the biggest sales payoffs.

_____ 12. A contract carrier includes all those transport companies that must serve the general public.

_____ 13. Since the 1950s, the use of pipelines has increased tremendously.

_____ 14. Shippers' associations serve the same function as freight forwarders, except that they work on a profit basis for members of the same industry.

_____ 15. The economic order quantity specifies the amount of stock that costs the most to keep on hand in order to meet the average level of demand.

_____ 16. Market-positioned warehouses are usually chosen by manufacturers with several plants and widely scattered markets. The warehouses gather the products of the various plants and mix them for shipment.

_____ 17. An automated warehouse is one with advanced materials handling systems under the control of a central computer.

_____ 18. Hidden costs show up on a profit and loss statement.

_____ 19. A private warehouse consists of the building, equipment, and labor that are company-owned or controlled.

_____ 20. Manufacturers must balance reasonable customer service with realistic cost outlays.

CHAPTER SOLUTIONS

Key Concepts

1.	f	7.	x	13.	a	19.	v	25.	z
2.	p	8.	b	14.	k	20.	h	26.	cc
3.	i	9.	g	15.	s	21.	e	27.	j
4.	aa	10.	t	16.	y	22.	o	28.	l
5.	m	11.	n	17.	d	23.	c	29.	q
6.	u	12.	r	18.	bb	24.	w		

Self-Quiz

1.	a	5.	b	9.	b	13.	T	17.	T
2.	c	6.	d	10.	c	14.	F	18.	F
3.	c	7.	a	11.	T	15.	F	19.	T
4.	a	8.	b	12.	F	16.	F	20.	T

CHAPTER 14
MARKETING COMMUNICATION: THE PROMOTIONAL MIX

CHAPTER SUMMARY

1. Developing an effective promotional campaign is a tough challenge for the
    marketer. Very few goods or services can survive in the marketplace with-
    out effective promotion. Some products seem to sell themselves. Other
    products need to be heavily promoted. Promotion is one of the most
    dynamic and influential areas of marketing. Promotion is the marketing
    communication activity that attempts to inform and remind individuals
    and persuade them to accept, resell, recommend, or use a product, service,
    idea, or institution. The key elements of this definition are that
    promotional communication should inform, remind, and persuade a variety
    of publics. Often a company will attempt to accomplish several of these
    tasks simultaneously. Informative promotion is generally more common
    during the early stages of the product life cycle. Reminder persuasion
    is used to keep the brand name in the public's mind and is common during
    the maturity stage of the life cycle. Persuasive promotion is designed
    to stimulate purchase or action and is often used in the growth stage
    of the product life cycle. In marketing communication, a seller attempts
    to transmit information to a buyer. In order for communication to be
    effective, it must gain the attention of the receiver, it must be under-
    stood by both the receiver and the sender, and it must stimulate the
    needs of the receiver and suggest an appropriate method of satisfying
    those needs.

2. Communication is an exchange process in which thoughts or ideas are
    expressed. There are six basic elements in the communication circuit:
    the source, or originator of the message; the receiver, the ultimate
    destination of the message; the medium of transmission, the means by
    which the message moves from the sender to receiver; encoding, or putting
    the message into understandable form by the source; decoding, or trans-
    lating the message into understandable terms; and feedback, whereby the
    receiver signals understanding. On occasion, the message may not be
    understood at all, or it may be interpreted not quite in the intended
    manner. The source effect occurs when the reputation of the source
    affects the way the message is received. Often receivers do not get
    the message that the source sends out. Individuals often see and hear
    what they want. Multiple transmitters can occur when individuals mis-
    take the words of a message, whether spoken or in print, for the whole
    message. Decoding errors can occur when receivers do not always get the
    message that a source sends out. Noise is interference that is either

deliberately or accidentally introduced and blocks or distorts transmissions. There are three types of noise. Internal noise is the kind that characterizes the message itself. External noise is introduced accidentally from outside the communication process. Competitive noise is deliberately introduced by another source to gain a competitive advantage. Inadequate feedback occurs when there is a lack of sufficient feedback to the source that can stand in the way of future communications.

3. An organization can use a variety of different promotional activities to communicate with potential customers. The elements of the promotional mix include advertising, personal selling, sales promotion, publicity, and packaging. Advertising can be defined as any paid form of nonpersonal presentation and promotion of ideas, goods, or services by an identified sponsor.

4. Personal selling is the oral presentation of a tangible or intangible product by a seller to a prospect for the purpose of completing an exchange. Selling involves a one-to-one or face-to-face method of promotion. It gives the salesperson the opportunity to develop a presentation suited to the needs of the target market. Personal selling includes such things as a salesperson explaining a product's features, demonstrating a new device, or even distributing free samples of a product while describing its ingredients. In addition, it can provide immediate feedback and reaction of customers to the sales talk. The price of a personal sales presentation can be very expensive. To offset the large expenditure, marketers often have to rely on sales promotion tools as well as mass selling.

5. Publicity is any information relating to a manufacturer or its products that appears in any medium on a nonpaid basis. In other words, publicity is a form of free information. This definition distinguishes publicity from advertising, which is paid for and clearly setoff from news in the media. It can be generated by the company or by word of mouth and can include such things as new items about products and companies, and the mention of brands and companies in books, plays, and television programs. Publicity can be good or bad. Companies have little control over its timing and content.

The chief advantages of publicity over advertising are its believability and comparatively low cost. Public relations attempts to generate a favorable attitude toward a company among employees, stockholders, suppliers, and the government, as well as among customers. It is an attempt on the part of a company to obtain goodwill and convey a positive image of itself. Publicity and public relations can both contribute to an effective promotional campaign at a relatively low cost and often can be more effective than advertising.

6. Sales promotion consists of all the other promotional activities of a firm that stimulate consumer purchases or aid dealer effectiveness. Coupons, trade shows, samples, rebates, and contests are examples of sales

promotion. Sales promotion can be aimed at consumers or middlemen and is intended as an aid or supplement to other forms of promotion. Sales promotion techniques often appeal to the "something for nothing" instincts in people and can be considered as a form of special inducement designed to stimulate immediate purchases. The main drawback of sales promotion techniques is that competitors tend to copy them, cancelling their effectiveness.

7. Effective packaging reflects one of the many decisions that market managers must make. A package can perform many promotional functions. Packages offer protection to the product and consumer, increase the use of the product, increase sales by adding a reuse value, and promote the product. In addition, packages can inform consumers about product benefits, offer suggestions or recipes, announce special value, sell other items in the same line, and highlight special product features. To enhance the promotional value, a package should be designed with the proper color in mind, styled accordingly, exhibit appropriate use of copy, and be formed or shaped to suit the needs of the user. Designers are relatively free to develop any package design that would satisfy consumer and distributor needs. A skillfully designed package will reinforce the information a consumer has already absorbed about the product through other promotional means. Recently, however, modern packaging practices have come under increasing attack from environmentalists and consumer groups that believe the packaging revolution has had harmful side effects. Many groups believe that packaging practices waste resources and pollute the environment. Marketers must be aware of social pressures and seek solutions to the problems of waste avoidance and its economical disposal.

8. Marketers should develop an appropriate combination of the promotional mix to achieve the company's goals. Promotional tools should be used to communicate a message to a person or appropriate target and should be measurable. Effective promotional planning entails setting objectives and devising strategies to meet them. A plan involves setting objectives, or goals, and then designing the strategies to meet those objectives. A company must first set very general communication objectives and then, after research, quantify them for each promotional tool used. One approach may be to suggest that the goals of promotion coincide with the stage of product knowledge of the prospective buyer or, to put it another way, to conform to the AIDA sequence. The AIDA sequence consists of those steps that reflect the usual path that most consumers follow before making a purchase decision. Promotion should create awareness, arouse interest, create desire, and stimulate action. Promotional objectives give marketers a goal; strategies, on the other hand, tell them how to get there. Promotional managers may use a push strategy or pull strategy in designing a promotional program. A push strategy involves pushing, or urging, members of a market channel to sell a product or to give it adequate display. Promotional tools are often directed at wholesalers and retailers to get them to handle the products. A pull strategy attempts to create demand for a product within a channel of

distribution by appealing directly to the consumer. This develops a
high degree of consumer awareness, interest, and desire for the product
by urging retailers to stock it. Often a company may use a combination
strategy, a balance of selling, advertising, and other promotional
techniques to achieve sales goals. In choosing the right strategy, one
has to consider the product type, the customers in the target market,
and the strategies of competitors.

9. Many companies find it very difficult to determine the level of promotional expenditures needed to meet goals and objectives. One of the
reasons for this is because of the interactive effect among the marketing
mix variables.

   There are a number of economic considerations that a marketer has
to consider in preparing an appropriate promotional budget. The percent-
of-sales-approach fixes the amount to be spent for promotion as a percentage of last year's sales or of anticipated sales for the coming
year. The fixed-sum-per-unit method calls for putting aside a specific
amount for each unit produced. The competitive comparison method is
designed to meet competition by spending as much on promotion as the
leading firms do. The objective and task method is based on meeting
future objectives, not on past sales. After promotional objectives are
set, the tasks necessary to reach those objectives and their costs are
worked out for each form of promotion to be used. Other costs, such
as those for research, are then added in; and all costs are totaled to
arrive at a budget. This method guides management toward the future by
its emphasis on goals and eliminates rote spending justified by past
budgets.

10. Marketers often attempt to evaluate the effectiveness of a promotional
strategy. This attempt at evaluation often fails because it is difficult to determine which promotional effort created the desired effect.
Another reason is that outside factors may complicate measurement.
Finally, measurement is difficult because all promotional efforts suffer
from time lag. However, marketers often attempt to measure indirect
effects. Such indirect effects can be measured prior to, during, or
after a promotional campaign is launched. Pretesting is measuring a
promotional campaign's effectiveness before spending on a large scale.
Concurrent testing is securing information while a promotional effort
is under way. Posttesting takes place after a full-scale campaign has
been completed.

11. Marketers must be especially sensitive to the social issues surrounding
the elements of the promotional mix. For example, there has been a
number of complaints from environmentalists that modern packaging
wastes resources and pollutes the environment. Other social issues
involve how much information promotion should convey, whether or not
promotion (especially advertising) should be aimed at vulnerable groups,
and whether or not marketers should promote less consumption of material
goods.

LEARNING GOALS

After reading this chapter, you should be able to:

1. Define promotion and describe how it is used as a form of communication.
2. Know what is necessary to develop effective promotional communication.
3. Understand how communication works and be able to describe some complications such as the source effect, multiple transmitters, decoding errors, and inadequate feedback.
4. Describe and define the elements of the promotional mix including advertising, personal selling, publicity, sales promotion, and packaging.
5. Know the importance of promotion objectives and strategies; be able to distinguish between the pull, push, and combination strategies; and list the factors in choosing the right strategy as it relates to product type, customer, and competition.
6. Understand the importance of budgeting for promotion; distinguish between the percent-of-sales approach, the fixed-sum-per-unit method, the competitive comparison method, and the objective and task method.
7. Explain the need for evaluating and controlling promotion, including the use of indirect measurement.
8. Understand the role of social responsibility in promotion.

KEY CONCEPTS

From the list of lettered terms, select the one that best fits in the blank of the numbered statements that follow. Write the letter of that choice in the space provided.

(Answers to the key concepts appear at the end of the chapter.)

a. Sales promotion
b. Combination strategy
c. Pull strategy
d. Promotion
e. Objective and task budgeting
f. Personal selling
g. A receiver
h. Posttesting
i. Encoding
j. The medium of transmission
k. Pretesting
l. Percent-of-sales budgeting

m. Decoding
n. Fixed-sum-per-unit budgeting
o. The source effect
p. Feedback
q. Push strategy
r. Noise
s. Publicity
t. The source
u. Concurrent testing
v. Public relations
w. Advertising
x. Competitive comparison budgeting

1. _____ refers to creating demand for a product within a channel of distribution by appealing directly to the consumer.

2. _____ refers to the ultimate destination of a message.

3. _____ refers to the understanding signaled by the receiver to the source.

4. _____ is the means by which a message moves from sender to receiver.

5. _____ refers to the activities that attempt to generate a favorable attitude toward a company among employees, stockholders, suppliers, and government, as well as among customers.

6. _____ refers to the retranslating of a message into terms the receiver understands.

7. _____ refers to the strategy that emphasizes setting goals and then fixing costs of meeting those goals for each promotional task used.

8. _____ refers to interference that is either deliberately or accidentally introduced and blocks or distorts transmissions.

9. _____ is a plan to spend as much on promotion as leading firms do.

10. _____ refers to the originator of a message.

11. _____ is the measuring of a promotional campaign's effectiveness before spending on a large scale.

12. _____ refers to securing information while a promotional effort is under way.

13. _____ refers to the balance of selling, advertising, and other promotional techniques combining push and pull strategies to achieve sales goals.

14. _____ refers to the urging of members of a market channel to sell a product or give it adequate display.

15. _____ is any paid form of nonpersonal presentation and promotion of ideas, goods, or services by an identified sponsor.

16. _____ refers to the promotional activities besides selling, advertising, and publicity that stimulate purchases or aid dealer effectiveness.

17. _____ refers to the allocating of a specified amount for each unit produced.

18. _____ is the measuring of the effectiveness of a full-scale campaign after it has been completed.

19. _____ is any information relating to a manufacturer or its products that appears in any medium on a nonpaid basis.

20. _____ refers to putting a message into understandable form by the source.

21. _____ refers to marketing communication that attempts to inform and remind individuals and persuade them to accept, resell, recommend, or use a product, service, idea, or institution.

22. _____ is the sales approach that fixes amounts to be spent for promotion as a percentage of the previous year's sales or of anticipated sales for the coming year.

23. _____ is the oral presentation of a tangible or intangible product to a prospect for the purpose of completing an exchange.

24. _____ is the distortion of a communication resulting from the reputation of the source of a message.

PROGRAMMED REVIEW

The following self-teaching exercises consist of short statements that require you to make a response by filling in the blank (or blanks) provided. You will find the correct response printed in the margin to the left of the question.

a. awareness
b. interest
c. desire
d. action

1. List the four stages of promotion frequently referred to as the acronym AIDA.

   a. _____

   b. _____

   c. _____

   d. _____

reaction

2. The obvious advantage of a direct oral presentation is that it allows the salesperson to judge the _____ of consumers to the sales talk.

a. by color
b. by style
c. by copy
d. by form

advance

a. the reputation of
    the source
b. multiple transmitters
c. decoding errors
d. inadequate feedback

explicit
imply

a. to protect the
    product and consumer
b. to increase the use
    of the product
c. to increase sales by
    adding a reuse value
d. to promote the
    product

paid
nonpersonal

3. What are the four ways in which a package
    designer can distinguish his company's
    products from others on the same shelf?

    a. _____

    b. _____

    c. _____

    d. _____

4. The advantage of the fixed-sum-per-unit
    method is that the manufacturer knows
    the promotional cost per unit in

    _____.

5. What are four sources of misunderstanding
    in the communication process?

    a. _____

    b. _____

    c. _____

    d. _____

6. Promotion is often needed to make
    _____ what the other
    elements of the marketing mix only

    _____.

7. What are four functions of packaging?

    a. _____

        _____

    b. _____

        _____

    c. _____

        _____

    d. _____

        _____

8. Advertising is any _____ form
    of _____ presentation
    and promotion of ideas, goods, or ser-
    vices by an identified sponsor.

a. It is difficult to
    determine which pro-
    motional effort
    created the desired
    effect.
b. Outside factors may
    complicate measure-
    ment.
c. Almost all promotional
    efforts suffer from
    time lag.

9. What are the three reasons why measuring
    the effectiveness of a certain outlay
    by sales may fail?

    a. _____
        _____
        _____
        _____
    b. _____
        _____
        _____
    c. _____
        _____
        _____

before

10. Pretesting measures a promotional cam-
    paign's effectiveness _____
    spending on a large scale.

a. internal noise
b. external noise
c. competitive noise

11. Noise refers to interference that is
    either deliberately or accidentally
    introduced. What are the three types
    of noise?

    a. _____
    b. _____
    c. _____

favorable attitude

12. Public relations attempts to generate a
    _____
    toward a company among employees, stock-
    holders, suppliers, and the government,
    as well as among customers.

a. the percent-of-
   sales approach
b. the fixed-sum-per-
   unit method
c. the competitive
   comparison method
d. the objective and
   task method

13. What are four promotional budget tech-
    niques from which marketers can choose?

    a. _____
       _____
    b. _____
       _____
    c. _____
       _____
    d. _____
       _____

general communication
quantify

14. In setting promotional goals, an organ-
    ization must first set very
    _____
    objectives and then, after research,
    _____ them for each
    promotional tool used.

a. to inform
b. to remind
c. to persuade

15. What are the three purposes of promo-
    tional communication?

    a. _____
    b. _____
    c. _____

selling
advertising
other promotional
  techniques

a. the push strategy
b. the pull strategy
c. the combination
   strategy

16. The combination strategy uses a balance
    of _____, _____
    and _____
    to achieve company goals.

17. What are the three strategies that are
    often used in achieving promotional
    objectives?

    a. _____
    b. _____
    c. _____

one-to-one

18. Selling, unlike advertising, involves a
    _____ relationship
    with a customer.

a. the source
b. the receiver
c. the medium of trans-
   mission
d. encoding
e. decoding
f. feedback

moves

a. advertising
b. sales promotion
c. publicity/public
   relations
d. personal selling
e. packaging

creative

a. what product type
b. what customers
c. what about competi-
   tion

19. What are the six basic elements of the
    communication circuit?

    a. _____

    b. _____

    c. _____

    d. _____

    e. _____

    f. _____

20. The medium of transmission is the means
    by which the message _____
    from sender to receiver.

21. What are the five promotional activities
    or tools?

    a. _____

    b. _____

    c. _____

    d. _____

    e. _____

22. Advertising often captures attention
    because it is often quite _____.

23. What are the three factors that must be
    weighed in choosing the right promo-
    tional strategy?

    a. _____

    b. _____

    c. _____

215

a. It must gain the attention of the receiver.
b. It must be understood by both the receiver and the sender.
c. It must stimulate the needs of the receiver and suggest an appropriate method of satisfying those needs.

24. What are the three objectives that are necessary in order for a communication to be effective?

a. _____
   _____
   _____

b. _____
   _____
   _____

c. _____
   _____
   _____
   _____

a. pretesting
b. concurrent testing
d. posttesting

25. What are the three indirect measurements used to measure the effectiveness of sales results as reflected by promotional effort?

a. _____
b. _____
c. _____

MARKETING RIDDLE

The purpose of this exercise is to find the missing word that solves the riddle. Each of the statements requires you to make a response by filling in the blank (or blanks) for the appropriate missing word. Each statement contains a key letter which, when combined with the other key letters, will provide you with the solution to the riddle. Correct solutions to the riddle questions can lead to valuable prizes. See instructions for more information.

One of the major advantages of stating promotional objectives in measurable terms is that it allows the organization to
$\overline{}\ \overline{}\ \overline{}\ \overline{}\ \overline{}\ \overline{}$ the effectiveness of its promotional mix.
1 2 3 4 5 6

1. External noise is introduced __ __ __ __ __ __ __ __ ☐ __ __ __.

216

2. Communication only works if the receiver of the information
_ _ _ _ _ ☐ _ _ _ _ _ what the sender is trying to say.

3. The receiver is the ultimate _ _ ☐ _ _ _ _ _ _ _ _.

4. A skillfully designed package will _ _ _ _ _ _ _ _ _ ☐ the information a consumer has already absorbed about the product through advertising, sales promotion, or publicity.

5. An advantage of advertising is that is allows perfect reproduction of
the _ _ ☐ _ _ _ _ message.

6. The requirement that packages be both attention-getting and functional
puts a heavy burden on _ _ ☐ _ _ _ _ _ _ _.

EXPERIENTIAL EXERCISE

Marketers are so concerned with packaging that it has become over a $50 billion-
a-year industry in the United States. It has often been said that the
package may be more important than the product it contains. The purpose of
this exercise is to help you determine if the packaging functions and design
features are being met.

A package on the retailer's shelf may be surrounded by many more packages
competing for the consumer's attention.

Visit a local supermarket and select a product that you would like to evaluate
concerning packaging and design characteristics.

1. Do you believe that the package successfully protects the product as well
as the consumer? How?

_____

_____

_____

_____

_____

2. Does the package help to increase the use of the product? How?

_____

_____

_____

_____

_____

3. Does the package increase sales by adding a reuse value? How?

_____

_____

_____

_____

_____

4. Does the package help to promote the product? How?

_____

_____

_____

_____

_____

5. Is the package properly designed? How has color, style, and copy con-
   tributed to the product's marketability?

_____

_____

_____

_____

_____

6. What other benefits does the package provide?

_____

_____

_____

_____

_____

SELF-QUIZ

Multiple Choice

____ 1. In establishing promotional budgets, which method allows for
        putting aside a specific amount for each unit produced?
        a. the competitive comparison method
        b. the fixed-sum-per-unit method
        c. the objective and task method
        d. the percent-of-sales approach

2. Which testing method takes place after a full-scale campaign has been completed?
   a. posttesting method
   b. pretesting method
   c. concurrent testing
   d. campaign testing

3. In the communication circuit, what is the term that describes the practice of putting the message into understandable form by the source?
   a. medium of transmission
   b. retranslating
   c. encoding
   d. feedback

4. Which type of noise or interference is deliberately introduced by another source to gain an advantage?
   a. internal noise
   b. interference noise
   c. external noise
   d. competitive noise

5. It is believed that a pull strategy is far more common for what type of goods?
   a. industrial goods
   b. convenience goods
   c. specialty goods
   d. consumer goods

6. The promotional effort in which information relating to a manufacturer or its products appears in any medium on a nonpaid basis is known as
   a. publicity.
   b. advertising.
   c. personal sales.
   d. public relations.

7. The stages frequently referred to by the acronym AIDA stand for
   a. action, interest, desire, and attention.
   b. awareness, interest, desire, and action.
   c. action, innovation, decline, and attention.
   d. attention, interest, desire, and activity.

8. The strategy most familiar to consumer goods companies and that uses a balance of selling, advertising, and other promotional techniques is known as
   a. combination strategy.
   b. push strategy.
   c. pull strategy.
   d. push-pull strategy.

_____ 9. According to the Department of Labor, about _____ million people are engaged in sales occupations.
   a. six
   b. ten
   c. thirteen
   d. twenty

_____ 10. The method that recognizes that promotion leads to future sales, not to past sales, is known as
   a. the fixed-sum-per-unit method.
   b. the competitive comparison method.
   c. the objective and task method.
   d. the percent-of-sales approach.

True-False

_____ 11. Feedback is generally much more immediate and therefore more useful in shaping future messages for television ads and publicity talks than for personal selling and cents-off coupons.

_____ 12. In general, the more complex a product, the more appropriate a pull strategy.

_____ 13. A budget guides a manager in purchasing the selling, advertising, and other services needed.

_____ 14. Promotion is a form of communication practiced by both business and nonbusiness organizations.

_____ 15. The medium of transmission reflects the means by which the message moves from sender to receiver.

_____ 16. A push strategy attempts to create demand for a product within a channel of distribution by appealing directly to the consumer.

_____ 17. Pretesting is concerned with securing information while a promotional effort is under way.

_____ 18. Packaging experts are now paying more attention to environmentalists complaints.

_____ 19. The objective and task method recognizes that promotion leads to future sales.

_____ 20. Sometimes the reputation of the source affects the way a message is received.

CHAPTER SOLUTIONS

Key Concepts

1. c	6. m	11. k	16. a	21. d
2. g	7. e	12. u	17. n	22. l
3. p	8. r	13. b	18. h	23. f
4. j	9. x	14. q	19. s	24. o
5. v	10. t	15. w	20. i	

Self-Quiz

1. b	5. b	9. a	13. T	17. F
2. a	6. a	10. c	14. T	18. T
3. c	7. b	11. F	15. T	19. T
4. d	8. a	12. F	16. F	20. T

CHAPTER SUMMARY

1. Advertising is one of the most obvious forms of marketing activity
    dating back to ancient times. Advertising's importance has increased
    dramatically over the past few decades, accounting for about $115 billion
    in 1987. Advertising is by no means a tool only of large companies.
    To the contrary, organizations of every size use it in some way. Today,
    we find many professionals such as lawyers, accountants, and even dentists
    using advertising to tell their stories. However, we find that adver-
    tising is more important in certain markets--especially final consumer
    markets. Though creativity is an essential input, consistently effective
    advertising comes about because of well-thought out decision-making activ-
    ities.

2. The advertising objectives largely determine the types of advertising to
    use. Selective or brand advertising consists of messages that try to
    increase consumer preference for a particular firm's product. It may be
    aimed at the final users or channel members. Primary demand advertising
    increases the total demand for products without distinguishing between
    brands. Association advertising is a special way of increasing primary
    demand and occurs when members of a trade association pool funds to
    promote a class of products or services. Institutional advertising is
    a paid message designed to build long-range goodwill for a firm rather
    than to sell specific goods. Its objective is to improve the advertiser's
    image, sales, and relations with the various groups the company associates
    with. Noncommercial advertising consists of advertising placed by non-
    profit organizations. This form of advertising is relatively new and
    rapidly growing. Its four chief users are public interest groups, fed-
    eral and state governments, nonprofit hospitals and universities, as well
    as political parties.

3. Organizations have many varied reasons for advertising. Most firms
    advertise in order to inform and persuade the public. In addition, ads
    also work for firms by reminding consumers of a company's products or
    services and reassuring buyers they have made the right purchase. Ads
    can also provide leads for salespeople, help obtain desirable outlets,
    provide ongoing contact with target customers, and provide immediate buy-
    ing action.

4. An advertising campaign can be handled by advertising departments and/or
    agencies. The advertising department is responsible for setting the
    advertising objectives of a campaign and its budget. Depending on the
    size of the advertising program, an advertising department may consist
    of a few persons or a large number of individual specialists. The

department may be organized by function, media, product, end use, or geographical location. The advertising agencies, especially the larger ones, are useful because they bring together highly skilled specialists who are independent of the advertiser and have an outside viewpoint. Agencies are capable of providing various services for their clients including the design of entire campaigns, determining objectives, selecting and contracting development with media, designing themes and appeals, as well as creating copy design. As specialists, agencies often can do the job more economically than a company's own department. For their efforts, the large established agencies are paid by commission, usually 15 percent of the dollar value of the media they purchase for a company.

5. There are many decisions to be made before the basic content and form of the advertising message is prepared. The first decision is concerned with the objectives of the advertising campaign. The objectives of any campaign must be in keeping with the broader promotional objectives set by the company. The second decision is concerned with the establishment of a budget. In preparing a budget, the nature of the company, the product, and the stage of the product life cycle have to be considered. The third decision is concerned with product positioning. The theory of positioning states that to sell a product, a company must create a unique niche, or position, for it in the consumer's mind. It is concerned with defining a class of competitors and finding a way to distinguish the product in that class.

6. The fourth decision is concerned with the creation of a message to effectively promote the product. Message development involves making decisions about the theme, copy, and format. Creative copy and presentation can greatly increase the ad's effectiveness. The image sell stresses the importance of creating an exclusive image for a product in ads. The direct sell relies on uncovering one unique product benefit and then hammering it home through repetition. The humorous, or soft sell, uses ads that joke about the product. The competitive sell, or comparative advertising, is the creative style that uses the names of competitors.

7. The fifth decision is concerned with the selection of media in which the ad should run. In seeking an effective communications channel, a firm has to consider how much to spend on various media types and what specific media to use. Media are all the different means by which advertising reaches its audience. An advertising budget should be developed for the various media in relation to their potential for effectively conveying the intended message to the target market. Matching target customers and media is the major problem in effective media selection. In preparing a media plan, media experts should consider various qualities. Among the most important are selectivity, flexibility, life span, production quality, and reputation. The most popular advertising medium is newspapers. They account for about 26 percent of the total advertising dollar. Advantages of newspaper advertising include its wide use, short

lead time, and flexibility in reaching local markets. Its disadvantages include cost, short life, and limited reproductive capabilities. Magazine advertising accounts for 5.4 percent of the total advertising dollar. Advantages of magazine advertising include long life, segmented audiences, good reproduction, and prestige. Its disadvantages include early closing dates and inflexibility. Television advertising accounts for 21.9 percent of the total advertising dollar. Advantages of television advertising include the ability to offer sight, sound, and motion, wide reach, and the ability to provide a captive audience with a good attention span. Television can be purchased on either a nationwide, regionwide, or local basis. Its disadvantages include its high-dollar costs, nonselective audience, extensive clutter, and short exposure. Radio advertising accounts for 6.9 percent of the total advertising dollar. Advantages of radio advertising include its relatively low cost per exposure, segmented audiences, wide reach, and the ability to change the message quickly. Its disadvantages include its lack of visual capabilities, weak attention, and short exposure. Direct-mail advertising accounts for 16.4 percent of the total advertising dollar. Advantages of direct-mail advertising include the ability to personalize, flexibility, and the use of selected audiences. Forms of direct mail include the use of sales letters, catalogs, postcards, and house organs. Its disadvantages include its high cost per contact, considered to be "junk mail" by many, and criticized as an invasion of privacy. Outdoor/transit advertising accounts for 2.8 percent of the total advertising dollar. Advantages of outdoor/transit advertising include its flexibility, low cost, and the opportunity for repeat exposure. Forms of outdoor/transit advertising include the use of billboards, blimps, and taxicabs. Its disadvantages include very short exposure, short messages, and the lack of demographic selectivity.

8. The sixth decision is concerned with the measurement of the ad's effectiveness. It is very difficult to determine whether a particular ad produced a certain sale. Often advertisers try to measure such things as whether the intended audience was exposed to, is aware of, or can recall their message. Increasing advertising costs, more intense competition, and advancements in computer technology has inspired companies to develop sophisticated mathematical tools as measuring devices. Advertisers should try to determine whether a campaign accomplished its advertising objectives; evaluate the effectiveness of several advertisements as they apply to copy, layout, and illustrations; and evaluate the strengths and weaknesses of various media. Advertisers often use a number of techniques to measure advertising effectiveness. Pretesting is conducted to evaluate advertising before the campaign begins. Pretesting techniques include opinion and attitude tests, mechanical laboratory methods, and projective techniques. Concurrent testing is conducted in an attempt to evaluate television and radio advertising at the time it is aired. Concurrent techniques include the use of the Nielsen audimeter and consumer diaries. Posttesting is conducted in an attempt to evaluate advertising after it has appeared in various media. Posttesting techniques include the use of readership (recognition) tests, recall tests, and attitude change measures.

9. Advertising is probably the most controversial component of marketing. The criticisms vary, but the most serious ones fall into the categories of deception, manipulation, wastefulness, and irritation. In addition, many individuals question advertising's cost and effect on prices. Despite its criticisms, advertising is a necessary marketing component in the overall marketing mix.

10. Marketers use sales promotion for a variety of reasons. Sales promotion is the added inducement that can aid personal selling, advertising, and publicity. Sales promotion activities are quite varied and their use depends upon the situation; but all of them attempt to get the sales force, intermediaries, and customers to handle the product. Annual sales meetings, contests, and gifts are common forms of sales promotion targeted specifically for wholesale intermediaries and retailers. A trade show is an exposition that allows salespeople to display their new products to dealers, to make new contacts, and to develop mailing lists for future use. Point-of-purchase (POP) materials include posters and signs, display racks, banners, price cards, interactive videos, and displays that emit product aromas. Advertising allowances are reimbursements provided to retailers, and sometimes wholesalers, when they run the company's ad in a newspaper or on local broadcast media. The reimbursement can be paid in part by the manufacturer. Sales promotions can also be targeted to consumers. Coupons allow a number of cents off the price of an item. Most coupons are distributed through the mail, in newspapers and magazines, within a package, or on the back of cash register tapes. Samples are offered by manufacturers as giveaways in a trial size for products whose benefits cannot be fully conveyed through advertising. Premiums are items offered free or at a low cost as a reward for buying a product.

11. Businesses employ publicity for a variety of reasons. Publicity refers to any information relating to a manufacturer or its products that appears in any medium on a nonpaid basis. It is often used to make people aware of a firm's products, brands, or activities. Publicity can also be used to maintain a certain level of visibility and image. Publicity consists of news stories and personal appearances and carries a high degree of believability. Because it is free, publicity is less controllable than advertising. Publicity tools also include feature articles, press conferences and personal appearances, records and films, and editorials. In addition to publicity, organizations have extensive public relations programs. They may include opinion research, lobbying, public affairs, and fund raising. Like other forms of promotion, a publicity program should begin with objectives consistent with the overall marketing program. Public relations refers to a company's attempt to communicate and maintain effective relations with its many publics including suppliers, stockholders, employees, society, and the government. Because it is difficult to measure the effectiveness of a public relations campaign, organizations often attempt to measure results by using controlled market comparisons, direct response, and by communicating with the sales force.

LEARNING GOALS

After reading this chapter, you should be able to:

1. Describe the nature and growth of advertising and describe the many varieties of advertising, including selective or brand advertising, primary demand advertising, institutional advertising, and noncommercial advertising.
2. Understand the specific reasons for advertising.
3. Discuss the organization of advertising, including the advertising department and advertising agency.
4. Discuss the marketing decisions involved in the advertising campaign, including the setting of advertising objectives, establishing a budget, and postioning; the importance of creating the appropriate message, including the use of image sell, direct sell, humorous or soft sell, and competitive sell; the importance of selecting the right media, including newspapers, magazines, television, radio, direct mail, and outdoor/transit media; and the importance of testing advertising effectiveness.
5. Discuss advertising criticisms and constraints.
6. Understand the role of sales promotion, including the importance of promoting to the sales force; to the intermediary by the use of trade shows, point-of-purchase materials, and advertising allowances; and to consumers by the use of coupons, samples, and/or premiums. You should also know the importance of carefully selecting and blending the various sales promotion tools.
7. Describe the role of publicity and public relations.

KEY CONCEPTS

From the list of lettered terms, select the one that best fits in the blank of the numbered statements that follow. Write the letter of that choice in the space provided.

(Answers to the key concepts appear at the end of the chapter.)

a. Media
b. A sample
c. An advertising allowance
d. Positioning
e. Comparative advertising
f. Point-of-purchase materials
g. A premium
h. Noncommercial advertising
i. A trade show
j. Selective or brand advertising
k. Institutional (or corporate) advertising
l. Association advertising
m. A coupon
n. Primary demand advertising

1. _____ consists of giveaways in a trial size for products whose benefits cannot be fully conveyed through advertising.

2. _____ is creative style that uses names of competitors.

3. _____ consists of messages that try to increase consumer preference for a particular firm's product.

4. _____ consists of advertising aimed at increasing the total demand for products without distinguishing between brands.

5. _____ is a paid message sponsored by nonprofit organizations.

6. _____ is a theory holding that to sell a product, a company must create a unique niche, or position, for it in the consumer's mind.

7. _____ consists of a sales promotion tool aimed at consumers that offers a certain amount off the price of an item.

8. _____ is an exposition that allows salespeople to display their new products to dealers, to make new contacts, and to develop mailing lists for future use.

9. _____ consists of all the different means by which advertising reaches its audiences.

10. _____ are promotional tools such as posters, display racks, and price cards.

11. _____ provides for reimbursement by a manufacturer for part of the cost of local advertising run by retailers and wholesalers.

12. _____ is an item offered free or at a low cost as a reward for buying a product.

13. _____ consists of advertising sponsored by a trade association to promote a class of products.

14. _____ consists of a paid message designed to build long-range goodwill for a firm rather than to sell specific goods.

PROGRAMMED REVIEW

The following self-teaching exercises consist of short statements that require you to make a response by filling in the blank (or blanks) provided. You will find the correct response printed in the margin to the left of the question.

227

a. selective or brand
   advertising
b. primary demand
   advertising
c. institutional
   advertising
d. noncommercial
   advertising

annual sales meeting

a. public-interest
   groups
b. federal and state
   governments
c. nonprofit hospitals
   and universities
d. political parties

display
contacts
mailing lists

a. reminding consumers
   of a company's prod-
   uct or services
b. reassuring buyers
   they have made the
   right purchase

selective
long life span

1. What are four types of advertising?

   a. _____

   b. _____

   c. _____

   d. _____

2. Perhaps the most common form of sales
   promotion to the sales force is the
   _____.

3. Who are the four chief users of noncommercial advertising?

   a. _____

   b. _____
      _____

   c. _____
      _____

   d. _____

4. The main purpose of a trade show is to
   allow salespeople to _____
   their products to dealers, to make new
   _____, and to develop
   _____ for
   future use.

5. In addition to informing and persuading,
   what two other benefits do ads provide?

   a. _____
      _____
      _____

   b. _____
      _____
      _____

6. Besides being relatively inexpensive,
   outdoor media are _____
   of local audiences, and they have a
   _____.

228

a. news releases
b. feature articles
c. press conferences
d. records and films
e. editorials

7. What are five commonly used publicity tools?

   a. _____

   b. _____

   c. _____

   d. _____

   e. _____

$100,000

8. The cost of producing a single uncomplicated TV commercial can run to about _____ .

a. opinion research
b. lobbying
c. public affairs
d. fund raising and
   membership drives

9. What are four areas that may be included in an organization's public relations program?

   a. _____

   b. _____

   c. _____

   d. _____

   _____

objectives
budget

10. As they do with advertising, marketers should begin a sales promotion campaign by establishing _____ and a _____ .

a. oversee the planning
   of all campaigns
b. act as go-between
   in ad agency-company
   relations
c. control expenses

11. What are three functions of the advertising manager's job?

   a. _____

   _____

   b. _____

   _____

   c. _____

duplicated
short-term

12. Unfortunately for the initiator, most sales incentives are easily _____ and, therefore, may have only a _____ effect before competitors' defensive maneuvers erode any sales increases.

a. by function
b. by media
c. by product
d. by end use
e. by geographical
   leader

manufacturers
retailers

a. the image sell
b. the direct sell
c. the humorous or
   soft sell
d. the competitive
   sell

type
stage

assist

13. What are five ways that an advertising
    department can be organized?

    a. _____

    b. _____

    c. _____

    d. _____

    e. _____

14. Cooperative advertising occurs when
    _____ give
    _____ promotional
    money to promote their brands.

15. What are four creative styles that are
    used in presenting advertising messages?

    a. _____

    b. _____

    c. _____

    d. _____

16. Informing and persuading the public are
    among the primary reasons most companies
    advertise. The mixture of information
    and persuasion varies with the _____
    of advertising and the _____
    in a product's life cycle.

17. Sales promotion often is designed to
    _____ the efforts of the
    sales force.

a. what the objectives
   of the campaign are
b. what the budget is
c. how the product
   should be positioned
d. what message should
   be used
e. what media should be
   used
f. how its effectiveness
   can be measured

18. Before an advertising campaign can be
    mounted, what are six issues that must
    be addressed?

    a. _____
       _____
    b. _____
       _____
    c. _____
       _____
    d. _____
       _____
    e. _____
       _____
    f. _____
       _____

mind

19. The theory of positioning states that
    to sell a product, a company must
    create a unique niche, or position, for
    the product in the consumer's

    _____.

a. selectivity
b. flexibility
c. life span
d. production quality
e. reputation

20. What are five qualities that media
    experts look for in determining the
    strengths and weaknesses of the media?

    a. _____
    b. _____
    c. _____
    d. _____
    e. _____

radio

21. With television rates reaching astronom-
    ical figures, many analysts believe
    that _____ will emerge
    as an even stronger medium in the
    future.

a. more consumer income
b. greater consumer willingness to spend on services and pleasures
c. more competition
d. more products and outlets for shopping
e. a rapid movement to self-service retailing

mature
market share

a. deceptive
b. manipulative
c. wasteful
d. irritating

a. newspapers
b. magazines
c. television
d. radio
e. direct mail
f. outdoor/transit signs

22. What are five principal reasons for the growth of advertising?

a. _____
_____
b. _____
_____
c. _____
_____
d. _____
_____
e. _____
_____

23. The theory behind most selective advertising is that a product in the _____ stage of its life cycle must be kept before the public to maintain its _____.

24. What are four accusations that have been used to describe advertising?

a. _____
b. _____
c. _____
d. _____

25. What are the six major media commonly used by advertisers?

a. _____
b. _____
c. _____
d. _____
e. _____
f. _____

232

MARKETING RIDDLE

The purpose of this exercise is to find the missing word that solves the riddle. Each of the statements requires you to make a response by filling in the blank (or blanks) for the appropriate missing word. Each statement contains a key letter which, when combined with the other key letters, will provide you with the solution to the riddle. Correct solutions to the riddle questions can lead to valuable prizes. See instructions for more information.

Advertising is costly and requires many $\underline{}\,\underline{}\,\underline{}\,\underline{}\,\underline{}\,\underline{}\,\underline{}\,\underline{}\,\underline{}\,\underline{}$
 1 2 3 4 5 6 7 8 9 10

decisions based on judgment and creativity rather than just on hard facts.

1. People ☐ __ __ __ __ __ out a great many of the ads they see, so breaking through their attention barrier is a real feat.

2. In establishing an advertising budget, the __ __ __ ☐ __ __ of the company is probably the foremost consideration.

3. The quality that magazines lack most is __ __ __ __ __ ☐ __ __ __ __ __ .

4. The humorous or soft sell approach uses ads that ☐ __ __ __ about the product.

5. Association advertising is a special way of increasing primary __ ☐ __ __ __ __ .

6. Despite the large overall audience, most magazines are highly targeted because they appeal to __ __ __ ☐ __ __ __ interests.

7. Comparative advertising is the creative style that uses the names of __ __ __ __ __ ☐ __ __ __ __ .

8. In the hotly competitive advertising business, the message is just as important as the __ __ __ ☐ __ __ __ __ for success.

9. Primary demand advertising is used mainly for __ __ __ __ ☐ __ __ __ __ __ products in the first stages of their life cycle.

10. Although the number of major media is small, the decision as to which to use can be __ __ __ __ __ ☐ __ .

EXPERIENTIAL EXERCISE

In promoting their products or services, organizations can select from a wide variety of media. The success or failure of advertising media depends on how well it helps the company to achieve its promotional objectives, including the importance of creating consumer awareness and increasing sales.

In each of the six media, select a particular product or service that you recently were exposed to and discuss the reasons why you were able to recall the ad, the message content effectiveness, the choice of ad location in a broadcast program or print medium, and the ad timing. Indicate whether you believe the message was informative and whether your opinion, attitude, or behavior was influenced in any way.

1. Newspapers

_____
_____
_____
_____
_____
_____
_____
_____

2. Television

_____
_____
_____
_____
_____
_____
_____
_____

3. Radio

_____

_____

_____

_____

_____

_____

_____

_____

4. Magazines

_____

_____

_____

_____

_____

_____

_____

5. Direct Mail

_____

_____

_____

_____

_____

_____

_____

6. Outdoor/Transit

_____

_____

_____

_____

_____

_____

_____

SELF-QUIZ

Multiple Choice

_____ 1. What media is known to be relatively inexpensive and has a long
life span, often 30 days or more?
a. radio
b. newspapers
c. magazines
d. outdoor/transit

_____ 2. When people associate advertising with messages that try to increase
consumer preference for a particular firm's product, it is called
a. selective or brand advertising.
b. primary demand advertising.
c. association advertising.
d. institutional advertising.

_____ 3. What media is the most popular in terms of dollar expenditure?
a. newspapers
b. television
c. radio
d. magazines

_____ 4. Traditionally, what percent of the dollar value of the media
purchased do established advertising agencies receive as a commission?
a. 10 percent
b. 15 percent
c. 20 percent
d. 25 percent

5. The approach that relies on uncovering one unique product benefit and then hammering it home through repetition is known as
   a. the image sell.
   b. the competitive sell.
   c. the direct sell.
   d. the humorous or soft sell.

6. What type of advertising do we generally find for mainly innovative products in the first stages of their life cycle?
   a. cooperative advertising
   b. primary demand advertising
   c. noncommercial advertising
   d. selective advertising

7. It is estimated that nonprofit organizations now account for about _____ percent of all money spent for advertising.
   a. 5
   b. 8
   c. 10
   d. 15

8. Which media appears to be experiencing one of the most innovative and competitive periods in its history?
   a. television
   b. magazines
   c. outdoor/transit
   d. radio

9. In an attempt to look at the strengths and weaknesses of media, what is the term used to determine how much time in advance an ad must be placed?
   a. production quality
   b. selectivity
   c. flexibility
   d. reputation

10. The promotional tool that relies on posters and signs, display racks, banners, and price cards is called
    a. point-of-purchase material.
    b. a trade show.
    c. a coupon.
    d. advertising allowances.

True-False

11. Advertising by nonprofit organizations is relatively new and rapidly growing.

12. Publicity is very popular because it is free and is more controllable than advertising.

237

_____ 13. Sales promotion can be used to assist the sales force, stimulate middlemen, or motivate consumers.

_____ 14. Advertising as we know it today began after World War I.

_____ 15. Most people do not screen out a great many of the ads they see, thus advertisers are able to maintain one's attention barrier.

_____ 16. The two organizations that employ the most people in the advertising field are advertising departments and agencies.

_____ 17. The theory of positioning states that to sell a product, a company must create a unique niche, or position, for it in the consumer's mind.

_____ 18. After an advertising budget is established, objectives should be set.

_____ 19. Humor seems to be making a comeback in advertising.

_____ 20. Although the number of media is small, the decision as to which to use can be complex.

CHAPTER SOLUTIONS

Key Concepts

1. b	4. n	7. m	10. f	13. l
2. e	5. h	8. i	11. c	14. k
3. j	6. d	9. a	12. g	

Self-Quiz

1. d	5. c	9. c	13. T	17. T
2. a	6. b	10. a	14. F	18. F
3. a	7. c	11. T	15. F	19. T
4. b	8. d	12. F	16. T	20. T

CHAPTER SUMMARY

1. Just stop and think about what could happen to our economy if people
    stopped buying goods and services. Each sale generates many supportive
    jobs and provides a livelihood for over 8 million people. Selling is a
    vital and necessary part of our American economy. Almost all organiza-
    tions employ salespeople and many firms spend more money on personal
    selling than on any other component of the promotional mix. Personal
    selling is the oral presentation of a tangible or intangible product by
    a seller to a prospect for the purpose of completing an exchange. Per-
    sonal selling can allow for flexibility and adaptibility in meeting the
    needs and wants of specific targets. By proper use of selling tech-
    niques, personal selling can provide for a detailed explanation of prod-
    uct or service features, leading to the last stage in the purchaser's
    decision-making process. In addition, it can provide for immediate
    feedback to a firm as to the success of its marketing program. On the
    negative side, personal selling can accomodate only a limited number of
    prospective customers, it can be quite expensive on a per customer basis,
    and generally has a negative image in the eyes of many customers.

2. There are many types of sales jobs which are often categorized by degree
    of creativity. Sometimes companies utilize one type of salesperson,
    others a combination of all the five types. Merchandise deliverers are
    individuals who have no responsibility for creative selling, but they
    provide essential support to the sales effort by seeing that buyers
    receive their purchases. Order takers are salespeople who may suggest an
    article for purchase but whose main function is to write or ring up
    orders. Missionaries are salespeople whose job is to build goodwill or
    to educate potential customers rather than to make a direct sale. Tech-
    nical salespeople are technicians in sales positions who act as consul-
    tants and sometimes help to design products or systems to meet a client's
    needs. Creative salespeople are those individuals charged with determin-
    ing customer needs, helping them solve problems, and getting orders.

3. Once the decision is made to field a sales force, its objectives, struc-
    ture, and size must be determined. The role of the sales force is deter-
    mined by establishing objectives which can include such areas as presales
    and post-sales activity, technical assistance, and problem-solving advice.
    However, the major goal is persuasion or the ability of converting con-
    sumer interest into a sale. Once these are set, a sales manager must
    determine the sales force structure to ensure that sales tasks are
    achieved effectively. The structure can be established by territory,
    product, market, or by an organizational combination. Once a structure
    has been set, the next important consideration is the size of the sales

force. This can be achieved by noting the company's sales forecast for a given period for individual districts or regions. Then, based on area potential, a salesperson or group of salespeople can be determined. Another method is to determine the number of accounts and then to categorize them on the basis of their sales and potential importance. Another possibility is to observe total sales and add a salesperson based on a specific dollar amount. Carefully established guidelines can be quite valuable in reducing travel time and the ultimate cost of sales calls. In staffing a sales force, it is important to select the most qualified individuals. A sales manager has to decide on such issues as the size of the sales force and the number of people to hire in a given period. The overall productivity of the sales force has to be evaluated and where necessary, new sales presentation techniques considered. The sales force selection process should be based upon the job description and should include an analysis of such personal attributes as mental, physical, and personality characteristics; product knowledge; and the nature of the customer's buying task. The interaction of all these variables can often determine whether or not a sale is made. Thus, characteristics of the salesperson can be an important dimension in a sales situation. Companies use application forms, tests, and interviews to recruit and select a sales force. Sales trainees can be recruited from nonselling jobs within a company, direct from competing companies, recommendations from current employees, college campuses, employment agencies, or from submitted resumes.

4. The sales manager is an important part of a firm's success because the sales force is responsible for sales revenue. The sales manager is responsible for translating the goals and objectives set by management into results. His basic function is to maximize sales at a reasonable level of cost. Sales management involves recruiting, selecting, and training salespeople; supervising and motivating them on the job; and evaluating their performance. After a recruit has been hired and given a brief orientation, training begins. Sales training should be an ongoing part of any sales-oriented organization. Training should be provided not only to new recruits, but also to experienced personnel. The type of training program and its length can vary from company to company. It can be systematically organized or consist of mainly on-the-job training. Training can equip the salesperson with the necessary tools for selling. Role playing occurs when one person acts the part of salesperson and the other the customer. Factual information often stressed in a training session includes knowledge of the company, product, and competition. In addition, sales reps are often expected to learn about the AIDA theory of selling and the want-satisfaction theory. The AIDA theory suggests that promotional goals be keyed to the stage of product knowledge of a prospective buyer. The want-satisfaction approach stresses that the salesperson must first determine what a buyer really wants or needs before launching a sales talk. The salesperson encourages the buyer to do most of the talking in an attempt to gather selling points which are then used in the sales presentation. The want-satisfaction method takes longer to master

and is most effective in creative and technical selling jobs. Other forms of training can include lectures, demonstrations, and films. A good training program can build confidence, improve morale, increase sales, and develop better customer relations.

5. The various sales situations necessitate the use of different selling techniques. However, most sales presentations consist of six stages. The first stage of the sales presentation includes prospecting and qualifying. In prospecting, the salesperson actively seeks out buyers from available sources including the use of unsolicited phone calls, referrals, directories, conventions, newspapers, recommendations, and cold canvassing. In qualifying, the salesperson tries to determine whether prospects have the authority to buy and the money to pay for the purchases. To avoid wasting time and money, the salesperson needs to identify the buying authority before making a presentation. Often an organizational chart can provide the information. Determining ability to pay can often be obtained from credit rating reports or other financial reporting services. Based on this information, the salesperson can determine whether the buyer is a serious prospect or not worthy of further consideration. The second stage of the sales presentation is the approach, which is designed to secure attention and then to establish rapport and credibility with the client. This stage is important because first impressions can be quite significant in establishing rapport between buyer and seller. Making an approach can be achieved by a letter, unsolicited call, or telephone call. A good approach is one that results in the prospect's desire for additional information or contact. The third stage of the sales presentation is the presentation, whereby the salesperson demonstrates the benefits of the product in meeting the client's needs. The presentation is the heart of the selling process and is the stage at which a sale can often be made or broken. The salesperson jots down the product or service features and attempts to translate each of these into a benefit that the client may derive from the feature. The sales demonstration must attract and hold the prospect's attention in order to generate interest and assist in the sale of the product.

6. The fourth stage of the sales presentation is the handling of objections. The five categories of objections are delay or time objections, product objections, vendor objections, product service objections, and price objections. The salesperson should encourage and anticipate objections and then develop appropriate answers to them. A good salesperson should handle questions in a relaxed manner and view questions as a legitimate part of the purchase decision. The fifth stage of the sales presentation is the close, or the point at which a prospect agrees to buy or not to buy. The salesperson should constantly keep abreast of the presentation's progress in an attempt at a trial close if conditions warrant such action. If the prospect's objections are handled properly, there is no reason why the salesperson cannot ask for the sale. Some common closing techniques can include the direct approach, preference close, multiple acceptance approach, special offer close, last chance offer, list of features close,

fair minded approach, and assumption close. The sixth stage of the sales presentation is the follow-up, whereby the salesperson seeks continued contact by paying a return visit or calling clients to ensure customer satisfaction or determine why a prospect failed to buy. The follow-up represents one of the most important aspects of the salesperson's job. The salesperson must make sure delivery schedules were met, that the product or service performed as promised, and that the buyer's employees were properly trained in the product's use. A tickler file is composed of cards containing data on the sale and times to call back. To the salesperson, the file serves as a valuable tool in keeping adequate sales information.

7. To maintain an adequate sales force, a sales manager must develop an adequate compensation plan. Sales personnel are usually compensated by either a straight salary, commission, or some combination. A straight salary plan is a compensation method whereby salespeople are guaranteed a regular income. Salespeople are paid a specific amount for each pay period no matter what they accomplish. This method is widely used in industries where a salesperson has to perform functions other than creative selling. A commission is a plan in which salespeople receive a salary based on a percentage of sales for a specific period of time. A combination plan is one in which salespeople are paid a fixed salary and a commission based on their sales performance. The combination method is very popular in those activities where salespeople must divide their time equally between selling and nonselling activities.

8. Sales managers should be aware of the need for motivating salespeople. A good reward system will not only help motivate the sales force but will attract top salespeople to the firm. A sales manager can develop a high level of motivation by providing challenging opportunities and by developing lines of communication to top management. Sales task clarity is often used to determine the correlation between a salesperson's efforts and sales results. A systematic method of motivation should be designed to adequately achieve individual and company goals. Sales managers should also be aware that salespeople need guidance. Constructive criticism never hurt anybody. The evaluation of a salesperson's performance and the ability to take corrective action when necessary is another important responsibility of the sales manager. Often quotas are introduced, performance standards established based upon the quotas, and the results then compared with standards. A salesperson who does not generate desired results should then be directed to improve those areas that affect sales performance. Sales quotas are quantitative measures of the effectiveness of salespeople and are often determined on the basis of past records and sales forecasts. Other quotas used to measure sales effectiveness include gross-profit quotas, activity quotas, and expense quotas. In addition, the sales manager should also look at the daily activities of the salesperson as reflected by the call-record form.

9. The salesperson is responsible for communicating information to the sales manager. Because salespeople are constantly in the field, they are in a unique position to provide first-hand information about product effectiveness and competitive activity. Most field salespeople are required to write reports on a weekly or monthly basis. They include information on visits to potential customers and on sales expenses such as meals and transportation. Unfortunately, too much report writing has been a serious complaint by salespeople. In the near future, salespeople will be able to use computers, which will eliminate excessive paperwork.

LEARNING GOALS

After reading this chapter, you should be able to:

1. Describe personal selling's place in the promotional mix.
2. Understand the different types of sales jobs.
3. Explain the importance in making the proper sales force decisions concerning sales force objectives, sales force size, and the sales force structure.
4. Understand the need to properly staff the sales force.
5. Discuss the importance of managing the sales force.
6. Describe the six stages in the selling process.
7. Discuss the sales manager's responsibilities in developing compensation plans and the need to properly motivate and evaluate the sales force.

KEY CONCEPTS

From the list of lettered terms, select the one that best fits in the blank of the numbered statements that follow. Write the letter of that choice in the space provided.

(Answers to the key concepts appear at the end of the chapter.)

a. An order taker
b. The want-satisfaction approach
c. The approach (warm-up)
d. A sales quota
e. The presentation
f. Technical salespeople
g. A tickler file
h. Sales task clarity
i. Qualifying
j. Closing

k. A commission
l. Creative salespeople
m. A merchandise deliverer
n. A missionary
o. The follow-up
p. Role playing
q. Sales management
r. Prospecting
s. Straight salary

1. _____ is a salesperson whose main function is to write or ring up orders.

2. _____ is a pay plan under which salespeople are guaranteed a regular income.

3. _____ refers to the point of the selling process at which a prospect agrees to buy or decides not to buy.

4. _____ refers to the sales theory that stresses that the salesperson must first determine what a buyer really wants or needs before launching a sales talk.

5. _____ is the actively seeking out of buyers.

6. _____ is the pay plan under which salespeople are paid a percentage of the sales they close.

7. _____ refers to the beginning of the sales presentation and is intended to secure attention and to establish rapport and credibility with the client.

8. _____ is the marketing function that embraces recruiting, selecting, and training salespeople; supervising and motivating them; and evaluating their performance.

9. _____ are those individuals charged with determining customer's needs, helping them solve problems, and getting orders.

10. _____ refers to a quantitative measure of the effectiveness of salespeople.

11. _____ refers to the training method for salespeople in which one person acts the part of the salesperson and the other takes the part of the customer.

12. _____ is the stage for determining whether prospects have the authority to buy and the money to pay for the purchases.

13. _____ is the stage of the selling process during which a salesperson checks to see that orders have been filled and the customer is satisfied.

14. _____ is the stage of the selling process during which a salesperson translates the features of a product into benefits the customer can understand.

15. _____ is the salesperson who sees that buyers receive their purchases.

16. _____ are those technicians in sales positions who act as consultants and sometimes help to design products or systems to meet a client's needs.

17. _____ refers to the visible relationship between a salesperson's efforts and sales results.

18. _____ is a salesperson whose role is to build goodwill or to educate potential customers rather than to make a direct sale.

19. _____ is a reminder file, often composed of cards, containing data on a sale and times to call back.

PROGRAMMED REVIEW

The following self-teaching exercises consist of short statements that require you to make a response by filling in the blank (or blanks) provided. You will find the correct response printed in the margin to the left of the question.

a. the goals of the sales force
b. the size force the company requires
c. how the sales force should be structured

1. What are three decisions that a company will have to make in establishing a sales force?

a. _____
_____

b. _____
_____

c. _____
_____

straight

2. The _____ salary plan is widely used in industries in which a salesperson has to perform functions other than creative selling.

a. knowledge of the company
b. knowledge of the product
c. knowledge of the competition

3. During a training program, what three types of factual information are stressed?

a. _____
b. _____
c. _____
_____

paperwork

a. recruiting, selecting, and training sales-people
b. supervising and motivating salespeople on the job
c. evaluating the sales force's performance

consultants
design

a. the AIDA theory of selling
b. the want-satisfaction theory

diversity

4. The number one complaint of the sales force has been that there is too much _____.

5. What are the three tasks of the sales manager?

a. _____
   _____
   _____

b. _____
   _____
   _____

c. _____
   _____

6. Technicians in sales positions act as _____ and sometimes help to _____ products or systems to meet a client's needs.

7. What are the two sales approaches that salespeople often learn?

a. _____
   _____

b. _____
   _____

8. Because there is such a _____ of selling jobs, the qualities that make for a good salesperson in one field may not work in another.

a. prospecting/qualifying
b. the approach
c. the presentation
d. handling objections
e. the close
f. the follow-up

9. What are the six stages of the sales
    process?

    a. _____

    b. _____

    c. _____

    d. _____

    e. _____

    f. _____

knowledge
sales

10. During the training program, companies
     try to impart both _____
     and _____ skills.

a. application forms
b. job interviews
c. various tests

11. What are three methods that companies
     use to screen applicants for sales
     positions?

     a. _____

     b. _____

     c. _____

creative
support

12. Merchandise deliverers have no responsi-
     bility for _____ selling,
     but they provide essential _____
     to the sales force by seeing that
     buyers receive their purchases.

a. delay or time
    objections
b. product objections
c. vendor objections
d. product service
    objections
e. price objections

13. What are the five categories of objec-
     tions?

     a. _____

     b. _____

     c. _____

     d. _____

     e. _____

compensation

14. As might be expected, the more knowl-
     edge, creativity, and responsibility a
     sales job requires, the greater will be
     its _____.

a. sales-volume quotas
b. gross-profit quotas
c. activity quotas
d. expense quotas

15. What are the four methods that sales managers use to evaluate the performance of salespeople?

a. _____

b. _____

c. _____

d. _____

time
territory

16. Executives surveyed in over 400 indus- tries indicated that, for the future, sales managers will emphasize the importance of _____ and _____ management to their sales personnel.

a. the nature of the product
b. the number and location of buyers
c. the type of selling required

17. In an attempt to determine the amount of territory that an individual sales- person can cover effectively, what three factors must be considered?

a. _____
   _____

b. _____
   _____

c. _____
   _____

a. merchandise deliverers
b. order takers
c. missionaries
d. technical salespeople
e. creative salespeople

18. What are the five groups of sales jobs that are often categorized by the amount of creativity they require?

a. _____

b. _____

c. _____

d. _____

e. _____

efforts
sales

19. Sales task clarity enables salespeople to see the correlation between their _____ and _____ results.

248

a. straight salary
b. commission
c. combination salary
   and commission

20. What are the three ways in which sales-
    people are customarily compensated for
    their work?

    a. _____

    b. _____

    c. _____
       _____

goodwill
educate

21. A missionary is a salesperson whose job
    is to build _____ or to
    _____ potential cus-
    tomers rather than to make a direct sale.

a. by territory
b. by product
c. by market
d. by an organizational
   combination

22. What are the four ways in which a sales
    manager must determine how to organize
    the sales force for maximum efficiency?

    a. _____

    b. _____

    c. _____

    d. _____
       _____

customer relations
company reputation

23. In selecting candidates for sales
    positions, a company must make its
    selection carefully in order to avoid
    damage done to _____
    _____ and _____
    _____ by a poor sales-
    person.

a. nonselling jobs
   within a company
b. "pirated" from
   competing companies
c. college campuses

24. What three sources are sales trainees
    primarily recruited from?

    a. _____
       _____

    b. _____
       _____

    c. _____
       _____

want-satisfaction

25. For most creative and technical selling jobs, training in the _____ _____ theory is probably best.

MARKETING RIDDLE

The purpose of this exercise is to find the missing word that solves the riddle. Each of the statements requires you to make a response by filling in the blank (or blanks) for the appropriate missing word. Each statement contains a key letter which, when combined with the other key letters, will provide you with the solution to the riddle. Correct solutions to the riddle questions can lead to valuable prizes. See instructions for more information.

Personal selling has several advantages over other forms of promotion. One advantage allows for the salesperson to
___ ___ ___ ___ ___ ___ a message to the motivations and interests of the
1 2 3 4 5 6
prospect.

1. Sales task clarity allows salespeople to see the
___ ___ ___ ___ ___ ___ ___ ☐ ___ ___ ___ between their efforts and sales results.

2. The ___ ☐ ___ ___ ___ ___ approach occurs when a company prepares a standard presentation for trainees.

3. Besides getting attention, the approach should also establish rapport between seller and buyer by ___ ___ ___ ___ ___ ___ ☐ ___ ___ the prospect in the sale.

4. The follow-up is an important part of a salesperson's job. To remind themselves, salespeople sometimes keep a ___ ___ ___ ___ ☐ ___ ___ ___ ___ ___ ___ ___, composed of cards containing data on the sale and times to call back.

5. ___ ___ ☐ ___ ___ ___ ___ ___ ___quotas encourage salespeople to sell high-profit products instead of concentrating on low-profit items that may be easier to sell.

6. One method of determining the size of the sales force is to use the company's sales ___ ___ ☐ ___ ___ ___ ___ ___ for a given period to determine sales potential for individual regions or districts.

EXPERIENTIAL EXERCISE

Most salespeople are hardworking professionals who try to sell goods and services in an attempt to meet customers' needs, wants, or desires. Assume you are employed by a publisher of encyclopedias and assigned the responsibility of selling encyclopedias. By using the six sales presentation stages, describe what you would do, or how you would act in an attempt to secure a sale.

1. Prospecting/Qualifying

_____
_____
_____
_____
_____
_____
_____
_____

2. Approach

_____
_____
_____
_____
_____
_____
_____

3. Presentation

_____
_____
_____
_____
_____
_____
_____

4. Handling Objections

_____

_____

_____

_____

_____

_____

_____

_____

5. The Close

_____

_____

_____

_____

_____

_____

_____

_____

6. The Follow-Up

_____

_____

_____

_____

_____

_____

_____

Multiple Choice

_____ 1. What percentage of the nation's businesses rely exclusively on commissions for compensation?
   a. 6 percent
   b. 10 percent
   c. 12 percent
   d. 18 percent

_____ 2. Those charged with determining customer's needs, helping them solve problems, and getting orders are called
   a. technical salespeople.
   b. merchandise deliverers.
   c. creative salespeople.
   d. missionaries.

_____ 3. What percent of all companies use a straight salary plan in which salespeople are guaranteed a regular income?
   a. 17 percent
   b. 35 percent
   c. 50 percent
   d. 65 percent

_____ 4. What category of sales personnel are in sales positions and act as consultants and sometimes help to design products or systems to meet a client's needs?
   a. order takers
   b. merchandise deliverers
   c. technical salespeople
   d. missionaries

_____ 5. As might be expected, the more knowledge, creativity, and responsibility a sales job requires, the greater will be its
   a. sales.
   b. motivation.
   c. territory assignment.
   d. compensation.

_____ 6. For most creative and technical selling jobs, training in what theory is probably the best?
   a. technical theory
   b. want-satisfaction theory
   c. creative theory
   d. AIDA theory

_____ 7. The process of determining whether prospects have the authority to buy and the money to pay for purchases is known as
a. prospecting.
b. qualifying.
c. the follow-up.
d. demonstrating.

_____ 8. In measuring sales performance, the quota that sets the number of calls to be made, orders to be gotten, and displays to set up is known as the
a. expense quota.
b. gross-profit quota.
c. sales-volume quota.
d. activity quota.

_____ 9. The closing technique that gives the prospect a choice is known as a
a. preference close.
b. direct approach.
c. multiple acceptance approach.
d. last chance offer.

_____ 10. When a prospect presents an objection with the statement "I have to talk it over with my wife," which objection is being used?
a. product objection
b. vendor objection
c. delay or time objection
d. product service objection

True-False

_____ 11. Companies never make any attempt to screen out those who are obviously unsuitable for the kinds of selling they require.

_____ 12. Missionaries are salespeople who may suggest an article for purchase but whose main function is to write or ring up orders.

_____ 13. Prospecting is that part of the sales presentation in which salespeople actively seek out buyers.

_____ 14. Regardless of the type of company, training is not a great expense.

_____ 15. Most companies agree that video presentations are no replacement for personal contact.

_____ 16. Besides aiding memory, demonstrations do not help maintain interest during the presentation.

_____ 17. The sales task clarity reflects the correlation between the salesperson's efforts and sales results.

_____ 18.   The number one complaint of the sales force has been that there is too much paperwork.

_____ 19.   Sellers who are expected to create new business often work on a straight salary basis.

_____ 20.   The AIDA theory takes longer to master, allows for limited company control, and usually results in more profitable sales.

CHAPTER SOLUTIONS

Key Concepts

1. a	5. r	9. l	13. o	17. h
2. s	6. k	10. d	14. e	18. n
3. j	7. c	11. p	15. m	19. g
4. b	8. q	12. i	16. f	

Self-Quiz

1. a	5. d	9. a	13. T	17. T
2. c	6. b	10. c	14. F	18. T
3. a	7. b	11. F	15. T	19. F
4. c	8. d	12. F	16. F	20. F

CHAPTER 17
INTERNATIONAL MARKETING

CHAPTER SUMMARY

1. A company's business activities and markets are not limited to its nation's
    borders. In recent decades, the world has seen a high increase in inter-
    national trade unlike any other in history. Many American firms obtain
    a large portion of their sales and profits from international activities.
    In some instances, more sales and profits are derived from international
    trade than from domestic activity. It would be very difficult to find a
    country that has not purchased American products or services. Interna-
    tional marketing is the performance of marketing activities across national
    boundaries. Firms seek markets overseas because they are being pushed
    out of their home market or because they are pulled by promising market
    prospects abroad. Amongst the many factors that can influence the move-
    ment, we can find heavy competition at home, unfavorable government poli-
    cies, excess production capacity, and the desire of a company to produce
    greater quantity, thus the potential for additional profit. Although
    international marketing presents many complex and diverse challenges, a
    careful analysis of foreign markets can enable firms to plan appropriate
    marketing strategies and thus respond to potential worldwide demand for
    their products. Foreign trade involves home production and the export of
    products across national boundaries. Foreign marketing is a mode of
    international marketing in which firms operate within the foreign country
    where goods are to be sold. Multinational marketing is the integration
    of marketing activities that are carried out in a number of countries.
    The multinational corporation is a company with business investments,
    production operations, and management personnel in several countries.
    About half of all sales by multinationals are made by American-based firms.
    The present time appears favorable for U.S. firms to continue their pur-
    suit of foreign markets because countries in Europe, Latin America, and
    the Far and Near East have grown considerably in the last three decades
    and now possess a high level of demand for many types of U.S. industrial
    and consumer products.

2. There are many routes of expansion abroad, including exportation, licens-
    ing, joint ventures, and direct investment. Marketers must choose a
    route based upon the amount of time and resources they want to commit
    and the level of risk they are willing to bear. Exporting is the selling
    of goods and services to other countries. Firms that engage in exporting
    can use middlemen or they may choose to sell directly to buyers. Export-
    ing is usually the first step in international marketing because it
    requires the smallest financial commitment. Licensing is an arrangement

in which a company grants a foreign firm the rights to patents, trade-marks, and the use of technical processes in exchange for a royalty or fee for use. The main advantages of licensing are that a firm risks no capital in granting a license and that it gains direct access to foreign markets. However, the licensor must be certain it can control the licensee's activities necessary to insure proper quality levels, pricing structures, and adequacy of distribution. Another route is a joint venture, or partnership with a foreign firm. Both partners invest money and share ownership and control in proportion to their investment. The partners may share patents, trademarks, or control over production and marketing. This in turn can allow a company to share risks with another, take advantage of another company's existing lines of distribution, and allow a new company to enter a market faster, thus providing a head start or at least allowing it to keep up in a fast changing environment. How-ever, joint ventures can present problems in such areas as conflicting objectives, the lack of total control, and the risk of investment loss. The key to any successful joint venture is the selection of the right partner and then maintenance of effective communications. A direct investment can provide total control of production and sale of goods in a foreign country. Direct investment can sidestep trade barriers, take advantage of cheap labor, and overcome the inflated prices of American exports relative to other nation's currencies. Direct investment in wholly owned companies offers the greatest potential rewards because it allows a company superior control over operations. However, direct invest-ment can present problems in such areas as the exposure to expropriation, or seizure of facilities, and the possibility of discouragement by some countries.

3. The development of a successful international trade program requires an understanding of many environmental issues. Gaining an understanding of foreign environments can be quite difficult, because marketers are not often familiar with economic, cultural, and political/legal character-istics of the marketplace. Consequently, high priority and funding must be allocated towards intelligence gathering. A country's economic con-dition and potential for development are important issues. In order to appreciate business opportunities, or lack of them, it is helpful to investigate a country's economic growth and technical development. One way to measure this is to use per-capita income, which is a country's gross national product divided by its population. Very often countries may be classified according to their industrial structure which can provide information as to where people desire employment and income. Subsistence economies are found in those countries where most people engage in simple agriculture and consume most of their output. This group offers limited opportunities for exporters. Raw-material-exporting economies are found in those countries which are rich in natural resources and receive most of their revenue from exporting them. These countries present good markets for tools, supplies, and heavy equipment. Indus-trializing economies are found in those countries in which manufacturing accounts for about 10 to 20 percent of the economy and a small middle

257

class if forming. As manufacturing increases, the country can rely on many imports. In addition, a new rich class and a small, but growing, middle class can emerge. Industrial economies are found in those countries which are major exporters of manufactured goods and investment funds and have large middle classes. The large and diverse manufacturing activities of this group and their sizable middle class make them extremely valuable for all sorts of goods. Economic infrastructure studies can also provide information on facilities such as paved roads, communication and transportation services, banks, and distribution organizations that make marketing possible.

4. A second environmental issue relates to cultural differences. Culture basically consists of the beliefs, values, and customs shared by members of a society. Failure to take account of cultural differences is responsible for many, if not most, marketing failures abroad. It is important to know the many variations of culture including language, aesthetic perception, social organization, and values. Language presents such problems as translation errors, multilingual packages and labels, and often diverse languages and dialects. Aesthetic perceptions are concerned with beauty and good taste and are almost as internationally varied as languages. Culture can also form the basis for social organizations, including the role of the family and the educational system. Values can refer to a religious or moral belief or merely a practical attitude that sums up a person's experience.

5. A third environmental issue relates to political and legal differences. Marketers must be aware of the political atmosphere of the countries that are being considered for marketing activity. All countries have laws that regulate business activities. However, foreign governments will often apply a different set of laws or regulations to foreign firms than to their own businesses. Companies have to keep up with this vast and expanding body of laws because their success in the marketplace often depends on it. Governments can control marketing activity by imposing a number of controls. Tariffs are taxes on imports brought into a country. Import quotas, or restrictions, can be placed on the number of goods entering a country. Other controls can include restricting the amount of currency that can be taken out of a country by a foreign multinational and by setting maximum prices on goods sold within their borders. Some firms have been accused of dumping in the United States, or selling products in the United States for less than in the company's domestic market. While evaluating the risk of foreign outbreaks, marketers should consider both subjective and objective means. Subjective means include talks with political and business leaders and assessments by educated experts. Objective means include extrapolation, or estimating possible action based upon past events. International laws do exist in the form of treaties, conventions, and agreements among nations. The General Agreement on Tariffs and Trade (GATT) is designed to reduce the level of tariffs. Its two main principles include the issues of nondiscrimination and consultation.

6. With an understanding of the advantages and disadvantages of international marketing activities and an analysis of how external variables can affect the marketing mix, a firm can be in a better position to explore the vast potential of international trade. Marketers must engage in market research and use secondary data to determine the demographic, sociological, and psychological characteristics of international customers. The first step in creating a marketing mix is to develop an understanding of the target market. Multinational marketing occurs when an organization chooses to develop a marketing mix aimed at certain nations or groups within nations. Global marketing occurs when the organization tries to identify needs held in common around the world and to design a single marketing mix to meet those needs. Once the target market has been identified, the marketing mix can be developed. With proper research, product, price, placement, and promotion, policies can be designed to meet the needs of customers. Marketers must determine whether to sell the same product abroad as at home, modify it for the new market, or develop an entirely different product. The physical makeup of the product, service, and brand name choice are areas of concern. As more countries become industrialized, they have turned towards the service industry for assistance. Banking, transportation, consulting, insurance, franchising, and computer services represent additional marketing challenges for many American firms.

7. Marketing managers have to decide how to price exports as well as how to price component parts or goods transferred between a company and its overseas subsidiary. Often higher export prices may be justified because there may be additional taxes in the form of tariffs, special packaging, greater documentation, or higher inflation abroad. In other instances, lower prices may be justified and implemented. The second major pricing issue is concerned with the amount to charge subsidiaries. A transfer policy reflects pricing within the corporate family. In recent years, firms have been using an arm's-length policy, which requires the subsidiary to charge or be charged the same price as any buyer outside the firm.

8. There are many placement issues that also have to be considered. The degree of control needed and the volume of exports are key factors in placement decisions. Marketers can use resident buyers within this country who work for foreign firms, overseas representatives of foreign firms, or independent intermediaries who either buy goods for sale abroad or arrange to bring buyers and sellers together. Distribution problems can include such issues as the degree of control desired and problems associated with the economic and physical infrastructure.

9. Promoting goods and services abroad is not like promotion in the United States. Promotion programs in different countries require widely varying approaches. Language barriers, translation problems, and cultural difference have created numerous promotional problems. In addition, advertising messages and media, as well as different national attitudes toward

advertising and sales promotion, can even carry over into the field of personal selling and cause consumer confusion, As a result of these problems, it may be advisable to select international advertising agencies to serve as advisors and assist American firms in creating a positive image and avoid marketing blunders. In view of the fact that it is difficult to standardize a firm's advertising program, it may be best to develop new promotional themes in foreign countries.

10. In some instances a uniform marketing strategy across national boundaries is possible. <u>Standardization</u> is the practice of transferring all parts of a successful marketing mix from one country to another. This may be desirable because costs can be kept down if one product can be produced and sold in the same way in many markets, products can be identified easily by travelers, and planning and control can be simplified by a uniform marketing mix. A <u>modified standardization approach</u> can be used when cultural, economic, and legal differences make standardization undesirable or impossible. This approach provides for the changing of one or more elements of the marketing mix. The modified strategy is used by leading American multinationals in Europe. Marketers have to consider many factors before an appropriate marketing strategy is adopted within the international market scene.

LEARNING GOALS

After reading this chapter, you should be able to:

1. Understand the importance of marketing abroad and differentiate between foreign trade, foreign marketing, and multinational marketing.
2. Explain the routes of expansion abroad including the importance of exportation, licensing, joint ventures, and direct investment.
3. Describe the environment of marketing abroad, including economic and cultural differences such as aesthetic perceptions, social organizations, and values; and explain the political and legal differences, including the political life abroad and specific legal restrictions.
4. Understand important strategic planning issues concerning the research of foreign markets.
5. Discuss the importance of selecting international target markets and the problems associated with developing the market mix.

KEY CONCEPTS

From the list of lettered terms, select the one that best fits in the blank of the numbered statements that follow. Write the letter of that choice in the space provided.

(Answers to the key concepts appear at the end of the chapter.)

a. Multinational marketing
b. Standardization
c. A tariff
d. Foreign trade
e. Licensing
f. A joint venture
g. Direct investment
h. Foreign marketing
i. Dumping
j. Economic infrastructure
k. An import quota
l. International marketing
m. An arm's-length policy
n. A modified standardization approach
o. Per-capita income
p. Transfer pricing

1. _____ is concerned with the integration of marketing activities carried out in a number of countries.

2. _____ is a partnership with a foreign firm under which both partners invest money and share ownership and control in proportion to their investment.

3. _____ describes the practice of selling goods overseas at a lower price than a company charges in its own home market.

4. _____ describes the practice of changing one or more elements of the marketing mix.

5. _____ refers to home production and the export of products across national boundaries.

6. _____ describes the performance of marketing activities across national boundaries.

7. _____ refers to pricing within a corporate family, perhaps used to avoid taxes.

8. _____ is the practice of operating within the foreign country where goods are to be sold.

9. _____ refers to a tax on imports.

10. _____ includes facilities such as paved roads, communication and transportation services, banks, and distribution organizations that make marketing possible.

11. _____ describes the practice of transferring all parts of a successful marketing mix from one country to another.

12. _____ refers to a country's gross national product divided by its population.

13. _____ describes the total control of production and sale of goods in a foreign country.

14. _____ describes restrictions on the number of goods entering a country.

15. _____ refers to the policy that requires a firm's subsidiary to charge or be charged the same price available to any buyer outside the firm.

16. _____ is an arrangement under which a company (the licensor) grants a foreign firm (the licensee) the rights to patents, trademarks, and the use of technical processes in exchange for a royalty or fee for use.

PROGRAMMED REVIEW

The following self-teaching exercises consist of short statements that require you to make a response by filling in the blank (or blanks) provided. You will find the correct response printed in the margin to the left of the question.

a. to sidestep trade barriers
b. to take advantage of cheap labor
c. to overcome inflated prices of American exports

1. Why have American firms invested heavily overseas during the mid-1970s to the mid-1980s?

a. _____
   _____

b. _____
   _____

c. _____
   _____

exports

2. Governments often restrict _____ in order to protect national security.

a. keep costs down
b. make products easily
   identifiable among
   travelers
c. simplify planning
   and control

financial

a. exportation
b. licensing
c. joint ventures
d. direct investment

competitive

3. What three benefits would standardization
   provide a marketer?

   a. _____

   b. _____
      _____

   c. _____
      _____

4. Exporting is usually the first step in
   international marketing because it
   requires the smallest _____
   commitment.

5. What are the four routes of involvement
   or penetration in international marketing?

   a. _____

   b. _____

   c. _____

   d. _____

6. Tariffs and quotas are intended to make
   goods and services produced within the
   country more _____
   with imports.

a. messages may have to overcome language barriers
b. to adapt to different values and attitudes
c. to reflect the availability and impact of various media
d. to respond to differing national attitudes toward advertising and selling
e. to accommodate income limitations and shopping habits

7. Describe five reasons why marketers have to modify promotions for foreign markets.

a. _____
_____
_____

b. _____
_____
_____

c. _____
_____
_____

d. _____
_____
_____

e. _____
_____
_____

time
resources
risk

8. Marketers often choose a route of expansion abroad on a variety of considerations, including the amount of _____ and _____ they want to commit and the level of _____ they are willing to bear.

a. because they are pushed out of their home markets
b. because they are pulled by promising market prospects abroad

9. What are the two reasons that firms often seek markets overseas?

a. _____
_____
_____

b. _____
_____
_____

antitrust

10. In addition to laws about international trade, _____ laws apply to U.S. firms marketing abroad.

a. subsistence economies
b. raw-material-exporting economies
c. industrializing economies
d. industrial economies

dumping

a. per-capita income
b. industrial structure
c. economic infra-structure

held in common
a single

a. heavy competition at home
b. unfavorable govern-ment policies
c. excess production capacity at home
d. a company can find it more profitable to produce in greater quantity

11. What are the four methods that are used to classify countries according to their industrial structure?

a. _____

b. _____
   _____

c. _____

d. _____

12. Some foreign firms have been accused of _____ in the United States, or selling products in the United States for less than in the com-pany's domestic market.

13. Describe three economic characteristics that marketers consider in evaluating international markets.

a. _____

b. _____

c. _____

14. With global marketing, the organization tries to identify needs _____ _____ around the world and to design _____ marketing mix to meet those needs.

15. What are four factors that often push companies out of domestic markets?

a. _____
   _____

b. _____
   _____

c. _____
   _____

d. _____
   _____
   _____
   _____

cultural

a. language
b. aesthetic perceptions
c. social organization
d. values

licensing

a. nondiscrimination
b. consultation

pride

a. pooling complementary
   areas of expertise
b. sharing risks with
   another
c. taking advantage of
   a company's existing
   lines of distribution
d. providing the oppor-
   tunity to enter a
   market faster than a
   new company alone

16. Failure to take account of _____
    differences is responsible for many, if
    not most, marketing failures abroad.

17. What are four examples of cultural
    differences that marketers must be aware
    of?

    a. _____

    b. _____

    c. _____

    d. _____

18. A company with a limited amount of
    money to invest but a need for greater
    control over marketing may try

    _____.

19. Describe the two main principles of the
    General Agreement on Tariffs and Trade
    (GATT).

    a. _____

    b. _____

20. National _____ sometimes
    stands in the way of statistical
    accuracy, and information about income
    levels or demand for a product may be
    exaggerated.

21. What are four benefits that companies
    can derive by forming joing ventures?

    a. _____

       _____

    b. _____

       _____

    c. _____

       _____

       _____

    d. _____

       _____

       _____

imports

a. by imposing tariffs
b. by setting import
   quotas
c. by restricting the
   flow of currency
   that can be taken out
   of a country by a
   foreign multinational
d. by setting maximum
   prices on goods sold
   within their borders

22. Governments often restrict _____ in order to protect domestic businesses.

23. Describe four ways in which governments can control marketing activities.

a. _____

b. _____
   _____
   _____

c. _____
   _____
   _____
   _____
   _____
   _____

d. _____
   _____
   _____

direct investment

a. whether to charge
   a different price for
   exports than for prod-
   ucts sold domestically
b. how much to charge
   foreign subsidiaries
   for goods or parts
   shipped to or from
   them

24. While American companies continue to invest overseas, a major trend in recent years has been _____ _____ by foreign companies in the United States.

25. Describe two pricing decisions that international marketers must make.

a. _____
   _____
   _____
   _____

b. _____
   _____
   _____
   _____

MARKETING RIDDLE

The purpose of this exercise is to find the missing word that solves the riddle. Each of the statements requires you to make a response by filling in the blank (or blanks) for the appropriate missing word. Each statement contains a key letter which, when combined with the other key letters, will provide you with the solution to the riddle. Correct solutions to the riddle questions can lead to valuable prizes. See instructions for more information.

> All countries have laws that regulate business activity. Generally, a product manufactured by a multinational firm that is central to a nation's economy is considered politically
> _____ and subject to special political
> ‾1‾ ‾2‾ ‾3‾ ‾4‾ ‾5‾ ‾6‾ ‾7‾ ‾8‾ ‾9‾ ‾10‾
> attention.

1. Ideas concerning beauty and good taste are almost as internationally
   ☐ _ _ _ _ _ as languages.

2. Advertising agencies often serve as advisers to international clients by helping them to create a positive image and to avoid
   _ _ ☐ _ _ _ _ _ .

3. Marketers must try to evaluate _ _ _ _ _ _ _ _ _ ☐ outbreaks before entering new markets.

4. Traditionally, the American philosophy has been to support free trade, that is, _ _ ☐ _ _ _ _ restrictions on importers and exporters.

5. Multinational corporations not only trade with but _ _ ☐ _ _ _ _ out of several countries and obtain much of their profit from such operations.

6. Exportation provides a company with the least amount of control, whereas _ _ ☐ _ _ _ investment allows maximum control.

7. About _ ☐ _ _ of all sales by multinationals are made by U.S. based firms.

8. Large multinational companies have legal staffs that keep up with a vast and expanding ☐ _ _ _ of laws in order to stay on top of legal developments.

9. True global marketing can require more creativity because marketers must go beyond the differences in what people say they want; instead, they try to identify _ _ _ _ _ _ ☐ _ _ _ _ needs.

10. The main advantages of licensing are that a firm risks no capital in granting a license and that it gains direct __ __ __ ☐ __ __ to foreign markets.

EXPERIENTIAL EXERCISE

As an American manufacturer of computers, select a country that you are familiar with and describe the opportunities and limitations that you would consider in the sale of computers.

1. <u>Why did you select this particular country?</u>

_____

_____

_____

_____

_____

_____

_____

_____

2. <u>What economic differences exist?</u>

_____

_____

_____

_____

_____

_____

_____

3. What cultural differences exist?

_____

_____

_____

_____

_____

_____

_____

_____

4. What political/legal differences exist?

_____

_____

_____

_____

_____

_____

_____

SELF-QUIZ

Multiple Choice

_____ 1. When companies sell goods overseas at a lower price than what they charge in their own home markets, it is called
a. dumping.
b. transfer pricing.
c. an arm's-length policy.
d. an embargo.

_____ 2. A tax levied on imported goods is called a(an)
a. quota.
b. embargo.
c. exchange.
d. tariff.

_____ 3. The practice of transferring all parts of a successful marketing mix from one country to another is called
a. exporting.
b. standardization.
c. adaptation.
d. balance of payments.

_____ 4. When a company expands into several countries, it should attempt to integrate all marketing activities. This practice is called
a. foreign trade.
b. foreign marketing.
c. multinational marketing.
d. licensing.

_____ 5. What percentage of American businesses are involved in the international marketplace?
a. 10 percent
b. 15 percent
c. 20 percent
d. 25 percent

_____ 6. In 1985 approximately how much did American companies export overseas?
a. $223 billion
b. $325 billion
c. $370 billion
d. $423 billion

_____ 7. Besides data on income level and distribution, marketers must also study facilities such as paved roads, communication and transportation services, banks, and distribution organizations that make marketing possible. This international marketing concern is called
a. per-capita income.
b. joint venture.
c. cultural considerations.
d. economic infrastructure.

_____ 8. One way in which the government can control or restrict the number of goods entering a country is by establishing
a. import quotas.
b. tariffs.
c. currency controls.
d. price maximization.

_____ 9. Approximately what percentage of our gross national product does the United States export?
a. 30 percent
b. 20 percent
c. 10 percent
d. 2 percent

_____ 10. A business partnership involving a foreign company and a domestic company is known as a
a. partnership.
b. direct partnership.
c. joint venture.
d. foreign license partnership.

True-False

_____ 11. About 95 percent of the world's population and three-quarters of its purchasing power exist outside the United States.

_____ 12. The distinction between nations on the basis of per-capita income is helpful in selecting markets, but it must be used with care.

_____ 13. In planning international marketing strategy, market research is not necessary.

_____ 14. Typically, the more developed and affluent the country, the higher the birth rate.

_____ 15. The use of media as we know it in the United States can be easily transferred intact to a foreign country.

_____ 16. When marketers decide to sell abroad, exportation is usually the first route of expansion because it requires the most financial commitment.

_____ 17. Direct investment refers to the total control of production and sale of goods in a foreign country.

_____ 18. Economically, some nations provide poorer marketing opportunities than others because they have developed infrastructures and higher levels of income.

_____ 19. The world population is approaching the 5-billion mark, of which only about 5 percent live within the United States.

_____ 20. According to the World Bank, about half of the world's population lives in countries with an average per-capita income of $500.

CHAPTER SOLUTIONS

Key Concepts

1. a	5. d	8. h	11. b	14. k
2. f	6. l	9. c	12. o	15. m
3. i	7. p	10. j	13. g	16. e
4. n				

Self-Quiz

1. a	5. a	9. c	13. F	17. T
2. d	6. c	10. c	14. F	18. F
3. b	7. d	11. T	15. F	19. T
4. c	8. a	12. T	16. F	20. F

CHAPTER SUMMARY

1. In the United States we find thousands of nonprofit businesses conducted
in the public interest. Nonprofit organizations manage billions of
dollars and employ many employees. It has been estimated that as much
as 20 percent of our economy operates for some reason besides making a
profit. As a result, they have great impact on the economy as well as
the quality of life. Nonprofit organizations generally operate in the
public interest or to support a cause and do not seek profits, market
share, or return on investment. The idea of applying marketing to nonprofit organizations is comparatively recent. Nonprofit organizations
face people and resource problems that marketers can help solve. When-
ever an exchange occurs, marketing principles can be applied. In addition to the many types of not-for-profit marketing organizations, persons and ideas can also be marketed. <u>Person marketing</u> involves an effort
to cultivate the attention, interest, and preference of a target market
toward a person. <u>Idea marketing</u> is the offering of a cause in exchange
for public acceptance. <u>Social marketing</u> is one particular type of idea
marketing which uses marketing techniques to increase the acceptability
of a social idea, cause, or practice in a target group(s).

2. <u>Organization marketing</u> represents the biggest share of nonprofit marketing and attempts to influence others to accept the goals of, receive the
services of, or contribute in some way to an organization. Nonprofit
organizations can be classified as service organizations, mutual benefit
associations, and government organizations. <u>Service organizations</u> are
institutions, such as hospitals, colleges, and museums, that provide a
service for clients, sometimes in exchange for a fee. This group attempts
to reach clients and donors for contributions or conduct fund-raising
efforts in order to make up cost differences. Service organizations rely
on clients and donors as their main constituencies. <u>Mutual benefit
associations</u> are organized for the benefit of members, not outsiders.
Political parties, unions, clubs, and churches fall into this category.
Marketing activities are carried on primarily to increase membership,
although they are also sometimes performed to win the support of others.
<u>Government organizations</u> serve the interests of the public at large.
Examples include all government agencies, including the post office, the
military services, and police and fire departments. Government organizations need professional marketing primarily to win goodwill and improve
their operations.

3. There are many differences between a profit and nonprofit organization
as well as a number of significant similarities. The first difference
is the dissimilarity in marketing objectives. A profit-making organization exists to make a profit and can do this by stimulating demand for

its products. Nonprofit organizations, however, generally work with limited resources and cannot afford to stimulate as much demand as possible. A second difference is concerned with the markets served. A profit-making organization meets its objectives by serving the buying public. A nonprofit organization may consider several markets. Client publics consist of those individuals who directly use the product exchanged by nonprofit organizations. General publics consist of those individuals who have an indirect interest in the use of the product exchanged by nonprofit organizations. Another difference concerns itself with control standards. A profit-making organization can use sales data and market share figures to guide it in meeting objectives. Nonprofit organizations have difficulty in finding similar measures.

4. There are similarities between nonprofit and profit-making organizations. Both need to plan objectives and analyze their environments to operate efficiently. The basic aim of nonprofit organizations is to obtain a desired response from a target. The responses sought could be a change in values, financial contributions, the donation of services, or some other type of exchange. Both need to know their clients to serve them well. Unfortunately, goals, and sometimes clients, are difficult to define. Both work with the Four "Ps" in serving customer needs, and both need to check on whether objectives are being reached and marketing programs implemented.

5. Nonprofit organizations, as well as profit-making organizations, develop organizational objectives which direct the organization as a whole and marketing objectives which state what marketers can do to support the overall objectives. However, nonprofit organizational objectives are reflected toward the public to be served and not stated in terms of a product or service offered. For example, objectives can include the number of clients to be served, the amount of service to be provided, and the quality of service needed. Once flexible organizational objectives are determined, marketing objectives to meet overall goals can then be set. Three environmental levels must be analyzed to determine whether objectives are realizable. The internal, operating, and general environments affect the operation of profit and nonprofit organizations alike. The internal environment, consisting of the tangible and intangible resources an organization needs to operate, can make or break the marketing effort of a nonprofit organization. The operating environment is concerned with competition and changing values which are becoming more intensive. The general environment is concerned with economic developments, technological advances, legal and governmental actions, and social expectations and values.

6. Nonprofit organizations, as well as profit-making organizations, are concerned with target marketing. Nonprofit organizations are increasingly turning to marketing to help them realign their services to better meet the needs of their target markets and to improve their financial resources. Nonprofit institutions that cater to both the client and general public

must distinguish market segments. It can choose to concentrate its marketing effort on one segment or serve many segments. The proper development of the marketing mix strategy can limit alternatives and direct marketing activities toward achieving organizational goals. Profit-making organizations look at a product as a complex entity. In nonprofit organizations, a product can be difficult to define because very often what is offered for exchange is completely intangible. The marketing of ideas and concepts is more abstract and requires much effort to present benefits. The concept of price varies depending on what is being marketed in the nonprofit sector. Very often the price is nonmonetary when ideas are marketed. Service organizations, which have both donor and client markets, charge both a monetary and nonmonetary price. In setting a monetary price, the goal is usually to cover costs. The goal in determining nonmonetary price is to encourage involvement, and its charge is usually psychological or intangible. Since most of the products marketed by nonprofit organizations are ideas or services, their distribution or placement tends to be direct, without the use of intermediaries. Distribution usually is examined as it relates to decisions about product and promotion. Since most nonprofit products are ideas and services, the distribution decisions relate to how these ideas and services will be made available to clients. Promotion is another area used by both nonprofit and profit-making organizations. Advertising and publicity are used widely by nonprofit organizations to communicate with clients and the public. However, the most important promotional element is often personal selling, provided free by volunteers.

7. Unlike profit-making organizations, the most difficult job for nonprofit marketers in the control phase is to find measurements that indicate progress toward objectives. Marketers have to focus on using information obtained in the marketing audit to make sure goals are achieved. The purpose of control is not only to uncover errors and mistakes, but also to change organizational goals and marketing objectives as necessary. Marketers should seek out and develop the proper tools to measure the effectiveness of marketing efforts. The process of control involves setting well-defined objectives, measuring actual results against planned results, finding reasons for deviation from the plan, and taking corrective action. Currently nonprofit organizations use such measures as total marketing response, market share, cost per dollar of marketing response, and marketing attitudes.

8. Marketing has an important role to play in nonprofit marketing. Even though the nature of nonprofit organizations differs from profit-making businesses, marketing concepts, ideas, and strategies play an important role in the economic growth and development of nonprofit organizations.

LEARNING GOALS

After reading this chapter, you should be able to:

1. Describe the scope of nonprofit marketing.
2. Differentiate between the various types of nonprofit marketing which can include person, idea, and organization marketing.
3. Describe the differences and similarities between profit and nonprofit marketing organizations.
4. Explain the importance of establishing marketing objectives and the environment of nonprofit organizations, including the internal, operating, and general environments.
5. Describe target marketing for nonprofit organizations.
6. Explain how the marketing mix variables can be applied to nonprofit organizations.
7. Describe marketing control for nonprofit organizations.

KEY CONCEPTS

From the list of lettered terms, select the one that best fits in the blank of the numbered statements that follow. Write the letter of that choice in the space provided.

(Answers to the key concepts appear at the end of the chapter.)

a. A mutual benefit association
b. Client publics
c. Person marketing
d. General publics
e. Idea marketing
f. Organization marketing
g. A government organization
h. A service organization
i. Social marketing

1. _____ involves an effort to cultivate the attention, interest, and preference of a target market toward a person.

2. _____ is a nonprofit organization that serves the interests of the public at large.

3. _____ consist of those individuals who have an indirect interest in a nonprofit organization's goods or services.

4. _____ is the offering of a cause in exchange for public acceptance.

5. _____ is a nonprofit organization that is organized for the benefit of members, not outsiders.

277

6. _____ consist of those individuals who directly use the product exchanged by nonprofit organizations.

7. _____ reflects the biggest share of nonprofit marketing and attempts to influence others to accept the goals of, receive the services of, or contribute in some way to an organization.

8. _____ refers to the use of marketing techniques to increase the acceptability of a social idea, cause, or practice in a target group.

9. _____ refers to an institution, such as a hospital, college, or museum, that provides a service for clients, sometimes in exchange for a fee.

PROGRAMMED REVIEW

The following self-teaching exercises consist of short statements that require you to make a response by filling in the blank (or blanks) provided. You will find the correct response printed in the margin to the left of the question.

a. total marketing response
b. market share
c. cost per dollar of marketing response
d. marketing attitudes

1. What are four important measures needed in the nonprofit sector?

   a. _____
   b. _____
   c. _____
      _____
   d. _____

competition

2. The factor of most concern in the operating environment of nonprofit organizations is _____.

a. in marketing objectives
b. in the markets served
c. in establishing control standards

3. Nonprofit and profit-making organizations have a number of dissimilarities. What are three differences between them?

   a. _____
      _____
   b. _____
      _____
   c. _____
      _____

public at large
goodwill

a. person marketing
b. idea marketing
c. organization
   marketing

client

a. setting well-
   defined objectives
b. measuring actual
   results against
   planned results
c. finding reasons for
   deviation from the
   plan
d. taking corrective
   action

cause

4. Government organizations serve the interests of the _____.
   They need professional marketing primarily to win _____ and
   improve their operations.

5. What are the three basic types of nonprofit marketing?

   a. _____

   b. _____

   c. _____

6. Those who directly use the "product"
   exchanged by nonprofit organizations are
   called _____ publics.

7. What are the four steps in the control
   process?

   a. _____
      _____

   b. _____
      _____

   c. _____
      _____

   d. _____
      _____

8. The essence of idea marketing is the
   offering of a _____ in
   exchange for public acceptance.

a. Both need to plan objectives and analyze their environments.
b. Both need to know their clients to serve them well.
c. Both work with the same marketing elements in serving consumer needs.
d. Both need to check whether objectives are being reached and marketing programs implemented.

9. Nonprofit and profit-making organizations are more similar than dissimilar. What are the four major similarities between them?

a. _____
_____
_____

b. _____
_____
_____

c. _____
_____
_____
_____

d. _____
_____
_____
_____

intangible

10. In nonbusiness organizations, a product can still be difficult to define. Often what is offered for exchange is completely _____.

a. general organizational objectives
b. marketing objectives

11. What are two kinds of objectives that interest marketers?

a. _____
_____

b. _____

goodwill

12. In a sense, nonprofit organizations must be even more environmentally sensitive than businesses because their existence often depends on the _____ of donors and taxpayers, as well as the public they serve.

280

recent

a. service organiza-
   tions
b. mutual benefit
   associations
c. government
   organizations

a. economic develop-
   ments
b. technological
   advances
c. legal and govern-
   mental actions
d. social expectations
   and values

direct

a. clients
b. donors

personal selling

a. client publics
b. general publics

13. The idea of applying marketing to non-
    profit organizations is comparatively
    _____.

14. What are the three categories into
    which nonprofit organizations can be
    classified?

    a. _____

    b. _____

       _____

    c. _____

15. What are the four most important factors
    in the general environment?

    a. _____

    b. _____

    c. _____

       _____

    d. _____

       _____

16. Since most of the products marketed by
    nonprofit organizations are ideas or
    services, their distribution tends to
    be _____, without the
    use of intermediaries.

17. What are the two large markets that
    service organizations must reach?

    a. _____

    b. _____

18. In the nonprofit sector, the most impor-
    tant promotional element is often
    _____.

19. In serving markets, what are the two
    "publics" that are served by "nonprofit
    organizations"?

    a. _____

    b. _____

measurements

20. For nonprofit marketers, the most difficult job in the control phase is to find _____ that indicate progress toward objectives.

a. internal environment
b. operating environment
c. general environment

21. What are the three distinct environmental levels that must be analyzed to determine whether objectives are realized?

a. _____

b. _____

c. _____

general publics

22. Those who have an indirect interest in the use of the "product" exchanged by nonprofit organizations are referred to as _____.

a. monetary price
b. nonmonetary price

23. What are the two types of price that service organizations have?

a. _____

b. _____

members
outsiders

24. Mutual benefit associations are organized for the benefit of _____, not _____.

a. attention
b. interest
c. preference

25. What are the three goals that "person marketing" attempts to cultivate?

a. _____

b. _____

c. _____

MARKETING RIDDLE

The purpose of this exercise is to find the missing word that solves the riddle. Each of the statements requires you to make a response by filling in the blank (or blanks) for the appropriate missing word. Each statement contains a key letter which, when combined with the other key letters, will provide you with the solution to the riddle. Correct solutions to the riddle questions can lead to valuable prizes. See instructions for more information.

Nonprofit organizations are frequently expected, or even required, to serve market segments that a profit-oriented organization would find ___ ___ ___ ___ ___ ___ ___ ___ ___ ___ ___ ___.
 1 2 3 4 5 6 7 8 9 10 11 12

1. In general, nonprofit organizations work with limited
   ___ ___ ___ ___ ☐ ___ ___ ___ ___ and cannot afford to stimulate as much demand as possible.

2. For nonprofit organizations that are supported by the same members they serve, it pays to consider ___ ___ ___ ___ ___ ☐ ___ ___ ___ ___ ___ ___ if members have different needs.

3. Mutual benefit associations conduct marketing activities primarily to increase ___ ___ ___ ___ ☐ ___ ___ ___ ___ ___, although they are also some-times performed to win the support of outsiders.

4. Social marketing is the use of marketing techniques to increase the
   ___ ☐ ___ ___ ___ ___ ___ ___ ___ ___ ___ ___ ___ of a social idea, cause, or practice in a target group(s).

5. A typical example of person marketing occurs in the
   ___ ☐ ___ ___ ___ ___ ___ ___ ___ arena.

6. Nonprofit organizations are making increased use of
   ___ ___ ___ ___ ___ ___ ___ ___ ___ ___ ___ ☐ ___.

7. When the product is highly intangible, as in the case of an idea, mar-keters may try to embody it in a more ___ ☐ ___ ___ ___ ___ ___ ___ form.

8. Occasionally nonprofit pricing is ___ ___ ☐ ___ ___ ___ oriented rather than cost oriented.

9. The ☐ ___ ___ ___ ___ ___ ___ ___ environment, consisting of the tangible and intangible resources an organization needs to operate, can make or break the marketing efforts of a nonprofit organization.

10. Besides personal selling, nonprofit marketers have found advertising to be a highly effective way of ___ ___ ___ ___ ___ ___ ___ ☐ ___ ___ ___ ___ ___ with the public.

11. Organizations that are product oriented may become locked into limited objectives and disappear as conditions change. Firms that are public oriented may ___ ___ ☐ ___ ___ to a changing world.

12. In addition to competition, the operating environment of nonprofit organ-izations is concerned about changing ___ ___ ☐ ___ ___ ___.

EXPERIENTIAL EXERCISE

Nonprofit marketing is performed by companies that operate for the betterment of the public or in support of a cause.

In each of the following categories, select a nonprofit organization and describe its objectives, source of funds, market served, and control standards being used.

1. Service Organization

_____

_____

_____

_____

_____

_____

_____

_____

_____

_____

2. Mutual Benefit Association

_____

_____

_____

_____

_____

_____

_____

_____

_____

_____

3. Government Organization

_____
_____
_____
_____
_____
_____
_____
_____
_____
_____

SELF-QUIZ

Multiple Choice

_____ 1. Approximately what percentage of the U.S. economy operates for some
          reason other than making a profit?
          a. 10 percent
          b. 20 percent
          c. 30 percent
          d. 40 percent

_____ 2. In the nonprofit sector, the most important promotional element is
          often
          a. advertising.
          b. sales promotion.
          c. publicity.
          d. personal selling.

_____ 3. The nonprofit sphere in this country is
          a. holding steady.
          b. slipping.
          c. large and growing.
          d. not important to marketers.

_____ 4. The nonprofit organization category that includes institutions,
          such as hospitals, colleges, and musuems, that provide a benefit
          for clients, sometimes in exchange for a fee, is known as
          a. service organizations.
          b. mutual benefit associations.
          c. government organizations.
          d. charitable organizations.

5. The effort to cultivate the attention, interest, and preference of a target market toward an individual is known as
   a. person marketing.
   b. the client publics.
   c. indirect groups.
   d. the general publics.

6. The classification with the biggest share of nonprofit marketing is
   a. service organizations.
   b. mutual benefit associations.
   c. organization marketing.
   d. person marketing.

7. What percentage of workers in the United States is emloyed in the nonprofit sector?
   a. 10 percent
   b. 20 percent
   c. 30 percent
   d. 40 percent

8. The offering of a cause in exchange for public acceptance is known as
   a. person marketing.
   b. servicing.
   c. client publics.
   d. idea marketing.

9. Those individuals who have an indirect interest in the product exchanged by nonprofit organizations are known as
   a. indirect groups.
   b. general publics.
   c. person marketing.
   d. client publics.

10. The nonprofit organization category that includes political parties, unions, clubs, and churches is known as
   a. charitable organizations.
   b. government organizations.
   c. mutual benefit associations.
   d. service organizations.

True-False

11. Even though organizations may be supported by the same members they serve, it pays to consider segmentation if members have different needs.

12. In nonbusiness organizations, a product is easy to define.

_____ 13. Setting prices when both monetary and nonmonetary considerations are involved is quite difficult.

_____ 14. Persons, ideas, and organizations can be marketed just as a physical product can.

_____ 15. The nonprofit sphere in this country is small and appears to have peaked.

_____ 16. Nonprofit marketers must establish specific objectives and test their feasibility in light of prevailing environmental conditions, just as marketers for business must.

_____ 17. The essence of idea marketing is the offering of a cause in exchange for public acceptance.

_____ 18. Service organizations have only the client market to reach.

_____ 19. Mutual benefit associations serve the interests of the public at large.

_____ 20. Both profit-making and nonprofit organizations work with the same marketing elements in serving their customers.

CHAPTER SOLUTIONS

Key Concepts

1. c	3. d	5. a	7. f	9. h
2. g	4. e	6. b	8. i	

Self-Quiz

1. b	5. a	9. b	13. T	17. T
2. d	6. c	10. c	14. T	18. F
3. c	7. a	11. T	15. F	19. F
4. a	8. d	12. F	16. T	20. T